Methods
of Family Therapy

Methods
of Family Therapy

Luciano L'Abate
Georgia State University

Gary Ganahl
West Virginia University, School of Medicine

James C. Hansen
State University of New York at Buffalo

Prentice-Hall, Englewood Cliffs, New Jersey 07632

Library of Congress Cataloging-in-Publication Data

L'Abate, Luciano, 1928-
    Methods of family therapy.

    Bibliography: p.
    Includes index.
    1. Family psychotherapy.   I. Ganahl, Gary.
II. Hansen, James C. III. Title.   [DNLM: 1. Family
Therapy—methods. WM 430.5.F2 L114m]
    RC488.L3   1986   616.89'156   85-21484
    ISBN 0-13-579376-9

Editorial/production supervision and interior design: Lori L. Baronian
Cover design: Ben Santora
Manufacturing buyer: Barbara Kittle

Printed in the United States of America
10 9 8 7 6 5 4 3 2 1

ISBN 0-13-579376-9   01

Prentice-Hall International, (UK) Limited, *London*
Prentice-Hall of Australia Pty. Limited, *Sydney*
Editora Prentice-Hall do Brasil, Ltda., *Rio de Janeiro*
Prentice-Hall Canada Inc., *Toronto*
Prentice-Hall Hispanoamericana, S.A., *Mexico*
Prentice-Hall of India Private Limited, *New Delhi*
Prentice-Hall of Japan, Inc., *Tokyo*
Prentice-Hall of Southeast Asia Pte. Ltd., *Singapore*
Whitehall Books Limited, *Wellington, New Zealand*

Contents

SECTION III
HELPING FAMILIES GROW

Preface

The field of family therapy is currently rich in clinical techniques but poor in specific methodology. A method is a special procedure that can be replicated while a technique involves the therapist's individual style in applying a method. The purpose of this book is to describe the key methods of family therapy. The astounding growth in the use of family therapy suggests the need for a theory-free, comprehensive, simply written, method-oriented collection of interventions specifically designed for families in need of help. In our training of various mental health professionals, we have not found one single source that contained the various methods to be used. Consequently, we have deemed it useful to put them all under one cover.

Since family therapy is free from professional affiliations, we hope that this collection of methods will be useful to students in the various mental health disciplines as well as to professionals who want to update their skills. Emphasis throughout the book will be on practical applications rather than theory, and on concrete practices rather than on abstractions.

The book begins with a chapter presenting the characteristics of methods and emphasizes the place of methodology in learning family therapy. Section I focuses on understanding the family. One chapter conceptualizes the family as a system. It is important to understand families from a systems perspective as well as functional and dysfunctional characteristics of families. Another chapter examines the concepts and methods used in assessing family functioning. These conceptual chapters are a foundation for the therapist in selecting and implementing methods to change families.

Sections II and III present chapters on specific methods. The chapters are arranged according to two stages: helping families change and helping families grow. The methods presented in this book vary along four different dimensions: (1) verbal to nonverbal, (2) relatively passive to relatively active, (3) most tried to least tried, and (4) most simple to most complex. Clearly the risks involved are greater when one physically moves a family around, than they would be in terms of verbal positive reframing. Nonetheless, the four dimensions that we have covered governed our thinking in the organization of this book.

From verbal to nonverbal. It is clearly easier to talk than to act. A great deal of what a therapist does is talk. In fact, so much so that sometimes one wonders whether there can be any translation from the verbal to the non-verbal system. Yet, change is of a nonverbal nature. It is not only important what people say, but it is even more important what people do. For family therapists to expect that words will translate into action is tantamount to a shibboleth and to a crazy, illogical, unrealistic expectation. Translation from verbal to nonverbal does not happen without difficulty and over a period of time. Hence, verbalizations on the therapist's part have to be directed to a nonverbal behavior, and even better, nonverbal behavior should be used to change the verbal behavior. Consequently, both aspects, verbal and nonverbal, are emphasized here in terms of methods. Even though developmentally, the nonverbal is clearly earlier than verbal, it is assumed that verbalizations are the most common ones present in the relationships of families. Words are important if not necessary to achieve rapport, to relate, and to maintain a relationship. We are starting with the verbal because this is where most families start anyway. However, relying on the verbal alone leaves out important aspects of development as well as of functioning in most families.

From relatively passive to relatively active.   We have attempted to start gradually from the least amount of action to the most amount of action on the therapist's part. Most of the methods used in the change section (II) can be done with the therapist sitting in his or her chair. However, none of the nonverbal "growth" actions (III) can be implemented in this way. There is a need for the therapist to know role-playing techniques and to have experienced a great deal of self on a nonverbal basis using whatever methods may be at his or her disposal.

From most tried to least tried.   Clearly, we started with techniques which are much more common, such as positive reframing and prescription which are much better known than letters and homework assignments. By the same token, sculpting is better known than training.

From most simple to most complex.   We should recognize that none of the methods that we are presenting in this book are simple. Nonetheless, we have tried to present a gradual working up of methods whereby one method is necessary for the use of the next method in line. Prescriptions are based on positive reframing. Letters imply a knowledge of both positive reframing and prescriptions. Retraining is posited on the ability to role play, and role playing is posited on the ability to sculpt nonverbally a family.

Acknowledgments

We would like to explain how work on this book was divided among ourselves. All three of us collaborated on the first chapter. JCH was mainly responsible for Chapters 2 and 3, while GG was mainly responsible for Chapters 4, 8, and 9. LL was responsible for the rest. In addition we would like to express our appreciation to Peggy Mayfield for her help with the chapter on role playing. Many former students who are now colleagues, were generous in suggesting a variety of prescriptions, homework assignments, and examples of letters. In some cases we acknowledged them in the body of the book. However, we do want to recognize the help of Joseph Frey III, Marilyn Goodrich, Edgar Jessee, Michael O'Shea, Sadell Sloan, and Victor Wagner. If we have failed to acknowledge others, we ask them to forgive us.

L L
J C H
G G

Methods
of Family Therapy

1

Need for Specialized Methods

Something You Can Use

Family therapists aim to help a dysfunctional family change. Family therapy is generally based on the belief that a family is a system, and the therapeutic process involves treating the whole system or individuals and subsystems regarding their interaction within the whole system. A family therapist assesses the family's interaction and plans an intervention. What intervention? How does the therapist intervene? All too often an intervention is considered to be derived from a theory or associated with the technique of a charismatic spokesperson of an approach to family therapy. Practicing family therapists need methods that are appropriate with various theories and replicable by many therapists, but that also permit a therapist to later apply those methods with his or her individual style.

THEORY OR METHOD?

Even though some of these methods have some theoretical basis in family therapy, it would be relevant at this point to consider the separation of method and theory. We can have a method without theory, and we can have a theory without method. For instance, psychoanalysis developed as a theory as well as a practice. Family therapy has a variety of theories and a variety of practices. However, it would be very difficult to match a specific method with any particular theory. Hence, this book is as void of theory as possible because the reader can find plenty of theories elsewhere.

As Watzlawick (1976) commented in relation to theories in family therapy:

> Faced as we are, however, with the multitude of often incompatible and sometimes contradictory theories, the only meaningful question to ask is not which theory is more "correct" or respects reality better than the others, but which theory makes possible more effective and rapid results. (p. 120)

The issue, then, becomes one of choosing theories whose derived methods produce results in the most effective and long-lasting ways. However, at the present time there does not seem to be any theory that has developed methods specific to it alone. Several different theories often will predict the usefulness of the same method. Therefore, we need to choose the methods not on the basis of theory but on the basis of our experience of their individual effectiveness. We must look for methods which work with a minimal expenditure of time and energy in order to keep pace with the demands for our help. To the researcher and theorist, this abandonment of the deductive process may sound difficult to achieve and unworkable in any case. To the practitioner, who must achieve results now, such an eclectic approach may be more attractive. Certainly we cannot help but be influenced by theory in our search for new methods, but we may need to work our way back from method to more accurate theory.

METHOD OR TECHNIQUE?

A concern in the field of family therapy involves distinguishing between method and technique. These terms with two different meanings have been used synonymously and interchangeably. Their separate meanings, as defined by any dictionary, are:

1. *Technique:* The manner and ability with which an artist, writer, dancer, athlete, or the like, employs the specific skills of his or her particular art or field of endeavor.
2. *Method:* The body of specialized procedures and plans used in a specialized field, especially in an area of applied science.

Our usage in this book, as well as our orientation to the problem of method, follows the thinking of Buchler (1961). We distinguish method from technique by proposing that method is a more specific way of dealing with families than technique. Method implies a procedure for achieving a goal in a specified and systematic fashion with a minimum of intuitive qualities. Its purpose is to bring about order and predictability in a group of diverse elements or ideas. Technique, on the other hand, is by its very nature idiosyncratically and intuitively individual. It resides in the therapist's personal self or professional role. It connotes the manner or style in which he or she applies special and specific methods. Its purpose is to refine the application of method, to adjust it to fit the uniqueness of the situation and of the therapist. With increasing awareness and specificity, technique may evolve into method. Within technique may lie many new methods in embryonic form, waiting to be recognized and specified. Many of the "methods" presented here may yet be developed further to achieve greater specificity through continued use and experimentation.

The distinction between method and technique could best be explained through an analogy from music. Musicians can all reproduce the same music because musical notes and scores are understood by anyone who reads music. However, given three musicians reading from the same score, one may be faced with three different interpretations, although the basic melody may be the same. The point here is that before one becomes an artist she or he should be knowledgeable and competent in playing an instrument. One cannot interpret a piece of music unless one has mastered a knowledge of the musical score and of an instrument. In the family therapy field, many students would like to become instant professionals without undergoing professional training. Emphasis on individual style, that is, technique without knowledge of method, is just as dangerous as knowledge of method without appreciation of the importance of individual style. *Both are necessary.* Method is a matter of substance. Technique is a matter of style. Both substance and style are important.

REPLICABILITY

The primary quality of method which is of interest to us as teachers and researchers is its ability to be replicated by any well-trained professional. Method is relatively more communicable and repeatable than technique because it has characteristics of its own, independent of the therapist. It can be described, it can be recognized, and it can be followed. A technique, on the other hand, because of its relative reliance on the expertise and experience of an individual, is more difficult to replicate. Without knowledge, the experience and the personality of the therapist are hard to repeat. The expert may not even know what parts of his or her technique are crucial for his or her success. Methods can be broken down into their component parts and studied. It is much more difficult to break down a technique and to study it without also studying the personality of its practitioner. Techniques are too enmeshed with the idiosyncratic and unique characteristics of individual therapists for progress to take place. Methods have rules while techniques do not. As Buchler (1961) noted:

> A way without directions—rules of direction and identification—would lead nowhere and be no way at all. . . . Randomness in human activity may prevail on different levels and is subject to degree. When it obliterates purposiveness, it is the prime enemy of method. . . . The best methods attempt to fight vagueness of direction, but not to simplify . . . methodic activity, as distinguished from any other form, serves to render explicit things it takes for granted. (p. 35)

This emphasis on method does not differ much from Haley's (1976) problem-solving approach. If the therapist knows his or her methods he or she can be effective without undue overemphasis on personal style.

There has been sufficient preoccupation with techniques at the expense of methods, in spite of the fact that *both* are necessary for successful therapy (Keeney, 1983). Even though we may seem enamored of method, at no time are we thinking in mutually exclusive ways. Our emphasis on method is not done at the expense of technique. It is done to balance what we fear could become a wasteful blind alley for extent that therapy is *both* an art and a science, it is an exquisitely human activity.

NONOVERLAPPING METHODS IN FAMILY THERAPY

The whole field of psychotherapy is replete with techniques. References can easily be found to the varieties of viewpoints and techniques which can be used (Garfield & Bergin, 1978). There is clearly no lack of sources from which the budding therapist can learn the techniques of individual therapy. In the last ten years, with the great increment in the use and implementation of family therapy, there has been an increasing number of new methods developed specifically for use in family treatment. However, there are no specific sources where the student of family therapy can find all or most of the methods considered in this book. Consequently, we have tried to bring together those methods relevant to family work which do not overlap with individual methods.

Despite the great number of techniques already available from the literature of individual and group therapy, there is a need for methods of therapy specific to the family. In many cases what worked for the individual may be inappropriate or ineffectual when applied to the family. Furthermore, methods oriented to the needs of the individual may be antithetical to the needs of the family as a whole. One of the basic tenets of family practice has been that much of what passes for irrational behavior when viewed from outside the family context may be seen as particularly adaptive within the confines of the family. It may be disruptive to family life to change individual symptoms without considering their role in maintaining the equilibrium of the family. As clinicians we are sometimes reminded of this fact by family therapy, that is, the overemphasis on technique with insufficient attention to method. We in no way mean to detract from the personal qualities of compassion, sensitivity, introspection, empathy, warmth, and integrity that we feel are *sine non qua* for anyone working in this field. We assume, of course, a high level of professional integrity and personal maturity.

There are some dangers with methods. We acknowledge Buchler's (1961) warning against "methodolatry"—the militant and dogmatic exclusivity of one method or set of methods over other approaches. There is always the danger that methods may be used rigidly, indiscriminately, and inappropriately. To guard against such abuse we maintain that the best corrective is *technique!* Both method and technique are needed and each serves as a valuable corrective to the other.

In general we agree with Strupp (1976) in his conclusions regarding current themes in psychotherapy research:

> Modern psychotherapy is not, and can never be, the blind application of a set of techniques, and neither is it the unfettered, untutored influence of a charismatic mentor. It is a unique blending of personal qualities and technical skills that enables the psychotherapist to influence a patient's feelings, cognitions, or lifestyle for therapeutic purposes. Psychotherapy will perhaps always remain a clinical art, but at its best, it is an art in the hands of a highly skilled expert. (p. 219)

It is this emphasis on technique which makes therapy an art. It is the emphasis on method which will make family therapy a science. More adaptive families may merely substitute symptoms in a new family member to replace those taken away by therapy. In either case, the message is clear: It is important to have family therapy methods that do not overlap those used in other forms of therapy or that are dependent on the individual styles of the therapist.

Therapeutic methods can be classified according to four levels of complexity: (1) nonverbal approaches, dealing with physical arrangement in the home, like who sleeps with whom, where, and when; schedules for mealtimes and attendance to meals; nature of interactions before and after sleep and at mealtimes; distribution of labor and responsibilities (chores, routines about cleaning, bedmaking, meals, travel, etc.; (2) verbal-linear methods, which would consist of gradual training and graduated sequences of lessons, as discussed in Section III; (3) verbal-paradoxical methods, which will be considered in Section II; together with (4) symbolic-metaphorical methods. The latter two types of methods are usually more applicable at the beginning stages of family therapy, while verbal-linear and nonverbal methods are more applicable to secondary stages of therapy, after the initial crisis or the referring symptom have been successfully dealt with and brought under control.

Linear-Circular

Basic to our discussion is the linear-circular distinction. Linear methods generally are characterized by a gradualness that is probably appropriate when working with individuals and groups, but which does not seem to work with families. Given the greater capacity of the family to resist change and maintain sameness, the methods of family therapy must necessarily be of greater intensity than those used with individuals. With families a certain degree of shock or suddenness is useful, essentially to surprise the family. The shock functions to shake up its existing structure. Often a crisis is created which cannot be effectively handled by the previous way of doing things and requires it to try something new. Without this shock, the family may leave things well enough alone, but the shock gives an advantage to consider reorganizing a way of doing things. This crisis induction in the service of therapy has been advocated by several family therapists. The general strategy of blocking previous responses, thus requiring new approaches to problems, may be seen to underlie several of the methods presented here.

Not only must the therapist's comments or reactions to the family be fairly sudden, they must also be fairly unexpected in order to precipitate change. Many comments and interpretations that may be appropriate to individual therapy will appear irrelevant in family therapy, due to their obviousness. If two or three people fight, to say "You seem to be quite angry with each other" would not only be superfluous, but downright inappropriate. Furthermore, it would provoke a negative reaction to treatment on the part of the family members, who may be expected to ask themselves "What is this person telling us that we don't already know? We came here to hear something new." If the therapist can not tell the family something that the preacher, the neighbors, or their friends and relatives have not already told them, he or she will have a difficult time justifying the fee.* It is imperative, therefore, that the family therapist consider that his or her reactions to the family not only have to be fairly sudden, they have to be rather unexpected to obtain the result that she or he wants—change. Had the expected worked, the family would not now be in the office.

In searching for a novel effect, one that has not been tried and found wanting already, the family therapist should bear in mind that he or she may not only say something new, but may also *do* something new. Both modes of interaction may be usefully applied to the family and both will be treated in their own respective sections in this book. Saying and doing may also be used interactively to produce a novel effect. For example, the by now quite familiar lines of the family drama may be recited while the family is doing something quite different than the ordinary; or the lines may be placed on cue cards and held up rather than spoken. This latter intervention tends to emphasize quite dramatically the limited and repetitive nature of the interaction and leaves the family primed to say something new. More generally, doing or saying something familiar in a new context will create novelty and may bring change (Haley, 1963). And the change need not be large. The feedback systems of the family may amplify an initially small change until they create major changes in the family (Weakland, 1976).

---

*We should not overlook the fact that what is obvious to us as therapists may be unexpected to our families. They may not have a support system to give them the obvious advice, or they may have been given quite unusual advice. In any case, it is advisable to obtain a history of what advice they have been given and how they have tried to implement it to solve their problems before coming to us.

Status quo vs. change. The major dimension which is relevant to family therapy is that if the intervention is not appropriate, the family either will remain the same or will get worse. Therefore, it is important for the family therapist to think and act in ways which are designed to bring the desired goal of change for the better, *if this is what the family wants.* Clearly, some families do want change for the better. Therefore, for some families, change has to be achieved in the identified patient and not in terms of changes in the whole family system. Consequently, change for the better has to be a family goal, explicitly stated from the very beginning.

The Development of Specific New Methods for Family Therapy

The last ten years, with the great increment in the use and implementation of family therapy, have seen the creation of completely new methods which were not available to therapists previously. The methods presented here are recent and also specific to family therapy. In reviewing the possible methods available for family therapy, we have relied on a variety of disparate sources, scattered references, and fragmentary reports. How could we decide among what seem to be major and minor methods? This clearly was a matter of predilection on the authors' side as well as their own experience with the various methods. Of course, we attempted to choose those that seem to be more commonly used by most family therapists in practice. What may seem to be minor promising methods now may be the major methods of tomorrow. Nonetheless, our decisions were based on the presence of more than one source of any particular method.

CONCLUSION

In this introductory chapter, we have attempted to emphasize the importance of method, because the field of family therapy is replete with techniques. We would like trainees to learn methods from this book and techniques from the many other sources already available.

2

Family Systems

*Networks of
Relationships*

Problems in a family are an interpersonal phenomenon. The behavior of each person in the family directly affects the behavior of every other member. Therefore, to assess the family and select appropriate methods to intervene, a therapist needs to conceptualize the family system, be aware of the functional and nonfunctional aspects of the family, and view the family behavior in terms of its life cycle. This chapter explores those three aspects of the family.

THE FAMILY AS A SYSTEM

The process of family therapy should be guided by the therapist's conceptual thinking. The therapist needs a theoretical conception to guide his or her methodology. This type of conceptualization does not decrease the intuitive or artistic component of the therapist's contribution; however, a set of concepts functions as a cognitive map of the family's behavior and helps the therapist understand it. With such a conceptualization therapists are more likely to understand the chaos in a family's behavior and are more likely to develop diagnostic ideas about what is occurring. Such diagnostic ideas serve as guides for the therapist's methods. Freeman (1981) advocates having a broad conceptual map which helps therapists perceive the widest range of behaviors and suggests that systems concepts provide such an understanding. There have been numerous conceptualizations of human behavior. The mental health field has been predominantly influenced by theories of individual development and intrapsychic functioning. However, the family therapy field has come to embrace systems thinking and conceive of the family as a system.

Hoffman (1981) noted that family therapy is based on new assumptions about human behavior and human interaction. In terms of viewing the family as a system, Hoffman notes that there have emerged two identifiable streams of thought in family therapy. Devotees of the cybernetic model regard the family as a homeostatic system. They stress the notion that a symptomatic behavior has an equilibrium-maintaining function. The second line of thought derives from the work of theorists such as Paul Dell who has devised an "evolutionary" model based on early 1970s work from the natural sciences. This model views families not as equilibrium-maintenance systems but as evolving, changing, and transforming. Hoffman (1981) identifies circularity as the unifying notion of this new epistemology. This is a striking break from the linear cause and effect concepts of medical and psychodynamic models of mental illness. These models have traditionally seen mental illness as having a cause based on an anomaly of either genetic, biochemical, or intrapsychic origin. The symptomatic person was the focus of diagnosis and treatment. Instead of the linear model, the systems approach is circular. The communications and behavior of the symptomatic person affects and is affected by the members of the system in a part of what Hoffman calls a "recursive dance."

SYSTEMS THEORY AND THE FAMILY

A major contribution of general systems theory to family therapy has been the idea of understanding the individual in relation to his family system and to understand the family in relation to the community. It is important to understand how each subsystem interconnects and influences each larger system. It is equally important to acknowledge that the larger system interconnects and influences each of the subsystems.

According to French's (1977) definition of a system, the family is composed of a set of elements and a set of rules that determine the relationships among the elements and function in a way that makes the whole greater than the sum of its parts. In addition, structuralism's problem-solving power can be brought to bear on family problems because the family, like the formal structure, is characterized by: (1) wholeness, in that the whole is greater than the sum of its parts; (2) transformation, since it remains stable although individuals within it are continually changing according to the process defined by the family rules; and (3) self-regulation, since it maintains order during change.

The family can be seen as an open system that maintains a relatively constant state despite the fact of continuous flow of energy and material through the system. It maintains the constant state by maintaining communication from consequences to decision points, while a hierarchical feedback loop makes the system stable.

Freeman (1981) notes that a primary advantage of general systems theory is that "it provides a theoretical framework that is both broad enough and precise enough to bring together specific behavioral theories to conceptualize reality as a unified whole" (p. 31).

Allport (1968) defines a system as "a complex of elements in mutual interaction" (p. 344). The major concepts which expand this definition involve boundary, feedback, matter-energy, steady-state, progressive differentiation, and equifinality. Freeman discusses these major systems concepts.

Boundary. A system needs to have boundary structure, maintaining functions and developing processes. The boundary separates the system from the other elements of the environment making it a "distinguishable entity." This notion is useful in assessing family functioning as it allows the therapist to conceptually analyze particular systems one at a time, as they interact with the family as a system.

Freeman indicates how the boundary notion applies to practice. First, the therapist must note significant members of the family and their structural positions within the family's boundaries. This analysis includes consideration of the hierarchy within the family: norms, values, and rule patterns that guide intrafamilial and extrafamilial behavior; and how information is processed between family members and the external system. Second, the therapist needs to assess the structural, functional, and developmental components which comprise the family system at a particular developmental point in time. Finally, one needs to consider the degree of openness of the family boundaries: boundary flexibility, filtering devices for screening out and censoring information, the process of assigning family members the task of acquiring and encoding new information, and devices for maintaining the system's differentiation. Assessment of family boundary openness has important implications for the family's present competence as well as for its growth potential.

Feedback. "Exchanging of energy within and between systems boundaries . . . those processes which are responsible for receiving, interpreting, and transmitting information within the system boundary and its environment" (p. 38). The feedback system enables the family members to interact with each other and with the environment in an attempt to maintain a balance between internal needs and external demands. It does this by correcting errors, encoding environmental stimuli, and limiting input to what is helpful and useful to the system.

A system maintains itself via the use of feedback loops—mechanisms of information processing that allow the system to interact with the environment and then assimilate the results of this interaction to allow for correction of the organism's course of action.

To do this the system must have structures of communication, regulation of critical parameters, and change of the reference points from which the feedback loops operate. French claims that the organism uses these structures for three basic functions (1977):

1. *Type I Processes* (homeostasis or assimilation). These functions are involved in maintenance of the constant state of the organism (an open system) as it interacts with the environment in terms of a fixed set of reference points. These processes occur rapidly and with facility and therefore constitute the strategies of choice in a problem situation. If unsuccessful, Type II processes are tried.
2. *Type II Processes* (accommodation). These processes involve shifts in the fundamental reference structure with respect to which, the organism maintains its homeostatic balance. Type II processes are slow and laborious and thus should be considered only after all Type I changes have been considered.
3. *Adaptation* (This is the result of Type I and II processes). The family belief structure gives reference points regarding which corrective decisions to make. The family rules reflect the content of the belief as well as the criteria for changing the rules and the means for correcting deviation from the appropriate behavior. "Correction of these deviations with respect to constant reference points is homeostasis (Type I Process). A shift in the reference points, with respect to which homeostasis occurs, is accommodation (Type II Process). The end result of the two processes is adaptation" (French, p. 26). Freeman believes the therapist should consider the following in assessing feedback in the family communication pattern: (1) how family members communicate with each other; (2) the differences between each individual's understanding of the meassage; (3) the effect each person's feelings have on comprehension of the message; and (4) new methods of interfamilial and extrafamilial communication that avoid old dysfunctional patterns.

Matter-energy. This concept is useful in organizing the notions of what constitutes a family system and how it compromises a nonrandom whole. The members of the family system are the family system's "matter" and the feedback network is the "energy" which compels action. The interactional process of information flow is the device by which an exchange of energy occurs between matter (people) to result in "work," that activity which aids the system in accomplishing its goals.

Freeman contends that growth and development primarily are achieved via the exchange of energy from system to system (1981). The course of development is skewed when natural matter-energy exchanges are blocked by such events as overly rigid or loose boundaries when new information input is blocked out of a family's fear of upsetting homeostasis. The role of the practitioner, then, is one of providing new energy sources to facilitate change.

Steady State. The system works within a process of "steady state" to ensure that the openness, exchange of energy, and changes that occur are capable of being endured by the system. Steady state represents the simultaneous operation of several internal processes that combine to allow the system to change and develop over time while maintaining a degree of internal identity. Both the processes of homeostasis and morphogenesis are in operation. The homeostatic processes are directed at maintaining a stable balance while the morphogenetic processes aim toward growth and development. Thus, when the balance tips slightly toward morphogenesis, the system grows and develops in a tolerable fashion.

Freeman describes Rapaport's notion that the system attempts to achieve an acceptable homeostatic range within the steady state via the division of labor. When division of labor is rigid, it leads to regressive behavior in individual subsystems.

The therapist needs to determine how the family maintains a working balance. This is often accomplished via a multitude of equilibrium points, some of which are stable and some of which are unstable. The therapist needs to discern how individual family members operate within these components in their attempts to resist change, thrive on change, or mediate for an increased level of homeostasis. By supporting or challenging various family members, the therapist then effects change of the system.

Progressive Differentiation. "A universal characteristic of living systems is their tendency toward increasing complexity" (Freeman, 1981, p. 45). Progressive differentiation takes place in an evolutionary fashion as the system interacts over time with its environment. This energy exchange leads the system to expand its internal and external structural and functional relationships. The system enlarges its repertoire of feedback mechanisms, its division of labor, and the components within the system. A recognizable system emerges from an "amorphous mass" as the process of progressive differentiation occurs. Progressive differentiation explains the characteristic development sequences of complex systems.

This component of the family as a system stresses the need to view the family at a developmental point in time. One is then able to make some assessment of possible present areas of stress and some prediction as to what might be future stresses. Thus, intervention introduces a cognitive element whereby families can be alerted to impending change and view it as a part of a natural flow of events.

Equifinality. This process illustrates the goal-seeking tendencies of the organism. By equifinality we note that an open system is not "predetermined" by the initial state. Instead, the final state will be determined by the elements of the system itself which is goal directed. This principle directs us to attend to the ongoing, dynamic, interactional processes of the system rather than to the components of the initial state alone. Thus, we have a concept that intertwines past, present, and future behavior into a meaningful whole.

Commoner (1971) has summarized the notions of general systems theory into four useful rules. French (1977) has added the paraphrases which include a clinical application:

1. Everything is connected to everything else. (Everyone in a family is important.)
2. Everything has to go somewhere. (Unresolved tensions will always be expressed somewhere at some time even if in a disguised form.)
3. Nature knows best. (The family and each of its members has its own internal wisdom, with reasons for persistent patterns that need to be understood before change can be effected.)
4. There is no free lunch. (A trade-off of one problem for another is not a solution, just an inefficient delay tactic that may yield future unwanted complications.)

In applying these notions of systems theory to understanding families as systems, it is crucial to realize that the family's belief structure is the reference system from which family homeostasis is maintained. If this structure itself is ill-defined, then Type II problems will occur; if the belief structure of roles, rules, and communication patterns is clear, but family members cannot follow them, then Type I probems will occur.

It is important to have a definition of what a system is and a description of the structural, functional, and developmental aspects of systems behavior. The family can be viewed as a structural, functional, and developmental unit.

STRUCTURE OF THE FAMILY

Structure of the family is defined in terms of the family's subsystems, supra-systems, roles, norms, and values. The structure of the nuclear family system can be divided into four basic subsystems, each with its own boundaries, needs, and expectations: the individual, husband-wife, sibling, and parent-child. Freeman illustrates how the variety of intrafamilial and extrafamilial systems interact and interface with each other.

In order to operate effectively in daily living, families have to organize themselves in terms of a network of roles that is dependent upon the subsystem organization. Role assignment is closely intertwined with value judgments about who should do things and how they should be done. The role network can be divided into two types of roles and three levels of roles. Role assignment is either ascribed via the intrinsic characteristics of age and/or sex of the person (i.e., father, mother, daughter roles) or roles can be acquired due to the individual's social status or personal characteristics (scapegoat, leader). Freeman further divides the role network into three levels: individual roles, performed by an individual; subsystem roles, performed by a subsystem; and family roles, performed by the whole family as it interacts with the larger environment.

In addition, a system of norms and values develops as a part of the family system structure. These norms and values derive out of a blending and com-promising of the individual marital partners' previous experiences, particularly those with their own families of origin. These norms and values become the basis for a new set of principles. Societal values, family values, and individual values all operate to define the behavior in a family.

Function of the Family

There are two crucial aspects of family functioning. First, there are the functional responsibilities assigned to the family by the environment, that is, meeting basic needs for survival, education, and upbringing of children; the creation of a psycho-bio social environment for growth; social control of its members; and the nurturance of emotional bonds to enhance emotional growth. Second, there are the behavioral phenomena that occur within the family that move it into action. Family functioning will be discussed more thoroughly later in this chapter.

Development of the Family

The family experiences significant developmental stages in addition to the individual's stages of development, and if these two stages are in synchrony in terms of needs and issues, a system of mutual support can emerge. When the process of change is gradual and attention is given to preparation for life stresses, development proceeds smoothly. However, when attentions are diverted elsewhere, family dysfunction emerges. The stages of family development will be covered later in the chapter.

The Family as an Emotional System

Freeman (1981) discusses a variety of behavioral phenomena or processes that are pertinent to the family's functioning as an emotional system.

Loyalty. "Loyalty is the emotional commitment a person has to another or a group" (p. 60). The child from birth develops an identity intertwined with the family and its history. Reinforcers for family loyalty include freedom to exhibit behaviors not permitted outside the family, family stories, and relationships with family members. Loyalty issues are centered in two areas. First, the family loyalty may be seen as on a continuum from too restrictive and limiting to too loose and lacking in cohesiveness. Second, individual family members must find a balance between their own needs and the collective family needs without feeling they are breaching family loyalty. This is often a major issue of therapy.

Alliances. Subsystems in the family develop into alliances which may or may not be functionally adaptive. In the adaptive range, alliances facilitate communication and promote feelings of acceptance and belonging. Alliances become maladaptive when they involve collusions, coalitions, and/or triangulation of one or more parties.

Fantasies, Distortions, and Secrets. As the family is an emotional system a good proportion of the interactions which occur are centered around emotional issues. The more powerful these issues are, the more likely it is that distortions or fantasies will develop. Falsifications lead to confusion and alienation among family members because relationships are no longer seen as based in reality. True empathy is blocked as conceptions of each other get further and further from reality.

Secrets in the family system lead to conspiracies which are laden with power. A conspiracy to maintain a family secret is inherently powerful because the conspirators are then able to decide who and what is open for discussion in the family. A therapist who is drawn into a family secret becomes an agent of the power struggle and a part of the system.

Legends. Legends are a part of the individual's self-image and often evolve from the special circumstances of a child's birth into the family system. A child named after a deceased grandparent may be given expectations to become what the grandparent was. A person is shaped by the legend that is attached to him or her and his or her role assignment in the family.

Unpaid Dues and Ghosts. "Unfinished business" develops when a person decides that a debt is owed to someone in the family (usually a parent) and that person dies before the debtor is able to resolve the issue. This debt is then worked out through other members of the family's emotional system, often into the next generation.

Communication. The family as an emotional system survives and continues by the family's pattern of communication. Various family members are chosen to interpret communication from extrafamilial sources and relay it to the family. Nonverbal communication, subtle styles of speaking, and choices of phrasing serve to establish and strengthen family identity and isolate the family from the influence of others.

Differentiation of Self. Differentiation is seen as a person's ability to define himself as a separate being. An emotionally differentiated person is one who is characterized as "able to define who he is, what he wants, what he thinks, what his goals are, and what he is prepared to work on (and not work on), in a way that is minimally influenced by others" (p. 69). Freeman relies heavily on the work of Bowen (1966) for these notions. The process of differentiation begins at birth, a time when the infant is functionally indistinguishable from his or her parents. It is a never-ending process. In a family environment characterized by support, security, and consistency, a child can move toward a separation of self from the family ego mass. The process of differentiation involves conflict with the family at times, as the child must strive to be different, say "no," and perhaps do and say things with which the parents disagree.

In a developmental framework, Freeman notes two important periods in a child's process of differentiation occurring between the ages of two-and-a-half e and between the ages of thirteen to fifteen. The process of separation from the family ego mass is most pronounced during these times and a family that does not understand a child's need to be different will often perceive the child as a "problem" during these times.

During the course of life a person exists along a continuum of differentiation that is marked by three positions: differentiated, reactive, and undifferentiated. The differentiated person has a clear sense of self and is only minimally concerned with obtaining the approval of others. A reactive person functions in reaction to the demands and expectations of a significant other and is described as a pseudoself. The undifferentiated individual does not function separate from the significant other. All or most of his or her energy is invested in emulating, supporting, or seeking the approval of the significant other.

When anxiety escalates in a family system, one of the most common means of diffusing the tension is via the emotional triangle. That is, two people focus attention on a third person and that shift in attention reduces the tension. Triangles stabilize the system and reduce anxiety by maintaining the status quo. Triangling third parties also prevents further differentiation as the focus shifts from the self to the triangled person or object.

When differentiation is low, the thinking/feeling balance shifts toward feeling. That is, a person's objective (thinking) evaluation of a situation is deferred for an emotional response instead. With feelings predominating as a mode of understanding, there is a greater chance for distortion and fantasy to occur. The therapist's intervention into the system promotes the individuals to use their rational processes in dealing with family conflict.

When two persons with low levels of differentiation interact, they are likely to turn to each other for support. Often one person assumes the role of the inadequate one. In such a situation a cycle of overfunction/underfunction reciprocity is initiated where the adequacy of one person is balanced by the inadequacy of the other. These roles are intertwined and interdependent. If one person wants to change, the other will have to change as well.

Stress. French (1977) views symptomology as emanating from a family's unhealthy response to stress where stress is defined as ". . . anything that moves the organism away from homeostasis for a time and with sufficient force to prohibit the organism from reestablishing balance easily" (p. 28). An adaptive response to stress involves an organism (the family) responding without losing its sense of balance within the normal homeostatic process.

Mild or transient stress can actually promote the growth of the organism by leading to an increased ability to adapt and grow. Stress that is severe or extended requires an inordinate amount of the family's energy and may be irreversible, so that the family is never able to regain its balance. Often a family system's reaction to stress involves promoting symptomology in a child through balance bargains.

The family, as a system, is involved in simultaneously maintaining balance while minimizing energy expenditure. When a family is pushed beyond its adaptive limits by an unavoidable stress, it can respond by ignoring the stress (and facing destruction), or it can use vast amounts of energy to directly confront the stress. Third, it can strike a "balance bargain" which French defines as when "a maneuver experienced as stressful is either neutralized or experienced as useful or even essential" (p. 30). The difficulty with the "balance bargain" technique is that it is not a reversible process; the family cannot return to its original state. The consequence is that the family ends up with reduced capacities to handle future stress situations.

Thus, a family that scapegoats a particular child, rather than confront the marital discord directly, does in fact reduce the ostensible stress level. The symptomatic child, however, then becomes an intrinsic part of the family structure and future negotiations of the family take place with this added handicap and the concomitant reduction of adaptability.

French divides the symptoms that result from interactions with stress as either syntonic or dystonic. "Dystonic symptoms push the family apart and are a drain on the family's energies" (p. 33). "Syntonic symptoms pull the family together and are involved in the family structure through balance bargains." Syntonic symptoms are often not seen as symptoms by the family itself and may not become dystonic unless an outside agency (i.e., school) presents a case for looking at the behavior. By definition dystonic symptoms are regarded by the family as interfering with family functioning and the family will often declare a need to have these symptoms removed. Therapy, then, is seen as a way to clarify the connection between the two types of symptoms and transfer dystonic symptoms into syntonic.

FAMILY FUNCTIONING

French (1977) explained the operation of the family in systems terms and identified four important dimensions of family functioning. The first is anxiety. The presence of anxiety is not necessarily unhealthy but is a measure of stress in the family and indicates some need for transformation. The second dimension is the capacity for change. The family may need to change its reference points or rules and accommodate itself to new situations. The third dimension is the symptom-carrier role, which refers to the identification of a specific person as the problem; this identification may vary from one family member to another. The fourth dimension is power, which basically consists of a determination of who controls the assignment and operation of the first three dimensions. A powerful person in the family is the one who decides who gets anxious, who must change, and who will be defined as the problem. By using these four dimensions, one can get an impression of the family's healthy functioning.

Schulman (1979) describes the family system as a link in the chain between the individual and the larger society. Therefore, the family's role is that of a transmitter of societal messages and a negotiator and a cultivating agent between the individual and the society. As in all systems, the family is governed by two phenomena which are essential for its survival. The family system has to have enough stability, order, and predictability so that it can operate seperately from yet interdependently with the larger system or society. Therefore, families are described as having their own organization, distribution of power, and sets of rules in order to function. There are discernable boundaries that separate the family from the outside world. The second phenomena, and of equal importance, are the dynamic movements from the inside to the outside and from the outside toward the inside. This leads to change and growth. There must be constant communication transactions between both the individual and the family and the outside society.

According to David (1978) who presented a cross-cultural consideration of family health, effective problem solving is very important for healthy families. He suggested a definition of family health as "a family unit (whatever its concept in any given society) effectively coping with cultural-environmental, psychosocial, and socioeconomic stresses throughout the diverse phases of the family-life cycle" (p. 329). Healthy family functioning is based on the awareness of necessary choices as well as the recognition of alternatives and the degree to which the choices are based on realistic appraisals of the cost and consequences.

Classification of Family Functioning

Numerous classification systems have been proposed in an attempt to differentiate among the characteristics of various levels of family functioning. However, classifications of dysfunctional families have been typically based on the psychiatric diagnosis of one family member. This identified patient has been referred to the mental health or law enforcement agencies and the family has been labeled as a result. Such classifications based on psychiatric diagnosis of an identified patient fail to describe the characteristics of the families of origin. However, there are several classification models that do examine family characteristics.

Kantor and Lehr (1975) propose a model for understanding and classifying families based on a systems approach and their clinical observations. They emphasize that much of what characterizes a family involves the interaction between individuals and subsystems within the family, as well as the family and the social environment. Families regulate space, time, and energy in their striving for affect, power, and meaning. Families are classified as random, closed, or open according to how family members and the family as a system attempt to obtain their goals.

The random family uses dispersed space, irregular time, and has widely fluctuating energy. Its goal appears to be free expression, and it seeks to be original in its experiences. Individual choices are important, and power is dispersed laterally in terms of decision making. A closed family uses regular time, fixed space, and steady energy. Its structure of interactions is more stable, and staying in control is of importance. The power in this family is vertically organized with clearly established rules. An open family has an evolving structure with moveable space, variable time, and flexible energy. The family creates a dynamic system which can adapt to the needs of the individual as well as the family system. The goal is to share and be affectionate with each other. Power is handled laterally when appropriate and parents persuade rather than coerce.

The random family type finds meaning in being highly individualistic. The closed family believes reasoning, clarity, and precision are meaningful. The open family places high value on reasoning, relevance, affinity, and tolerance.

Beavers (1977) categorized families into three general groups according to a continuum of functioning: healthy, adequate (mid-range functioning), and dysfunctioning. He concentrated on the interaction of the family and the way its members handled both space and time. He felt that the oppositional-affiliative dimension is a critical dimension in families. One needs to consider whether the members look at each other as threats, being friends or foes. These feelings about family members are based on assumptions about human nature and about the nature of reality as relative or absolute. Healthy families seem able to handle the relative truth and still have somewhat arbitrary unbreakable rules. They also operate on ideas of multiple, circular, and relative causation. Beavers admits that change plays a role in family functioning, and many events beyond the family's control benefit or harm the family's situation.

The problematic family struggles for coherence, the adequate family for control, and the healthy family for intimacy. This forms a hierarchy of family needs. As a family improves its functioning, the members are able to move up this hierarchy and how they strive to improve together. The healthy family is affirmative in its attitudes and shows respect for the view of other family members. There is a firm parental coalition; however, they show openness as well as directness. Flexibility is demonstrated in the understanding of motivations and needs, and there is spontaneity in the interaction as members take initiative in showing unique, individual qualities. Healthy families use clear communication without excessive concern for clarity. Each family member is seen as capable of contributing, and the family shares values which allow separation, loss, and change to be handled. The family can negotiate differences and its members have respect for biological drives, expressions of intimacy, anger, and sexual feelings.

The adequate family shows considerable pain, and its interactional skills are often limited. There is a lack of spontaneity and frequent oppositional orientations with some strained parental coalitions. Communication may suffer from some confusion and there may be a mistrusting of feelings. The family can be energetic and purposeful but there is a predictable structure with the parents taking pride in trying to raise their family well. There is some pain in growth and the family has difficulty with separation and loss. As a result they try to cling to old relationships. Beavers suggests that the parents in such a family may have been raised in a family that had difficulties and are determined to do things better for their children.

The dysfunctional family is characterized by repetitive interaction, and the family members tend to form an undifferentiated cluster having little vital interaction with the outside world and allowing very little change in their own family. High hostility levels are frequent. There may be rather incongruous beliefs and the family often has difficulty coping with change, separation, and loss.

Fisher (1977) conducted a review of twenty years of literature about family classification. He emphasized that his report dealt with classification and not diagnosis; that there was not a distinction between normalcy and pathology. He tried to integrate the schemes according to five criteria: (1) styles of adaptation (expressive, repressive, defensive, paranoid, anxious, hysterical); (2) the developmental family stage, according to the major crises in the life cycle (marriage, child bearing, school age, empty nest); (3) initial problem or diagnosis of the identified patient; (4) family theme or dimension (uncontrolled, chaotic, or disintegrated families, rigid versus flexible or families with versus families without rules); (5) types of marital relationships (based on the dynamics of individual spouses, patterns of power and conflict within the marriage, and normal marital relationships). His integration of the literature led to six major family subtypes: constricted, internalized, objective-focused, impulsive, childlike, and chaotic.

The constricted family types were characterized by excessive restriction of a major aspect of emotional life such as the expression of anger or negative effect. A passive, depressed child or young adult was often the identified patient. There may be a concerted effort within the family to protect weak family members or the family relationships, and there may be adults with problems of low self-esteem or previous emotional difficulties.

The internalized families were inwardly focused and tended to view the world with fear, pessimism, hostility, and threat. These families were more isolated and enmeshed with well-defined role structure and strongly held values.

The object-focused families were characterized by an overemphasis on the children, outside community, or the self. The children may serve as a link between the spouses, maintaining their relationship. The externally focused subgroup turned outside the family for areas of interest and sources of support while the members of the self-focused subgroup would stay together to fulfill personal needs, but the emphasis was in favor of self as opposed to family issues. Family cohesiveness and closeness were low and the people were used for personal purposes which often resulted in explosions of anger and hostility when their needs were not met.

The impulsive family types were most frequently characterized by a troublesome adolescent who displaced his or her parent-based anger onto the community and acted in an inappropriate social manner. The adolescent may be an expressor for the adults' aggressive antisocial feelings.

The childlike family types were often young families with individuals who had not thoroughly separated from their families of origin. These individuals were dependent and needed to rely on their parents or other sources for decision making and even parenting of their own children.

The chaotic family type was described as more rare and was composed of poorly structured and decompensating families where chronic psychosis and deliquency were rampant. There were few rules for anything. Reliability of family members was quite low and the family members were constantly leaving or re-entering the family.

In an attempt to conceptualize healthy family systems, Barnhill (1979) reviewed the diverse theories of health and pathology in family functioning. From a comprehensive review he isolated eight basic dimensions of family mental health and pathology. Each of the eight dimensions is placed on a continuum such as individuation versus enmeshment. The eight dimensions of family functioning were grouped into four basic themes.

The first theme, identity processes, involves individuation versus enmeshment and mutuality versus isolation. At one end of the continuum individuation refers to a firm sense of autonomy, personal responsibility, identity, and boundaries of the individual. In contrast, enmeshment refers to a poorly delineated boundary of self with others in the system. Mutuality includes the joining, intimacy, and emotional closeness between individuals with clearly defined identities, while isolation refers to a disengagement from other members. Barnhill concludes that the first two dimensions are closely linked in an identity process.

A second basic family theme involves change and has two dimensions: flexibility versus rigidity and stability versus disorganization. Flexibility refers to the process of change and involves the capacity to adjust and be resilient in response to varied conditions. At the other end of the continuum, rigidity refers to the lack of flexibility or inappropriate and unsuccessful responses to varying situations. Stability involves consistency, security, and responsibility in family interactions, while disorganization involves a lack of these characteristics, and results in an atmosphere without predictability or clear responsibility.

A third area of basic themes involves information processing. The two dimensions that Barnhill categorized involve clear versus unclear or distorted perceptions and clear versus unclear or distorted communication. Clear perception involves a clear joint perception and conceptual validation of shared events, while lack of clear perception involves confusing or vague perceptions or perceptions that are distorted. Clear communication would involve a successful exchange of information between individuals that involves checking out the meaning and intention of the communication. In contrast, vague or confusing exchanges of information or paradoxical communication would lead to distortion.

The fourth basic family theme is called role structuring and includes the last two dimensions of healthy family functioning: role reciprocity versus unclear roles or role conflict, and clear versus diffuse or breached generational boundaries. Clear generational boundaries involves role reciprocity among family members despite differences between parent and child relationships. The individuals in each generation are allied more closely with their own generation. Diffused or breached generational boundaries refers to a lack of clarity between generational boundaries; alliances therefore may occur that blur the differences between the generations.

THE FAMILY LIFE CYCLE

The family life cycle is a concept that has become increasingly accepted in family therapy. Conceptualizing a family over a course of development places symptoms or dysfunctions in relation to normal functioning over the family's life span. A family can be observed in terms of the past patterns, the behaviors that are presently being maintained, and the projection to the future toward which they are moving. Carter and McGoldrick (1980) have emphasized that this perspective is crucial to understanding the problems that people develop as they move through life together. Haley (1973) described family stress as highest at transition points from one family stage to another and suggests that symptoms are more likely to occur when there is a disruption in the family life cycle. He believes that the symptoms indicate that the family is stuck and having difficulty moving through the transition into the next stage, and therefore therapeutic aids are used to help move the family in its normal developmental process. Other writers have also emphasized the importance of the family life cycle. Solomon (1973) described the tasks for the family at each of five stages and suggested that these can serve as a diagnostic base to understand the family and prepare a treatment plan. Hill (1970) emphasized a three-generation concept of the family life cycle which views the married children as the "lineage bridge" between the older and younger generations.

Carter and McGoldrick (1980) present a model of the normal family which includes a vertical and horizontal axis. The vertical movement of the family involves the patterns of relating and functioning that are transmitted down through the generations. It involves all the issues that are passed on in the family including the attitudes, taboos, expectations, and labels. The horizontal movement of the family involves the family moving through time dealing with the transitions in the family life cycle. This model emphasizes the enormous amount of vertical stress that can be passed down through generations of the family as well as the situational stresses that occur on the family as they are moving forward through the transitional stages. This view of the family recognizes the influence of the entire emotional system of at least three generations as well as the nuclear family as a subsystem reacting to the past, present, and even anticipating future relationships. With this concept, the therapist must understand the family themes, triangles, and labels involving the family over time as well as the dimensions of the current life cycle.

Stages of the Life Cycle

McGoldrick and Carter (1982) have provided a special service to the field by outlining the predictable stages of an American middle-class family. They acknowledge that cultural issues play a role in the family life cycle and that cultural groups vary greatly in their definitions of tasks for various life-cycle stages. In their general classification of life-cycle stages they describe the central, underlying process of expanding, contracting, and realigning the relationship system in a functional way. They also suggest changes required at each transition in order to procede developmentally. An important part of this model is the description of the required second-order changes. These involve the changes in the system itself. It is important for the young adult to make the second-order shifts in the relationship status in order to accomplish the transition process.

TABLE 2-1. The Stages of the Family Life Cycle

FAMILY LIFE CYCLE STAGE	EMOTIONAL PROCESS OF TRANSITION: KEY PRINCIPLES	SECOND-ORDER CHANGES IN FAMILY STATUS REQUIRED TO PROCEED DEVELOPMENTALLY
1. Between families: The unattached young adult	Accepting parent-offspring separation	a. Differentiation of self in relation to family of origin b. Development of intimate peer relationships c. Establishment of self in work
2. The joining of families through marriage: The newly married couple	Commitment to new system	a. Formation of marital system b. Realignment of relationships with extended families and friends to include spouse
3. The family with young children	Accepting new generation of members into the system	a. Adjusting marital system to make space for child(ren) b. Taking on parenting roles c. Realignment of relationships with extended family to include parenting and grandparenting roles
4. The family with adolescents	Increasing flexibility of family boundaries to include children's independence	a. Shifting of parent-child relationships to permit adolescents to move in and out of system b. Refocus on midlife marital and career issues c. Beginning shift toward concerns for older generation
5. Launching children and moving on	Accepting a multitude of exits from and entries into the family system	a. Renegotiation of marital system as a dyad b. Development of adult-to-adult relationships between grown children and their parents

TABLE 2-1.   The Stages of the Family Life Cycle (*Continued*)

FAMILY LIFE CYCLE STAGE	EMOTIONAL PROCESS OF TRANSITION: KEY PRINCIPLES	SECOND-ORDER CHANGES IN FAMILY STATUS REQUIRED TO PROCEED DEVELOPMENTALLY
		c. Realignment of relationships to include in-laws and grandchildren
		d. Dealing with disabilities and death of parents (grandparents)
6. The family in later life	Accepting the shifting of generational roles	a. Maintaining own and/or couple functioning and interests in face of physiological decline: exploration of new familial and social role options
		b. Support for a more central role for middle generation
		c. Making room in the system for the wisdom and experience of the elderly: supporting the older generation without overfunctioning for them
		d. Dealing with loss of spouse, siblings, and other peers, and preparation for own death. Life review and integration.

McGoldrick, M. & Carter E. (1982). "The Family Life Cycle," in Walsh, Froma (Ed.), *Normal Family Processes.* New York, The Guilford Press.

The Unattached Young Adult.   This model starts with the new family life cycle at the stage of an unattached young adult who has met the primary task of coming to terms with the family of origin. The manner in which he or she has resolved the developmental tasks with his family will influence whom, when, and how he or she marries and will influence the future stages in that life cycle. A primary task at this stage is to have the young adult separate from the family of origin and formulate personal-life goals in developing as an individual before joining with another person to form a new family system. Individuals who adequately differentiate themselves from their family of origin will experience fewer vertical stressors during their new family life cycle. During this stage, each person sorts out what they take from the family of origin and what they will change for themselves and build into a new family.

Problems in this family stage focus on either the young adult or the parents not recognizing the need for the shift to a less interdependent relationship. Typical problems involve parents encouraging dependence of their young children or of the young adult remaining dependent or breaking away through a pseudo-independent cut-off from their families.

The Newly Married Couple.   Forming a marital couple is a complex and difficult transition. Marriage requires that the couple renegotiate the personal issues that were defined by their parents and possibly redefined for themselves. The couple has to deal with daily tasks such as habits of eating, sleeping, having sex, celebrating holidays, working, vacations, and disagreements. In addition, the couple needs to renegotiate the relationships with their parents, siblings, and other relatives in view of this new marriage. The family of origin experiences stress as it tries to take a new member into its membership. It is apparent that it is not just the two individuals getting married who adjust to each other, it is the joining of two complex family systems. The problems encountered in the new marriage may involve the couple cutting themselves off from the families of origin or still being too enmeshed in their own families, causing difficulties in establishing themselves as a separate couple.

A Family with Young Children.   When the couple has children they must adjust the marital system to make room for the children and take on parenting roles. The couple now become caretakers of the younger generation. The realignments in the whole family system involve new parents in their roles and new grandparents in their roles. Parents who have difficulty in this role shift may struggle with each other regarding the responsibility of behaving as parents to their children. The parents may find it difficult to set limits with appropriate authority, or they may lack adequate patience to allow children to express themselves through behavior. Although problems with families at this stage are often focused on the children's behavior, therapy often is focused on helping the parents gain a view of themselves and deal with the tasks of parenting. Although this stage is focused on parents with young children, there are many phases of the family with young children. Therapists may encounter families with preschool children, those with children in early years of school, or those with children in the upper elementary grades. Children at each of these stages may present different types of problems.

A Family with Adolescents.   A family with adolescents has generally reached a stage in which the parents are approaching a midlife stage and the grandparents are in the later-life stage. That means the family has to modify the parent-child relationship to permit the adolescent to move in and out of the family system. The boundaries must be more permeable because the parents can no longer maintain complete authority. A major difficulty for families at this stage occurs because the parents continue to view the adolescents as children and keep the same expectations. The parents need to permit the adolescents freedom to develop and experiment with independence as well as provide a haven for them to be dependent when they are unable to handle things alone.

It is also important to note that adults must refocus their midlife marital and career issues. The parents may focus part of their attention on their own relationship as well as their examination of their career development. In some families there are concerns about the grandparents and additional attention is necessary to help their adjustment.

Launching Children.   This phase is noted for the number of exits and entries of family members. The exists involve the launching of grown children into education and careers and then has the entry of their new spouses and children. This period of time involves a renegotiation of relationships into adult-adult behaviors between the grown children and their parents. This also involves relationships that include the in-laws and the establishment of roles of the grandparents.

As children begin leaving home, the parents may have to renegotiate the martial system. After many years of being a family with a certain amount of energy focused on children, they once again are a dyad. Increasingly in our society, grown children are returning home. Therefore, the parents may need to readjust to having grown children back in the house. After having become a dyad, the adjustment to a parental role with adult children is a new substage with the major emphasis on the relationship of the adult to adult interaction between parents and grown children.

This is a long stage in the family life cycle and may last from the time when the children start leaving to enter college or a career to the time when the parents retire. This stage then involves the parents changing their own status and moving into a grandparent position. It also involves the type of relationship with their own parents. The older generation may become more dependent, requiring considerable caretaking responsibility. Because this is such a lengthy stage in the life cycle, families may actually pass through substages. There may be feelings of loss and depression over what is termed the empty nest, difficulties in restructuring the marital relationship or adjusting to adult children and grandparenting, or in the responsibilities to one's parents.

A Family in Later Life.   This stage in the family life cycle is an important one. At this time the parents may offer support to their grown children in the middle generation. Walsh (1980) reported that the majority of adults over sixty-five live with other family members and that over 80 percent live within an hour of at least one of their children. Therefore, most adults in their later years are still an intricate part of the family system. The older adults may need to deal with the loss of a spouse, siblings, or friends and do some preparation for their own death. This is often described as a period of life for review and integration. Although many older adults face some physiological decline, they are often active key members in the family system.

MAJOR VARIATIONS: DIVORCE
AND REMARRIAGES

Although the majority of families will go through the traditional life-cycle stages, nearly half of all American families experience divorce, and the rate of redivorce is also about 50 percent (Messinger, 1982). Therefore, divorce and remarriage need to be considered a major variation in the family life cycle. It produces a disequilibrium that is felt throughout the entire life cycle and necessitates changes in the family memberships. McGoldrick and Carter (1980) also chart shifts in this relationship status and the important emotional tasks that must be completed by the members of divorcing families in order for them to procede. Families that experience a divorce must go through one or two additional phases in the family life cycle. In the family in which the adult does not remarry, the family goes through one additional stage and can restabilize permanently as a divorced family. This involves the single parent family structure. The majority of individuals will remarry, however, and these families are required to renegotiate the phase of divorce and function as a postdivorce family before the second phase of remarriage.

Divorce. McGoldrick and Carter describe four steps in the divorce phase: the decision to divorce, planning the break-up of the system, separation, and the divorce. If the divorce is to be an effective situation for the adults and children in the family, they must cooperate to solve the problems of custody, visitation, and finances. Because the divorce affects the entire family, the extended family members need to be informed of the divorce. Kantor and Vickers (1983) describe divorce along the family life cycle. They indicate that divorce may be a progressive process in that individuals may be able to grow in self-differentiation that they were unable to in the marriage; however, in most situations, divorce is a regressive process in that it transforms the family in a way that prevents further differentiation of most system elements. They state that as formerly effective rules for regulating disturbances no longer work, conflicts become more arbitrary, and instability itself is institutionalized. Garfield (1982) writes about the mourning and its resolution for spouses who separate. He states that the separating adults experience a loss of a relationship rather than just the person. Much of the strain of the divorce involves the mourning process in the loss of that relationship. Garfield talks about the resolution of the mourning process which culminates in transforming the relationship with the ex-spouse. Huntington (1982) describes attachment loss as an issue in the divorce.

Postdivorce Family. In a postdivorce family one parent usually has custody of the children; the other parent makes up the noncustodial single parent family. The custodial single parent family needs to rebuild its own social network and function as an ongoing family. At the same time there must be recognition of the ex-spouse and parent of the children who continues to be a factor in the family. The noncustodial parent must find ways to continue to be an effective parent while remaining outside the normal parenting role.

Ahrons and Perlmutter (1982) state that the term "single-parent family" is a misnomer since both parents continue to function in parental roles. A divorce does create new households with single parents but it results in a single-parent family when only one of the parents has contact with the child. Divorce can be viewed as a process that results in a family's reorganization rather than its

TABLE 2-2.   Dislocations of the Family Life Cycle Requiring Additional Steps to Restabilize and Proceed Developmentally

PHASE	EMOTIONAL PROCESS OF TRANSITION: PREREQUISITE ATTITUDE	DEVELOPMENTAL ISSUES
DIVORCE		
1. The decision to divorce	Acceptance of inability to resolve marital tensions sufficiently to continue relationship	Acceptance of one's own part in the failure of the marriage
2. Planning the breakup of the system	Supporting viable arrangements for all parts of the system	a. Working cooperatively on problems of custody, visitation, finances b. Dealing with extended family about the divorce
3. Separation	A. Willingness to continue cooperative coparental relationship B. Work on resolution of attachment to spouse	a. Mourning loss of intact family b. Restructuring marital and parent-child relationships: adaptation to living apart c. Realignment of relationships with extended family: staying connected with spouse's extended family
4. The divorce	More work on emotional divorce: Overcoming hurt, anger, guilt, etc.	a. Mourning loss of intact family: giving up fantasies of reunion b. Retrieval of hopes, dreams, expectations from the marriage c. Staying connected with extended families
POSTDIVORCE FAMILY		
A. Single-parent family	Willingness to maintain parental contact with ex-spouse and support contact of children with ex-spouse and his or her family	a. Making flexible visitation arrangements with ex-spouse and his or her family b. Rebuilding own social network
B. Single parent (noncustodial)	Willingness to maintain parental contact with ex-spouse and support custodial parent's relationship with children	a. Finding ways to continue effective parenting relationship with children b. Rebuilding own social network

McGoldrick, M. & Carter E. (1982). "The Family Life Cycle," in Walsh Froma, (Ed.), *Normal Family Processes*. New York, The Guilford Press.

disintegration. Ahrons and Perlmutter describe the binuclear family as having two households, whether or not the households have equal importance in the child's life experience.

A Remarried Family. After a period of recovery of the loss from the first marriage relationship, the parent may become recommitted to marriage and forming a family with a new spouse. To develop effectively a remarriage family, the adults need to work through and openly establish a new relationship. A cooperative co-parenting relationship must be fostered with the ex-spouses, which can help the children deal with their fears and loyalties in establishing membership in two new systems. There will need to be some realignment of relationships with extended family members which will include new spouses and children. Obviously, there will still be maintenance of relationships with the family system of the ex-spouse.

Ahrons and Perlmutter (1982) describe the child as being in a binuclear family. When both parents have remarried, the child has two families with which to live. Successful development of the child depends on the relationship of the experience with four co-parents. The redefinition of the relationships in the binuclear family depends upon the interaction between the biological parents. The meaningful attachment between parents and children is dependent on the kind of relationship that develops between the parents and between step-parents and parents in the binuclear family system. "Each parent and step-parent must establish an independent relationship with the child, but the continuation of each parent-child unit requires the continued interdependence of the former spouses and step parents" (p. 39). The absence of clear boundaries can be a point of confusion and distress for both the children and the parents.

Remarried families have a major task of restructuring their boundaries and relationships. A common problem involves the "instant family" in which the parents have come together and essentially forced the blending of the families. Although the parents may be ready for this instant family, the children need a greater preparation. The most common problem is the development of the adversarial relationship between the new step-parent and the natural parent. Both individuals may feel some conflict and role strain, and if the children are caught in-between, it will be a negative factor in the children's development and the restructuring of the new family. Another problem that may occur in restructuring the family is a reversal of the hierarchy. At times this means the child who has been an important partner in the single-parent environment now takes a secondary position to the new spouse. In some families it means the new spouse has a lower position in the hierarchy than the child.

Whiteside (1983) has described a model procedure for weaving families together. During the first stage of courting in preparation for the remarriage, the adults need to resolve the issues from their first marriage and work through a period of modification while functioning as a single-parent household. A second phase involves the continued construction and consolidation that occurs after the wedding. The issues here involve cohesion and distancing rituals in that individuals coming together in a remarriage family need to become a cohesive unit and yet have individual amounts of distance. A third phase involves the established remarried family after three or four years. This family may experience the same difficulties as any other family with the addition of older children. Some families may be comfortable in the new structure that has been established and function as a stable unit. Other families may go through unhappy coalitions and experience a variety of difficulties. The birth of a child of the remarried family may be a positive force for the stability of the couple; at other times it may create difficulties in the restructuring of the family. As with any family with adolescents, the boundaries need to be more permeable. In a remarried family it is not uncommon for custody issues to arise when the child enters adolescence. A child who has been living with one parent and experiences difficulty either with the parent or at school may choose at that point to live with the other parent. This period of time requires tolerance and flexibility. It is possible that a change in custody could be a more appropriate adjustment for the needs of the adolescent, as well as for the families involved. If such a move occurs it requires changes in both households. The new custodial family must restructure to incorporate an adolescent within its boundaries, and the other family has to coalesce and deal with the loss.

CONCLUSION

The concept of the family as a system has been accepted in the field of family therapy. There are different ideas regarding the application of systems concepts to families. This chapter presented an overview of general systems theory to assist therapists in understanding how systems concepts can be applied to a family. Each therapist can select a specific theoretical approach: structural, strategic, systematic communications, or consult Haley, Minuchin, and Bowen for additional applications. Understanding family function as a system leads to diagnosis of the member interaction as well as of individual members. Examining characteristics of functional and dysfunctional families focuses additional attention on the family interaction, not the symptoms of one member. The knowledge of life stages places the family system in a time perspective. It suggests developmental tasks and helps the therapist develop hypotheses regarding why the problem is occurring. The material on the family system influences the methods of diagnosis and methods of treatment.

3

Assessment and Evaluation in Family Therapy

There has been a shift from the traditional clinical approach of assessing someone in terms of their individual pathology. A person is inseparable from the system which is the site of the pathology, and therefore assessment and diagnosis for family therapy involves the family system. Diagnosis means "to know," and understanding a problem situation can be called diagnosing. The process of diagnosing starts with observing data, forming concepts to the situation, and finally arranging the information in a particular way. All therapists have an epistemological base, and clinicians will diagnose differently according to that base. Keeney (1979) differentiated a traditional linear epistemology from an ecosystemic epistemology. Traditional linear epistemology follows the medical model and concerns itself with discrete elements in combination. An ecosystemic epistemology concentrates on the whole system, ecology, and relationships. Diagnosis based on this depends on the clinician seeing and knowing in an ecosystemic way. By bringing more people into therapy who are in the relational field of the identified patient, family therapy and diagnosis has moved more to the idea that the person within the system is a part of a relationship system.

MODELS OF DIAGNOSIS

Although most family therapists embrace systems concepts, there are various approaches to the process. Glick and Kessler (1974) outlined three approaches: one longitudinal in nature, one focusing on the family's present functioning, and another using the "here and now" within the therapy session. More recently, Levant (1983) gave an overview of three general diagnostic perspectives of dysfunctional families. The three models are: process models, structural models, and historical models. Theoretical models describe ideas about the family as an entity, while diagnostic models are especially used by therapists and are most often used with a theory of family therapy.

In order to make a diagnosis, a clinician obtains particular information in a certain way and organizes it according to the therapist's conceptual model. Levant examines three family contextual models. Family contextual models grew out of "ecosystemic epistemology" (Keeney, 1979) and are "concerned with patterns of relationship between parts within the whole system rather than with linear causal relationships" (p. 4). What causes a problem is circular and finding out about this is not as important as understanding a metaperspective on the family system.

The three types of family contextual diagnostic models build upon each other. The process models try to describe the symptom as a part of the dynamic family process. The structural models use this and add the organizational structure of the family. Historical models are the most inferential and add the generational development of the family.

The Process Models

The diagnosis which comes from a process model describes the family members' interactions in "real time" as described by Steinglass (1978). The three types of process models are: the behavioral approach, the communications and interactional approach, and the player-part model (Kantor & Lehr, 1975). The behavioral approach (Patterson & Reid, 1970) looks at the reinforcement system in the family and tries to determine what is supporting the symptom. The communications and interactional approach looks at the family's rule system in order to find the key interactional sequence (Watzlawick, Beavin, & Jackson, 1967). The player-part model is used by several different theorists to get a picture of the individual family members' roles in its interactions. There are two-, three-, and four-player models.

Marital interactions are described by the two-player model. The "over-adequate-inadequate reciprocity" (Bower, 1976) describes a situation where one partner is dominant, while the other is passive. The "distancer-pursuer" dynamic (Fogarty, 1976) describes a situation where one partner flees involvement while the other clamors for it. Similar to this is "abandonment" and "engulfment" (Karpel, 1976) and "rejection-intrusion pattern" (Napier, 1978). Cycles of conflict and emotional withdrawal leading to "emotional divorces" are described by Bower (1976).

Three roles are described in the three-player model: "persecuter," "victim," and "healer" (Ackerman, 1967). These three roles form a circular process. Bateson, Jackson, Haley, and Weakland (1956) also describe a three-player model. The healer role is replaced by someone who is distant or is another persecutor.

One four-player model grows out of Satir's (1972) belief that family members take on roles because they are not able to express their real feelings. The four generalized roles are: "blamer," "placater," "computer," and "distractor."

These roles are enduring. According to Satir "leveling" occurs when family members express what they are really feeling.

A second four-player model can be used for both functional and dysfunctional families. Kantor and Lehr (1975) have developed four parts of "mover," "opposer," "follower," and "bystander." Unlike Satir's roles, these roles can be situation specific.

The Structural Model

The structural model builds upon the process models by trying to define the family member's positions (family structure) which underly transactional patterns. Minuchin (1974) describes structure as "the invisible set of functional demands that organizes the ways in which family members interact" (p. 5). In order to arrive at a diagnosis, the therapist experientially takes on the role of family leader and observes the family's reactions and processes to him or her. Family structure is indicated by the position of family members.

Six elements are used in developing a structural map of the family. The first element is to assess the organizational structure underlying the family. The second element is concerned with the family's ability to change—their flexibility. The third element deals with the family's reactions to an individual member's change. This ranges from disengaged to enmeshed families. The role of the IP's (Identified Patient) behavior (or the symptom) is the fourth element. The fifth element is the family's "ecological context," and the sixth element is the family's developmental stage.

The characteristics of severely dysfunctional families usually have four constant features: (1) The intergenerational boundaries are not clearly defined and the boundaries around the triangular structure become rigid. Stable and unstable coalitions can form as can conflict-deterring patterns. (2) The family becomes rigidly bound. (3) Enmeshment, disengagement, or both (at different times) characterize the family. (4) The IP is part of that rigid triangular structure. Limitations to Minuchin's model are that it describes family life as being static. It is also not sufficient in its explanations of the extended family.

The Historical Model

Bowen's (1976) multigenerational model is used to represent the historical models group. This model builds on the process model and structural model by tracing several generations of a family in order to understand that family's generational structure.

Overadequate-inadequate reciprocity leads to turmoil and conflict. The triangular structures, as described in the structural model, are called the "family projection process" by Bowen. This means that the parental immaturity is transmitted to the children. The multigenerational transmission process is traced by generational maps of the clients' families-of-origin.

The three models go from the descriptive to the more inferential. The process model is more reliable, but it is also more limited in the range of formulation. The historical model has the broadest range with the most limited diagnosis. The structural model falls between the two.

For this reason, process models are best used with families where reliable diagnosis is needed for short-term work. Intermediate-term treatment is more suitable to the structural model, while long-term therapy—which would need a comprehensive diagnosis which evolves over time—would be best suited to the historical model (Levant, 1983).

DIMENSIONS OF DATA GATHERING

All families have symptoms of dysfunctionality—temporary or chronic—from time to time and possibly even a crisis. The symptom is a sign that the family is trying to get the problem under control and that a new interaction needs to be introduced to the system since the old interactions are not solving the problem. Caille (1982) suggested three conditions that need to occur prior to the family's entering therapy. First, the members of the family must agree that they have a problem; second, the problem must be beyond the capabilities of the family's ability to resolve; third, when the problem is presented to the therapist he or she must decide whether to work with this family.

The action of contacting a therapist may be complicated. The symptom and what it means to the family usually is not clear at first. The family member who calls the therapist nearly always has an explanation for the symptom and an idea of how it should be handled. Communication occurs on two separate levels (Watzlawick, Beavin & Jackson, 1967). Level one is defining the symptoms in a clear form. The second level is a personal metacommunication about the way the individual views the family and implies the relationship that the individual would like to have with the therapist. When family members start relating their positions in accord to the therapist, the implication is that a system is being formed.

So the therapist does not miss crucial information, it is important that he or she has a plan outlining what is necessary to understand in the dynamics of the family. Although therapists from different theoretical orientations may approach data gathering in a different manner, one way or another they are typically interested in similar types of information. The following outline for a family evaluation is presented as example information areas.

Current Phase of the Family Life Cycle

The family's developmental stage is easily ascertained and provides valuable information. By observing the family and asking a few questions about the developmental levels of the offspring, the therapist can ascertain in which stage the family is functioning and examine how well they are accomplishing or have accomplished the developmental tasks. Knowing the stage in the family life cycle helps the therapist to better understand the family and what difficulties are to be expected during that stage and the therapy process.

The therapist may wish to know why the family comes for treatment at the present time. Such information will help the therapist to understand how the family handles difficulties and other crises that have occurred, thus putting the situation in perspective.

The Current Problem

What is the current family problem? Each family member answers this question, with the focus being on the problem which brought the family to therapy. The therapist can get valuable information about the way in which the family interacts: who is blamed, who blames, and what role the identified patient plays in this system.

The therapist is looking to see how the symptom is defined and what function it serves (Caille, 1982). Usually the behavior of one member is described as a symptom; whether the problem behavior can be controlled is a clue as to whether the family sees the identified patient as sick or bad. An analysis of the symptom frequently proves it to be an attempt to extinguish or reduce a crisis. The symptom is maintained when the family agrees to continue cooperating in the existing family structure. The symptom provides a legitimate excuse for contacting a therapist. Family members may resist talking about the more threatening conditions for fear that they would break down the inner core of the family. The symptom is very important and the therapist will pay considerable attention to it during the initial sessions. The therapist also gains important information about the family structure by systematically mapping the symptom. This can be accomplished by examining what each person thinks about the problem including the symptom and the reaction of the family members to the behavior. The therapist may also inquire about the family members' definition of the problem generated by the symptom and explore the possible disagreements that different family members may have about the problem.

The Family Pattern

Caille (1982) comments that the circular interaction in the family's behavior pattern maintains the symptom. The solution to the problem seems to be beyond the capabilities of the family. The symptom's sequence seems unavoidable by the family members. The therapist needs facts about the interaction, including: how does it begin and end; where, when, and how often does it happen; when doesn't the symptom happen, even though it is expected; what does each family member do when this occurs? If the symptom happens continually, the questions can be asked in regard to intensity. The purpose of this is to get an idea of the circular interaction which leads to the occurrence of the symptom.

The therapist may wish to explore the background of the family problem. Such an exploration may include the composition and characteristics of the nuclear and extended family members. Some therapists will talk only about the background of this problem as it relates to earlier problems in the family, while other therapists may focus only on the present situation. Therapists who follow the historical model may use a genogram to look at the messages that are passed from the extended family through the nuclear family to the identified patient. By examining the composition and characteristics of the larger family system, the therapist may learn a great deal about the background of other family problems.

As a part of the exploration of the background the therapist can gain information about the developmental background about the husband and wife. By understanding the families of the two parents and following their courtship, marriage, and the development of their family, the therapist will have a clearer understanding of the family problem in terms of the larger family life cycle.

The therapist will examine the family relations prevailing at the time of the initial interview. These may include the relations within the extended nuclear family but also could include the family's interactions with other environmental sources. Differing amounts of information can be obtained depending upon the nature of the problem and the proposed course of treatment.

It is important to assess the intermember communication patterns and demands that family members place on each other. Having too many or too few demands can be problematic. It also could be important to find out about child care responsibilities, dependencies, discipline, money management, and sexuality, as these are all factors in the family's interaction. The family's organization, power structure, and alliances can affect the coping abilities of its members. To more fully understand the family, the therapist will seek knowledge about the unique family structure. Family alliances (both open and hidden), family history, and hierarchical construction need to be explored in order to more fully understand a family. Direct questions can be asked pertaining to the objective data of a family (i.e., births, deaths, ages). It is also important to note the subjective comments of family members while talking about this. More information about the nature of the relationships can be obtained through "organized gossip" (Caille, 1982). This occurs, for example, when one family member is asked to describe his or her opinion of the relationship between two of the other family members. By characterizing the information given by family members, more opinions and viewpoints might be accentuated. If this information does not fit, more clarification in the family will result (Caille, 1982). Added information can be found by directly observing the family and their behavior during therapy. Where do they sit and how do their interactions change when they are moved during therapy? Having an observer and a one-way mirror can be of great use for observing the total pattern of interaction.

Environmental influences are also important (Nelson, 1983). Performance in school and on the job is important to the self-esteem of family members. Having friends (or not having them) has an important influence on people. Family members cannot provide each other with all the necessary social interaction. Other factors which are important in the ways individuals identify themselves are: race, social-economic class, religion, geographic region, and ethnicity. Another environmental factor is the influence of other professionals on the family, i.e., doctors, tutors, teachers. Their influence needs to be taken into consideration.

Coping Abilities

It is also important to analyze the coping ability of the family members. Generally the therapist assumes that there is a disequilibrium between what is needed to be coped with and the coping abilities of the family (Nelson, 1983). When assessing this it is important to keep in mind the strengths and positive coping abilities of the family so that they can be utilized as a stress reducer. The needs, demands, and stresses of the family members that are to be coped with need to be looked at and considered, along with the demands that members make on each other. It is important to look at environmental, social, economic, cultural, and religious demands when analyzing what clients are coping with. How do clients deal with the needs, demands, and stresses which affect them? Each of these areas needs to be explored. When assessing a family it is important to note what strengths it has: health, intelligence, social skills, care and love for each other, relationships in and out of the family.

There are a number of stresses that people experience which are difficult for everyone, for example, adolescence, old age, health problems. Past experiences can cause guilt or rage, which can keep families from coping well on their own. Demands of one family member can constrain everyone's functioning. Not knowing how to cope is another constraint on coping abilities and can add to dysfunctional coping and family functioning. Family members may not know how to deal or cope with themselves, each other, and/or their environment.

Myths and Rules

Glick and Kessler (1974) suggest that examining the family's myths and rules will help in understanding the problem behaviors. Each family has a family theory and defends a myth about itself. The myth determines the family rules. The term "myth" is used to explain what is observed and is not affected by logical arguments. A family's myth may no longer be sufficient when there are changes in the world or new knowledge within the family. A crisis develops until a new myth is formed or the system dissolves (Caille, 1982). The information which makes up the mythical model is incomplete at first, as is the therapist's conception of it. How the family reacts to the therapist's remarks that try out ideas which fit into the mythical model, will help to better define it.

Overview of Family Dimensions

Fisher (1976) reviewed clinical assessment schemas and integrated a summary list of the most frequently used assessment criteria. The criteria were listed from four differing approaches to assessment: a single notion, a theoretical orientation, clinical lists, and empirical methods. Although the list is very large, Fisher found comparability among the criteria and outlined five general areas. Although these are simplistic categories, they summarize the major trends in the family assessment literature. The dimensions include the structural descriptors of the family, the controls and sanctions of rule reinforcement, the emotional climate of the family, the cultural and environmental stresses, and how these dimensions relate to the family's life stage. Although not related to any theoretical approach, the outline provides a general summary of important family information which would assist the therapist in understanding the family.

I. Structural Descriptors
    1. Role: complementarity, acceptance, confusion, adequacy
    2. Splits, alliances, scapegoating
    3. Boundaries: internal and external
    4. Patterns of interaction and communication: Rules and norms of relating
    5. Conflicts and patterns of resolution
    6. Family views of life, people, and the external world
II. Controls and Sanctions
    1. Power and leadership
    2. Flexibility
    3. Exercise of control
    4. Dependency-independency
    5. Differentiation-fusion
III. Emotions and Needs
    1. Methods and rules for affective expression
    2. Need satisfaction: giving and taking
    3. Relative importance of needs vs. instrumental tasks
    4. Dominant affective themes
IV. Cultural Aspects
    1. Social position
    2. Environmental stresses
    3. Cultural heritage
    4. Social and cultural views
V. Developmental Aspects: Appropriateness of Structural, Affective, and Cultural Aspects to Developmental Stage (Fisher, 1976, p. 379)

Past Treatment

The therapist will want to know the history of any previous attempts at problem solving. It is informative to understand the circumstances that led the family to seek help in the past, from whom they sought help, what assistance was rendered, and the outcomes. Such information may provide additional information about family dynamics and may assist the therapist in avoiding previous therapy traps.

If previous treatment involved individual therapy, the therapist may have to reorient the family to see the need for the whole family's participation. There is no need for the therapist to defend previous therapists or to feel superior by having been selected by the family. The comments and criticisms will provide clues to the family's goals and expectations of the therapist and the therapy.

Treatment Planning

To formulate a treatment plan, the therapist begins with the family's goals and expectations of treatment. Most families come with hopes and positive motivation, as well as some doubts and fears. Families typically come wanting to achieve short-term goals, that is, to solve the immediate problem. Other families may want confirmation of a solution they have already made. A few will come for long-term change in family functioning. The therapist should set short-term goals as well as final goals. In some approaches to therapy, these goals are discussed with the family, while in other approaches the therapist sets the goals and treatment plan.

After the assessment data have been gathered and formulated into hypotheses and goals, the therapist is ready to consider therapeutic methods. Again, some therapists discuss the treatment plan with the family, others simply implement the strategy.

USING INSTRUMENTS IN ASSESSMENT

The paradigmatic shift from a linear model to a systems model of family functioning has left a gap in the methods of assessment. L'Abate and Wagner (1985) have summarized their concerns about the problem of assessing families. They recognize that assessment devices that were designed for individuals have little or no utility for a systemic conceptualization. They call for a multidimensional battery of tests that is objective, can be administered and scored with ease, and that has more than one form to allow for pre- and postevaluation. This is no simple task because the assessment tools also need to be constructed so as to be appropriate for children as well as adults. They believe the stimuli used should permit the family members to report their observations of themselves and each other in terms of their "give and take" as well.

Numerous instruments have been developed. In their 1978 review, Strauss and Brown included 813 instruments. Although there was quantity, Strauss and Brown lamented the lack of quality.

There are times when a therapist may want to use an instrument as a part of the assessment process. Several instruments are presented which the clinician may find useful.

The Family Environment Scale (FES)

The Family Environment Scale (FES) was developed as one of a series of instruments that sought to assess the "personality" of a person's environment. The authors (Fuhr, Moos, & Dishotsky, 1981) describe how the FES can be used in treatment to: describe the "social milieu" of a family; and to give the family feedback that can facilitate the therapeutic process; and to evaluate that therapeutic process.

The FES is a paper and pencil technique comprised of ninety true-false items that are responded to individually by family members. There are ten subscales that give scores in three areas: Cohesion, expressiveness, and conflict assess how family members relate to each other. Independence, achievement orientation, intellectual-cultural orientation, active-recreational orientation, and moral-religious emphasis describe important developmental processes of growth and goal orientation. The third area, the structure, maintenance and change of the system, is assessed via the subscales of organization and control.

There is a forty-item short version of the FES (Form S), a Real form in which the individual is asked to describe the family as it actually is (Form R), an Ideal form where an individual responds to the items for his or her ideal family (Form I), and a reworking of Form R that assesses Expectations (Form E). It is a relatively quick and simple device to administer and score, but it may not be appropriate for children or others who are unable to read the items (Dreyer, 1978).

Fuhr et al. (1981) recommend the administration of both the Real (Form R) and Ideal (Form I) forms of the FES in the early stages of therapy. Form R can then be readministered several months later and at the end of therapy as an evaluative device. They also give a clinical example of a case where the marital couple filled Form R out twice at the beginning of therapy—once to describe their life alone together and once to describe their family life when the wife's antagonistic and demeaning brother came for one of his frequent extended visits. Raw scores for the FES are transferred into standard scores which can then be plotted for comparison among family members and between each individual's perception of the real and ideal family.

Fuhr et al. (1981) further delineate ways in which the FES can be used. First, the scale is organized around assessment of the family at present. Thus, it can facilitate introduction of a "systems" perspective and defocus the identified patient as the source of the problem. Second, it breaks family issues down into discrete, small, manageable parts. This helps to reduce the family's feeling of being overwhelmed and aids in focusing them on a topic. Third, the Ideal form (Form I) of the FES can be used as a mechanism by which family members participate in forming the therapeutic goals. When Form I and Form R are used together, there can ensue discussion on both the match of individual family member's perceptions of the present state of the family as well as on the differences and similarities of what is seen as desirable in a family. Finally, a repeated administration of the FES (Form R) can be used to evaluate the progress of therapy. This should be conducted cautiously, however, as an appropriate lapse of time needs to occur between readministrations of the same instrument, and there are no parallel forms of Form R available.

The Family Cohesion and Adaptability Scale (FACES)

The Family Cohesion and Adaptability Scale was developed from the circumplex model of family systems. The Circumplex Model of Marital and Family Systems is a well-thought-out model that was developed primarily by

David Olson, Candyce Russell, and Douglas Sprenkle (1983, 1979, 1982). They used a conceptual clustering of over fifty ideas from six social science fields, including family systems theory, to arrive at three dimensions they believe can adequately describe family functioning. Two of the dimensions, cohesion and adaptability, are conceived of as appearing on a continuum from high to low with the central regions representing the area of optimal family functioning. Gradations of these dimensions combine to form sixteen typologies. The third dimension, communication, is considered to be a "facilitating dimension" and is not included in their system of typologies.

Family cohesion is defined as "the emotional bonding that family members have toward one another" (Olson, Russell, & Sprenkle, 1983, p. 70) and includes such variables as: emotional bonding, boundaries, coalitions, time, space, friends, decision making, and interests and recreation. Extremely high cohesion is labeled "enmeshed" and is described as an over-identification with the family. At the other extremity of the continuum is disengagement which is marked by emotional, intellectual, and/or physical isolation. It is hypothesized that both ends of the continuum are potentially problematic. In the central ranges, low to moderate cohesion is described as separated; moderate to high cohesion is labeled connected. Both of these central areas describe optimal levels of family functioning.

The second dimension, adaptability, is defined as "the ability of a marital or family system to change its power structure, role relationships, and relationship rules in response to situational and developmental stress" (Olson, Russell, & Sprenkle, 1983, p. 70). Adaptability is seen as being composed of the concepts of family power (assertiveness, control, discipline), negotiation styles, role relationships, and relationship rules. Adaptability also encompasses four levels, from rigid (very low adaptability) at one end of the continuum to chaotic (very high) at the other end of the continuum, with both extremes again seen as representing pathology. The middle points on the continuum are structured (low to moderate adaptability) and flexible (moderate to high). Both of these represent areas of optimal functioning.

Olson and his colleagues developed the Family Cohesion and Adaptability Scale (FACES) to assess the cohesion and adaptability dimensions of their model. It is a 111-item self-report instrument that was revised and published as FACES II, a thirty-item self-report scale. FACES II was used in the National Survey of 1,000 families, thus it has the advantage of the availability of national norms. There is a form for families with and without children.

The authors of FACES II have begun the careful and tedious project of collecting reliability and validity data on their instrument. This information is summarized in the 1983 version of the test manual (Olson et al., 1983). The fifty-item version of FACES II was used in a national survey of 1,000 families (N = 2,412). Based on a factor analysis and internal consistency reliability data collected from this sample, FACES II was reduced to its present form of thirty items. Estimates of internal consistency reliability (Cronbach's alpha) for the total sample were Cohesion (.87), Adaptability (.78), and Total Scale (.90).

Authors report that test-retest data on the fifty-item version were collected in fall, 1981 with a four- to five-week lapse between administrations. Pearson correlations for Cohesion, Adaptability, and the Total Scale were .83, .80, and .84, respectively. These results, while encouraging, need to be interpreted with caution as they are based on the fifty-item version, not the simplified thirty-item version.

Evidence of validity of FACES II comes from a variety of studies conducted on the original 111 item FACES. Olson et al. (1983) summarize this work in the technical manual, although individual references are not listed. FACES was found to be able to discriminate clinic (55 families) from nonclinic families (117 families). Clinic families were more often at the chaotic, disengaged extreme than nonclinic families. FACES was also shown to discriminate between the same 117 nonclinic families and families with a runaway. These results are encouraging, but need to be extended by using the thirty-item version as well.

An advantage of FACES II is the availability of national normature data (Olson et al., 1983). These norms are based on subsamples of parents (N = 2,082) and adolescents (N = 416) from the National Survey. Separate norms are given for adults and adolescents with males and females combined in both cases.

Family Assessment Device (FAD)

The FAD is based on the McMaster Model of Family Functioning developed originally at McGill University by Westley and Epstein, as well as Sigal and Rahoff. Work shifted to McMaster University in the 1960s and 1970s and now has spread to Brown University. The model was recently described by Epstein, Bishop, and Baldwin (1982) and the most recent version of the assessment tool is described in Epstein, Baldwin, and Bishop (1983). Theirs is a systems theory that adopts the basic systemic tenets. They assume a family's primary function is to provide the environment where social and biological development and maintenance can occur. The family does this by competently handling basic, developmental, and hazardous (crisis) tasks (Epstein et al., 1982).

The FAD looks at six areas in assessing family functioning as the family deals with these tasks. These are:

1. Problem solving: the family's ability to resolve issues which threaten the integrity and functional capacity of the family.
2. Communication: the exchange of information among family members.
3. Roles: an assessment of whether or not the family has developed behavior patterns for handling functions: provision of resources, nurturance and support, supporting personal development, maintaining and managing the family systems, and providing adult sexual gratification.
4. Affective responses: assess whether individual family members experience appropriate affect.
5. Affective involvement: concerns the interest and value family members place on each other's activities and pursuits.

6. Behavior control: deals with the way in which a family communicates and maintains the behavior standards of family members.

In addition there is one scale, General Functioning, which purports to assess the overall health/pathology of the family. This scale was devised *ex post facto* by combining the items from each scale that correlated most highly with the other six scales and then choosing those items which correlated most highly with each other (Epstein et al., 1983).

The FAD is a paper-and-pencil instrument and consists of fifty-three items to be completed by each individual family member who rates how well a statement describes his or her family by responding to a four-point scale that ranges from "strongly agree" to "strongly disagree." The authors report that the instrument can be completed in fifteen to twenty minutes.

The FAD was developed as a theoretically based instrument. Each scale has between five and twelve items. Internal consistency reliability (Cronbach's alpha) ranges from .72 to .83 (General Functioning = .92). FAD has been shown to distinguish between a nonclinical and a clinical group of subjects with significant accuracy (Epstein et al., 1983).

The FAD appears promising as an assessment tool, but some cautions are warranted in its use. Epstein et al. (1983) note that it is only a "screening instrument" that merely identifies problem areas in the simplest and most efficient manner. Although the instrument is recommended for use with anyone at or above age twelve, the psychological "jargon" of some of the items may be confusing to a teenager (i.e., "We confront problems involving feelings"). The high subscale intercorrelation (all but one are in the .6 to .7 range) make reliance on the subscales as measuring distinct constructs somewhat unreliable.

Epstein et al. (1982) have attempted to extend use of the McMaster Model of Family Functioning to provide a description of the normal family. Equating normal with healthy, they have delineated normality for each of their six dimensions. A theoretical justification as well as behavioral characteristics are provided for each. For example, under Behavior Control, flexible behavior control is seen as most effective (therefore, healthy or normal) and chaotic behavior control is seen as least effective (unhealthy).

At present, the FAD appears most appropriate as a research tool which can be used as a global measure of outcome or to "screen" large population as Epstein et al. (1983) suggest. Use in individual case diagnosis should be done with caution, with visual inspection of individual item responses perhaps the most useful source of information.

A Visual and Verbal Test Battery

L'Abate's theory (1976), upon which he based his two assessment batteries, views optimal family adjustment as occurring as a result of the level of differentiation, appropriate ranking of priorities, and the congruence of communication patterns. L'Abate defines differentiation in relation to the continuing process of establishing clear boundaries between self and others. He reports that his own research has identified appropriate ordering of priorities in the family as follows: self, marriage, children, parents and in-laws, work, leisure, and friends. Congruence of communication patterns, the third variable, is defined by the degree of match between verbal and nonverbal messages. L'Abate theorizes that there are two dimensions to incongruent messages: punitiveness and degree of emotional control. Variations on these dimensions result in Satir's four patterns of communication: blaming, placating, computing, and distracting.

L'Abate and Wagner (1985) report on two theory-based batteries of tests that can be used in the assessment of families. The first, the Visual Battery, is composed of four separate "nonverbal" tests that are completely pictorial to allow for maximum participation by children and adults of various educational backgrounds. The second, the Verbal Battery, is composed of four tests that are verbal statements. The battery is designed for evaluation of the marital dyad and is not responded to by the children.

The Visual Battery

1. *Bell-Fagan Family Symbol Test* (BF): Fifty-two symbols which correspond to the emotions anxious/afraid, angry, sad, loving, quiet, and happy are placed on cards. Each family member is told to sort the cards into piles, each pile representing a family member, including self. A total score on each of the dimensions is obtained via a totaling of the responses of self and others.
2. *Description of Feelings in the Family Test* (DFF): Each member of the family is asked to choose from seventy-two cards of pictures depicting people in a sad, mad, distracting, or smug pose, those pictures which best represent family members. Total scores are obtained for each family member, plus self vs. others' comparisons of perceptions scores.
3. *Family Situations Pictures Series Test* (FSPS): Family members choose from a deck of 264 cards that illustrate one or two family members in one of Satir's four incongruent communication patterns. The free choice task is to select those cards that depict their family. Total and individual scores are obtained for comparison.
4. *Animal Concepts Pictures Series* (ACPS): Each family member is given a set of ninety animal pictures that have been assigned a value on ten bipolar scales. Each person in the family is asked to first sort the cards into piles for each person in the family including him or herself indicating how they actually are and then how they would like them to be. The assumption is that the animal pictures correspond to family members. Scores on the following ten dimensions are obtained for actual/ ideal, self/others perceptions comparisons: strong/weak, powerless/powerful, small/big, helpless/helpful, bad/good, slow/fast, quiet/noisy, dangerous/harmless, pleasant/unpleasant, and aggressive/passive.

The Verbal Battery

1. *Marital Questionnaire:* A true/false response format that obtains scores on six scales that represent L'Abate's theoretical notions of the family: Likeness (differentiation), ordering of priorities, and Satir's four modes of incongruent communication. A high score reflects optimal functioning.

2. *Likeness Grid:* A purported measure of self-differentiation. Twenty-four relatives of the respondent are listed and the task is to rate the self on a four-point scale from "completely the same as" to "completely the opposite of" each relative. The two extreme ratings are considered indicative of low differentiation and give no score on the differentiation scale, while the two midrange replies each contribute to the total "differentiation score."

3. *Priorities Inventory:* The respondent's task is to rate triads of items on their relative importance to the person. The items relate to categories of self, spouse, children, parents and/or in-laws, brothers and sisters, work, leisure, and friends. The respondent receives a point for assigning priorities in line with L'Abate's findings on the optimal ordering.

4. *What Would You Do?* (WWYD): This is comprised of twenty multiple choice problem situations based on Satir's four maladaptive response styles (blaming, placating, distracting, or computing). Based on the individual's replies, a characteristic pattern of responding is determined.

Wagner and L'Abate (1985) report on the results of several unpublished master's theses and doctoral dissertations in an attempt to provide evidence for the validity of their batteries. The results were not highly promising and indicate the fledgling status of the work. Most useful, at this time, are the Description of Feelings in the Family Test from the Visual Battery and perhaps the Likeness Scale of the Verbal Battery, once the issue of sex differences in verbal ability is resolved. Thus, while some of the tests in L'Abate's two batteries represent creative attempts to tackle the problem of assessment of families, they are by no means finished products and need further evidence of validity; reliability is not even mentioned as an issue.

Family-Concept Q Sort

Van derVeen and his colleagues, Hueber, Jorqeus, and Neja (1964) have developed a paper-and-pencil instrument that provides an overall rating of the family. The questionnaire has eighty items which ask for individual family member's perceptions of actual and ideal family functioning. These can be compared with provided data of the ratings of professional clinicians as to what constitutes an ideal family. The following scores are provided:

1. Family adjustment score: a comparison of an individual's rating of the family as it is compared to the clinicians' rating of an ideal family. Does not tell in what direction a family differs, only that it differs.

2. Family satisfaction score: illustrates the discrepancy between the individual's real and ideal family ratings.

3. Family congruence score: looks at the discrepancy between a husband's and wife's ratings of their real family.

4. Family compatability score: compares the marital couple's ratings of what an ideal family should be like.

The Van derVeen instrument in Q-sort form was shown to discriminate between low- and high-adjustment families (Van derVeen et al., 1964). Families that demonstrated "high adjustment" on such measures as school behavioral ratings also had higher family adjustment scores, greater correlation (for parents) between the real and ideal family, and greater agreement between parents on the real score of the Family Concepts Test. While this instrument may be useful for pre- and postevaluation, it has the disadvantage of offering little useful diagnostic information that would aid the therapist in designing treatment goals.

Reiss Card Sort

David Reiss (1980) assesses families through the use of direct observation as the family attempts to solve a structured problem task. Use of the task and a detailed scoring system are highly time-consuming for clinical use. The Reiss card-sorting technique has families sorting a group of fifteen cards, each of which shows a sequence of letters, into as many piles as they wish (up to seven) using whatever system they develop. This is done alone, then as a family and then alone again. A variety of scores can be obtained: problem-solving scores and similarity scores.

Reiss evaluates families in terms of a four-category typology that derives from two dimensions, each having two levels. Families are conceptualized in terms of high or low coordination and high or low configuration. Coordination refers to the harmony with which family members integrate their individual efforts into the solution of a family task. Configuration describes the extent to which the family process of problem solving facilitates understanding of that process in the individual family members. Families high in configuration benefit from working together as they are aware of the process and may modify it. Families low in configuration actually show deterioration as they work together. Combinations of these two dimensions are used to form four family types:

1. *Environment sensitive:* High in configuration and coordination, "it [the family] works together to amplify, explore, investigate, and understand the environment" (Reiss et al., 1980).
2. *Achievement sensitive:* High in configuration, but low in coordination. This group organizes to solve the laboratory tasks, but the work is characterized by competitiveness rather than cooperation.
3. *Consensus-sensitive:* High in coordination, but low in configuration. These families strive for consensus, but at the price of task achievement. Disagreements are avoided because they are considered a sign of weakness.
4. *Distance-sensitive:* Low in coordination and configuration. "They work separately and, as they work, their grasp of the problem deteriorates" (Reiss et al., 1980).

Reiss et al. (1980) have used this system to effectively predict successful engagement in a multiple-family group inpatient treatment program for adolescents. Environment-sensitive families were most quickly and effectively engaged in the group process of treatment, while the distance-sensitive families had the poorest attendance at sessions, remained "inconspicuous" in the group and felt little cohesion. Thus, while this system is cumbersome and difficult to use, it may be helpful in predicting families at "high risk" for therapy.

The Beavers Systems Model

W. Robert Beavers provides a fresh and interesting perspective to the problem of assessing family functions, as his experiences come from observing healthy families in the Timberlawn study (Lewis, Beavers, Gossett, & Phillips, 1976). Beavers uses two dimensions to typify different possible healthy and dysfunctional families. These are the continua of competence and of family style. Competence is seen as relating to eight variables that, in combination, represent optimal family functioning. These are:

1. *A system of orientation:* The family understands the interrelatedness of humans and does not attach blame in a cause-effect fashion.
2. *Clear boundaries:* This includes boundaries between the family and the external world, between members and across generations.
3. *Contextual clarity:* "When an optimal family interacts, it is generally clear to whom comments are addressed and what the relationship is between the speaker and the audience" (Beavers, 1982, p. 49).
4. *Relatively equal power and the process of intimacy:* At the basis of this area of competence is fear and how people react to this fear. In an optimal family, people can handle fear by relating, not controlling. They experience closeness, not coercion. While authoritarian control can sometimes be used (by parents), there is a tendency in optimal families to develop relationships rather than coercive controls.
5. *Encouragement of autonomy:* Autonomy is defined in terms of family members taking responsibility for their own thoughts, feelings, and behavior.
6. *Joy and comfort in relating:* Transactional relations in the optimal family would be marked by warmth, optimism, intensity, and empathy. Beavers looks for an affiliative orientation that is assessed on the basis of behavior, voice, tone, verbal content, and communicative patterns.
7. *Skilled negotiation:* "In shared tasks, optimal families excel in their capacity to accept directions, organize themselves, develop input from each other, negotiate differences, and reach closure coherently and effectively (Beavers, 1982, p. 51).
8. *Significant transcendent values:* A family is seen as needing a set of values and beliefs which transcend everyday life experiences. These values and beliefs offer the family comfort and solace in dealing with the inevitable losses of death and separation.*

These theoretical notions were transformed into a series of rating scales that were used by independent raters to evaluate videotaped segments of families interacting in a series of four tasks (Lewis et al., 1976). The four tasks involved discussing the family's main problems, planning an activity together, discussion of marital happiness and pain, and a family closeness task. The videotapes were judged in five areas, with a total of thirteen individual factors, as follows:

I.   Structure of the family
    A. Structure (power, pecking order)
    B. Parental coalitions
    C. Closeness
II. Mythology (congruence with reality)

*Reprinted with permission of the publisher.

III. Goal-directed negotiation (overall efficiency)
IV. Autonomy
    A. Communication of self-concept
    B. Responsibility
    C. Invasiveness
    D. Permeability
V. Family affect
    A. Expressiveness
    B. Mood and tone (from warm to cynical)
    C. Conflict (degree of unresolvable conflict)
    D. Empathy

Each factor was expressed in the form of a nine-point scale. Interrater reliabilities were found to be highly dependent on the training of the rater. Using a sample of twelve families, a social worker and psychiatrist were able to achieve significant interrater correlations on ten of the thirteen scales (Lewis et al., 1976).

As evidence of construct validity (although the authors do not use this term) a group of families of both healthy and psychiatrically hospitalized adolescents were given the Beavers-Timberlawn Family Evaluation Scales (Lewis et al., 1976). The Beavers-Timberlawn correlated appropriately with a global measure of health/pathology and a measure of adolescent psychopathology.

DIAGRAMS IN FAMILY ASSESSMENT

In addition to using observation and paper-and-pencil instruments, therapists can use diagrams to help understand family relationships. Two prominent methods of diagraming are theory related: the genogram (to Bowen's family system theory) and family mapping (to Munichin's structural approach). The genogram is used with the family members to picture the extended family and as a guide for therapy. The structural family map is conceived by the therapist, not shared with the family in the session, and serves as a guide to the structural changes to be made. Both diagram approaches use information from the family during the session.

Genogram

Guerin and Pendagast (1976) assert that the decision as to what method to use for evaluating a family is dependent upon the ideology of the therapist and the emotional state of the family. A family in crisis may need to reduce its "affective overload" before the therapist can begin a formal, structured process of information gathering. The genogram is a structured method of conceptualizing the family that may be used in the initial session or later in the therapy. Use of the genogram is based on Bowen's systems theory (1978). Guerin and Pendagast use the genogram to organize their data gathering about the family's physical and emotional boundaries, characteristics of membership, nodal events, toxic issues, emotional cutoff, closeness and openness, and availability of relationship options.

The first part of the information gathering concerns general contextual questions of how the family fits in with the larger social context of which it is a part. The therapist asks questions about the cultural and ethnic heritage, religious affiliations, and extent of the social network of the family. This information aids the therapist in forming a picture of the appropriateness of the family in its social environment, its level of isolation, or the extent of its support system and to what degree it is stressed by factors such as poverty, unemployment, or cultural isolation.

The second part of assessment involves compiling a genogram, which is defined as "a structural diagram of a family's three-generational relationship system" (Guerin & Pendagast, 1976, p. 452). There is a system of symbols to use in diagramming the family which facilitates the organization and interpretation of the material.

$\boxed{}$ = Male $\bigcirc$ = Female $\triangle$ = Child in Utero

A = Abortion or Stillbirth

——— = Marriage

| = Offspring

D/ = Divorce

X = Death

(From Guerin & Pendagast, 1976 p. 452)

In a discussion with the family, the therapist gathers data to produce this "family map" which includes such basic information as: names and ages of each family member (three generations); dates of marriage, divorce, birth, death; and cause of death or type of severe illness or disability.

Besides this basic factual data, information can be noted in several pertinent areas:

1. *Physical location of family members:* Physical distance can be a metaphor to emotional distance. Physical distance can be used to provide an emotional as well as a physical "cut-off" from a conflicted family with explosive tendencies. Conversely, some families have difficulty physically and emotionally separating and several generations may live within a two-block radius of each other.

2. *Communication patterns:* It is often revealing to find out who calls, visits and/or writes to whom. Often there is a "family switchboard" in the person of an oldest

child or grandmother through whom most communication of any importance must pass. This is a position of power and the death of such a person can lead to dramatic reorganization or disintegration of the family. Ritualized visiting and communication can be mechanisms to promote cutoff. Use of the telephone is an important clue to communication. Does one person always answer the phone or have the phone turned over to him or her immediately? The existence of triangles in the family signals the avoidance of conflict. When a dyad (usually parental) is threatened by conflict, they can bring a third party into the struggle and deflect their conflict on the third party.

3. *Territoriality:* Where are holidays spent or where does visiting occur? Are grandparents flexible enough to visit children as well as be visited? Territoriality reveals important boundary issues.

4. *Toxic issues:* Universal "hot" issues concern money, sex, and parenting, but issues such as alcohol, death, religion, education, and politics may also be toxic for a particular family. It is helpful for the therapist to discern if toxic issues are handled in an open or closed manner. Family secrets, often indicated by "gaps" in a genogram, indicate a closed system that does not resolve complicated issues.

5. *Family motto/message:* It is crucial to understand what messages and values the marital couple receive from their families of origin. How do these messages complement each other in the new family? Has the marital couple negotiated the differences in a new family?

6. *Nodal events:* Guerin and Pendagast define nodal events as "those crossroad times and events in the family life cycle that shape the future form and structure of the relationship process" (1976, p. 455). How has the family dealt with the developmental issues, crises, and catastrophes which occur? What supports have they used? What strengths or what maladaptive, rigid patterns?

7. *Sibling position:* Toman (1969) has emphasized that the role a person has taken on as a sibling is often the role he or she assumes initially or even permanently in a new relationship. What rivalries and alliances developed among the siblings and how these might affect relationships in a marriage or with peers are important factors to assess.

The genogram itself may look something like the one illustrated in Figure 3-1. This is the "map" of the family, but describes only the most basic material regarding the family. The possible significance and implications of this factual data may be summarized in a verbal report.

In the case illustrated by the genogram in Figure 3-1, the identified patient, Ann, is a married female (age twenty-nine) with problems of alcoholism. Ann, her husband, Joe, and their two children had lived in several locations around the country while Joe went through a variety of job and career changes, finally settling on a stressful, time-consuming position in their home town. They have few friends and rarely socialize because Joe maintains long hours at work. Presently, although they are well-off financially, they live in the family home with Ann's mother so that Ann's mother can "help out" when Ann is "sick." Ann does not work and has not since her marriage to Joe at age 19 (she was pregnant at the time with their eldest son).

Physical distance of various family members illustrates emotional distance. Ann and her mother, living in the same home, have a highly charged, conflicted,

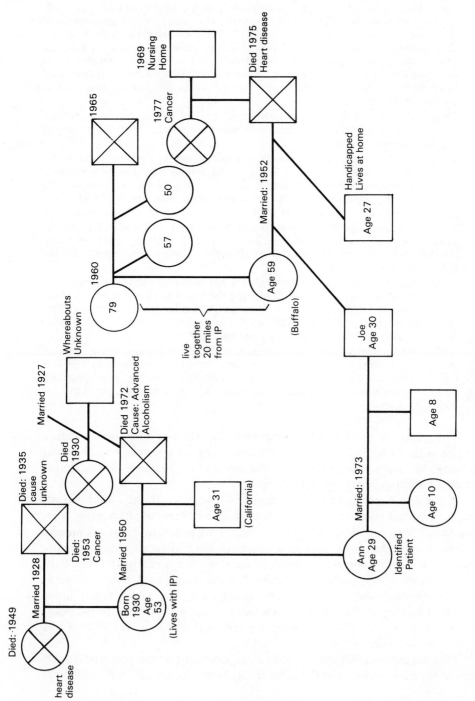

FIGURE 3-1.

54

enmeshed relationship where Ann is seen as infantile and incompetent. The bedroom she and her husband share, for example, is Ann's childhood bedroom. Joe maintains a rather distant position in the home when faced by the mother-daughter coalition. While Ann's mother idealizes her son who lives in California, the relationship is a distant one marked by brief ritualized visiting, and lavish gifts from son to mother. While Ann and her brother were growing up, a strong triangle existed among mother, father, and son. Mother and son united with secrets and privileged affections at the exlusion of father, who was characterized as a "mean drunk." Ann's mother feels Ann has "inherited" her husband's drinking problem.

Ann's mother has always maintained a central role in the communication patterns of the family. Ann and her brother rarely converse, all communications are handled through the mother. When Ann and her husband lived around the country, visiting always occurred at Ann's mother's home, and even now her brother visits his mother; she has never been to her son's home in California.

Joe's family was imbued with a strong Christian fundamentalist doctrine of moral living, helpfulness, and consideration. Joe at one point had considered the ministry but reconsidered due to the financial burden his handicapped brother already placed on the family. When asked her family's motto, Ann replied, "It's a cruel world out there." Her social isolation is a monument to her family's notion of a scary, unfriendly world; she finds comfort under Joe's moral, caring umbrella.

The divorce of her parents and the death of her father stand out in Ann's mind as the most impactful events of her life. She responded to the divorce by avoiding friends (feeling ashamed and different). She reports not being sure how she responded to her father's death, but notes she got pregnant, dropped out of a nursing program, and got married within a year. She feels she was "kept busy" by these events and had little time to think about her father's death. Thus, we can see Ann's pattern of handling life stresses by further isolating herself from friends, career, and personal achievement.

Sibling positions of Ann and her husband are interesting. Ann is a younger sister of an older brother, a position which further emphasizes her as helpless and in need of care. Joe is the older brother of a severely handicapped brother whom he was made to feel responsible for as he grew up. Thus, both partners have brought mutually reinforcing patterns to a marriage that characterizes Ann in a "sick" dependent role, needing to be cared for by both her husband and mother.

Mapping Families

Another type of diagraming used to understand family patterns is Minuchin's method of mapping. This map is used to present a picture of the family's structural behaviors.

Minuchin's structural model of families focuses on the interaction between the individuals in the nuclear family system. The family system operates through repeated transactional patterns of how, when, and with whom to relate (1974).

Each person belongs to different subsystems in which he or she plays different roles (i.e., father, husband, child), has varying levels of power, and learns differentiated skills. For proper family functioning the boundaries of subsystems must be clear. Boundaries can be diagrammed as clear (----), diffuse (....), or rigid (———). When family boundaries are diffuse, members are too enmeshed. Support is given when stress occurs in a family member but the response by other members is given with extreme speed and intensity. The map may look something like: $\underset{\text{cccc}}{\text{M}\ldots\text{F}}$ illustrating lack of a clear boundary. Where family boundaries are overly rigid, members are too separated, and people do not feel a sense of loyalty or belonging. This may be illustrated $\underset{\text{ccc}}{\underline{\text{M}\qquad\text{F}}}$ showing the rigid separation. The example of $\underset{\text{ccc}}{\text{M} - - - - \text{F}}$ shows there is a clear boundary but openness for interaction.

Relationships between members can be diagramed to show the type of transactions. An affiliation transaction is diagramed as =, while an overinvolvement is ≡. When there is a conflict between people, it is indicated by a slash, ≠. An example might be an affiliation between mother and father, mother's involvement with one child, and a conflict between the children: $\underset{\text{c} \neq \text{c}}{\overset{\text{|||}}{\text{M} = \text{F}}}$. If mother is overinvolved with one child, there may be conflictual transactions between the siblings.

When the boundaries separating the parental subsystem are crossed, inappropriate triads involving a child in spouse conflicts occur. In triangulation, each parent demands that the child side with him against the other parent. In detouring, the spouses submerge their own spouse subsystem problems by focusing on a child. They define the child as the source of family problems because he is bad or define him as sick and weak and unite to protect him. This is diagramed as $\underset{\text{C}}{\underline{\text{M}\qquad\text{F}}}$. Another form of the triad is the stable parent-child coalition in which one of the parents joins the child in a rigid alliance against the other parent, i.e., $\left.\begin{array}{l}\text{M}\\\text{C}\end{array}\right|\text{F}$.

Another facet of this scheme involves family adaptation to stress and conflict. Families can respond to stress or conflict by confronting issues and accommodating differences, by avoiding touchy topics altogether, or by endlessly fighting the same battle over and over. A family's capacity to adapt depends on its ability to keep the boundaries of the subsystems firm, yet flexible so that realignment can occur when circumstances change. Many structural family therapists use a map as a general hypothesis of the family's behavior pattern. The therapist can do things during the interview to check out the hypothesis. The map also shows suggested areas for change in the family structure and, therefore, is a guide for therapy.

4

Positive Reframing

See the Good Throughout

*If we take people as they are,
we make them worse. If we treat
them as if they were what they
ought to be, we help them become
what they are capable of becoming.*

Goethe

Reframing is the most frequently employed of all methods in psychotherapy, and the most often overlooked in training. In essence, reframing is the basis of much psychotherapy, i.e., the change of the client's world view to allow for more alternatives and less emotional interference in the conduct of one's life. Most forms of psychotherapy have a name for some form of reframing, though they are not all equivalent in function or in theory. In some cases the exact nature of the method is not clear, or is achieved with a method which has an altogether different rationale and purpose. This method has been more explicitly developed among family therapists, under a variety of names: relabeling (Haley, 1963; Minuchin, 1974); reframing (Watzlawick et al., 1974); content reframing (Bandler & Grinder, 1982); redefinition (Andolfi, 1979); seeing the good (L'Abate, 1975b); positive connotation (Palazzoli, Cecchin, Boscolo, & Prata, 1978); ascribing noble intentions (Stanton, Todd, & Associates, 1982); non-blaming (Alexander & Parsons, 1982); context markers (Viaro, 1980; Bateson, 1979), though there is much variation among them as well. The distinctions drawn in this chapter will aid the student in more clearly choosing and thinking through the use of these methods.

Since all the above terms refer to variations of the same general method, we use the term "reframing" throughout in a generic sense. Reframing is changing in the classificatory schema to which an activity (behavior, thought, statement, interaction, nonverbal reaction, or a sequence combining several of these) being considered belongs, thus changing the entire perspective. While the image is that of the dramatic effects which different picture frames can have on our perception of the picture enclosed, it is more useful to think of the different effects which arise with cameras when they are used to frame various aspects of a scene.

Closeups reveal very different aspects of a situation than long shots, which include many more details and make the material enclosed in the close-up seem very different now that they are seen as part of a bigger scene. One can also focus to reveal just the details of the foreground, just those of the background, or both.

A more extensive definition is given by Watzlawick et al. (1974).

> To reframe means to change the conceptual and/or emotional setting or viewpoint in relation to which a situation is experienced and to place it in another frame which fits the "facts" of the same concrete situation equally well or even better, and thereby changes its meaning . . . there is change while the situation itself may remain quite unchanged and, indeed, even unchangeable. What turns out to be changed is the meaning attributed to the situation, and, therefore, its consequences, but not its concrete facts (p. 95) . . . once something is seen as having a particular meaning or value, it is very difficult to see that same something in terms of its membership in another, equally valid, class . . . In its most abstract form, reframing means changing the emphasis from one class member of an object to another, equally valid class membership, or, especially, introducing such a new class membership into the conceptualization of all concerned. (p. 98)

Reframings may have a direct impact on our perception, or more accurately, on our construction of reality, which is intimately related to many other facets of our lives. Reframings bring with them changes in the salient features of an activity; the range, type, and likelihood of appropriate responses to the activity, including emotional responses; and may also trigger an automatic response sequence. Reframings change the context, or larger frame, around facts. From moral to medical, for example, as in the relabeling of alcoholics as sick rather than self-indulgent and weak; or from medical to moral, as in the labeling of anorexics as stubborn rather than as sick. They may also keep the same context, but change the meaning within that context; for example, from "crazy" to "developmentally delayed" within a mental health context, or from competitive to cooperative within a marital context. Once clients have been shown other alternatives, it is difficult for them to return to seeing just the image which they first perceived. Their alternatives have been increased. They can no longer perceive just the one image and ignore the possibility of the other. They can, however, by altering their frame of mind or their label, facilitate the perception of one particular image.

What is important is the basic cognitive activity of people. People do not passively perceive a reality which is waiting to be discovered, but actively participate in creating "reality." Much of this construction of reality is mediated by language. Recognized by Whorf (Carroll, 1956) as "linguistic determinism," this refers to the fact that one's language or symbol system determines how events, perceptions, and ideas will be cognitively processed and experienced. Weaker versions of the linguistic determinism hypothesis state that language symbols (words and sentences, grammatical structure) color one's perceptions and thoughts without completely determining them, and make some lines of thought easier than others.

When individuals become stuck, unable to construct a useful reality from their symbols, therapists may be able to help them fashion a somewhat different, more workable reality. Minuchin (1974, p. 216), for example, relabeled a mother's overcontrol as her concern for her children, a change which he believed served to "highlight submerged aspects of the woman's feelings towards her children" and "facilitate the appearance of new transactions between mother and child." In a family seen for an inpatient consultation by the author, a woman was interviewed who appeared to seek inpatient admissions at regular intervals as a way to gain solace from stress at home. When asked where else she might go for "vacations from the family," and what the alternative costs would be, she began to experience a refreshing feeling of self-control and view her situation more optimistically than in the recent past. Now having a different frame for her problem which allowed a different set of solutions, actually several different frames, she moved from involuntary symptoms to self-control; from a perspective which placed the problem focus on her alone to one which included the family situation; and from a self-suffering solution to one which allowed self-reward.

Theories of reality, determined by frames and labels, carry implications for how we should behave in a situation, for potential solutions to problems, for who should be responsible for solutions, and whether or not solutions are even to be attempted. Frames and labels help us to select a particular set of details from an amazing number of possibilities, organize them, organize our behavior in response to them in a habitual and possibly automatic fashion, and even determine the appropriate emotional tone for our experience. Physicians are now working with the power of labels and frames to improve patient response to medical procedures which vary from cancer operations to normal childbirth. Describing bone marrow transplant procedures as being an experience like vacuum suction reduces the usual sensations of pain associated with this novel though not particularly painful procedure (Grutsky & Srodes, 1984). Similarly, describing the breaking of water in cesarean childbirth as the sign that the baby will soon be available for the mother to hold reframes the meaning of this often anxiety-provoking physical experience (Cooper, 1984).

Labels, frames, or contextual cues may change clients' beliefs about their own actions and motivations, give a new set of action potentials, and increase clients' sense of self-control and self-esteem. New labels or frames may block old ones, so that only one frame will be experienced. This allows one set of details to be highlighted and another muted or blocked out entirely for some time. Problems may now appear under the control of the client and solvable for the first time, and intense emotions may be removed from the situation or increased in a way that motivates the client to achieve change. For the therapist, the essential feature is not the correctness of the reframe but its utility—what it makes possible for the client.

For example, a young male anorexic may be told that he has a "girl's disease." "Noncompliant" children may be defined as "deficient in attending skills," leading parents to behave differently than if they believe their children are truly noncompliant. Parents may try to get their children's attention when requesting cooperation, or do it in a different, more effective way. Parents with "hyperactive" children may look for different solutions than those who are told their children have a "high activity level" and need to have their activity directed, not dampened. Here it is also helpful to reframe the activity level from a moral frame of madness to a medical one of genetic control of temperament. This should serve to reduce anger, blame, and parental feelings of inadequacy and guilt, all of which probably hinder effective and flexible attempts to find new solutions.

Frames may also be enlarged so that a broader perspective is achieved, and those events which seemed so momentous a minute before may seem trivial. Wilhelm and Jung (1970) spoke in *The Secret of the Golden Flower* about such shifts.

> The greatest and most important problems of life are all in a certain sense insoluble. They must be so because they express the necessary polarity inherent in every self-regulating system. They can never be solved, but only outgrown. This "outgrowing" in further experience was seen to consist in a new level of consciousness. Some higher or wider interest arose in the person's horizon and through this widening of his view the insoluble problem lost its urgency. It was not solved logically, on its own terms, but faded out when confronted with a new and stronger life tendency. It was not repressed and made unconscious, but merely appeared in a different light, and so, did indeed become different. What on a lower level had led to the widest conflicts and to panicky outbursts of emotion viewed from the higher level of personality, now seem like a storm in the valley as seen from a high mountaintop. This does not mean that the thunderstorm is robbed of its reality, but instead of being in it, one is now above it.

Recognizing that the human situation is largely invariant puts a new emphasis on reframing. One becomes more interested in approaches which may turn liabilities into assets by pointing out different aspects of a situation or person. This is particularly important as the individual has direct control over himself and no such control over the actions of other people or circumstances, and what control he does have is mediated through his actions. Reframes and relabelings are especially useful in situations where the individual believes he cannot or should not change. While not willing to change basic aspects of the self or personal goals, individuals can still be helped to see new aspects of the self or new paths to their goals. In these instances change is accomplished or initiated at a cognitive level.

When one views problems as also being attempted solutions, one works to create new solutions to replace symptomatic attempts to achieve personal or family goals. The initiation of new behaviors will be more likely when clearly framed as attempts to realize the client's goals. An elegant example of this was a therapist who, when presented with a highly suspicious paranoid client, suggested that his client get closer to people so that the client would be privy to more accurate information than was available through careful, but distant scrutiny of people. The end result was an improvement in the client's social functioning and decrease in suspiciousness, all initially in the service of the client's wish to protect himself from other people.

IMPORTANCE FOR FAMILIES

The above considerations are as valid with families as with individuals, as families may be viewed as having important group realities which are mutually constructed. Reiss (1981) gives considerable evidence that it is useful to view families as operating from paradigms which control their vision of the world and their ideas about how the world is to be known and explored. This includes what conclusions can be drawn from one's experience, and how experience can be used to guide individual and family behavior. Such paradigms are not consciously available to the family members but rather are unquestionably accepted as indisputable features of life. One could debate such premises with the family, but it takes a good deal of work even to make the issue of the debate clear. It is wiser to accept some of these premises and work within them to create change, possibly leading to their own demise as in the example of the suspicious client given above.

Reframing seems to be particularly indicated in cases where the family is confronted with a situation it cannot change and must adjust to; in cases where frames are too limited; and in those cases where frames stand in the way of necessary action. Limited frames occur in a variety of forms. Families may have lost sight of the larger picture and be trapped in endless petty discussions and clashes with little remembrance of their initial goals and intentions. Families may have too few classifications for their experience, too few cognitive categories, all of which are black or white, bipolar, and overinclusive due to the paucity of concepts available. These latter families are usually referred to as rigid and resistant, working primarily in a moral frame of right/wrong, correct/incorrect, good/bad. Other families are unable to see the relationship aspects of their lives, and are involved in win-lose battles with partners, not seeing they must either hang together or hang separately. When frames are correctly adjusted, changes in symptoms may be achieved without hindering pursuit of the original goals. Or the context can be enlarged to give more appropriate or workable goals. Marital goals, for example, may be changed from the competitive frame of success or failure for the individual to the cooperative frame of success or failure of the relationship.

Bateson and Reusch (1951) long ago commented on people's way of construing reality in such a way as to confirm their own beliefs, as did Birdwhistle (1971), who pointed out that an essential feature of language and communication is to confirm the group's social beliefs rather than to convey new information. In those cases where family myths may be deadening, limiting, or prohibitive of personal development (Laing, 1965), reframing may make it harder for families to continue to see things from their limited perspectives. Several authors have noted the beneficial aspects of expanding the family's conceptual world, or blocking old, unilateral ways of seeing things by introducing new possibilities (Feynes, 1976; Watzlawick et al., 1974; Whitaker, 1975). The Milan associates (Palazzoli et al., 1978) make a habit of dealing only with "opinions" in sessions, and only current opinions at that. Their purpose is to undermine the concept that there is one truth—contained in the family ideology. Rather than oppose the family "truth" with their own version, they challenge the frame of unquestionable truth by introducing the frame of provisional truth, or utilitarian truth, that which helps the family progress at the moment.

Cases in which frames block individual action include those families which will not take necessary action because the action is labeled in such a way that it is inconsistent with a frame, and those which continue to take a problem-maintaining action because it is consistent with a frame. An example of an inconsistent label is the mother who does everything for the child who has recently left home. This action is undertaken to avoid abandoning the child and to help the child successfully make the break from home, but instead of helping, this behavior often serves to reinforce dependence. In this case what was previously seen as "neglect" of the son was relabeled as "selfless helping" since others might feel the mother was bad for not doing everything she could for her son. A case of a problem-maintaining label is a woman who sees herself as a supermother and will not take time away from her children for herself, is told she must recharge her own batteries regularly to operate at full effectiveness as a mother, or that she needs to set a good example for her children of how to enjoy adult life. It should be obvious from the above discussion that reframes can be important aspects of task assignment, where rationales to motivate the client for behavioral change must fit client frames.

It is important to emphasize that reframes are not sleight-of-hand tricks, but rather are different ways to account for the facts which clients present, or ways to highlight or add additional facts to the clients' experiences. The goal of reframing is not to seek the "truth," but a more useful way of viewing the world which blocks older, inhibiting ways. For the therapist, the essential feature is not the correctness of the reframe but its utility—what it makes possible for the client. Reframing is not an attempt to encourage clients to put on rose-colored glasses. Negative connotations can be as helpful as positive ones. They are both simply attempts to create more useful options for the client. The most important is their utility—what it makes possible for the client. For this reason reframes are not like analytic interpretations aimed at showing clients a more accurate way of seeing "reality," nor are they paraphrases into technical words. Technical words can be used to relabel and change frames, though, and to support the validity of the frame temporarily through impressive verbiage (Fisch et al., 1983, pp. 102–103).

Reframes are not always easily devised, but they become increasingly easy with practice and familiarity with examples. Listed below is a basic set of rules and guidelines for reframing which will become less formidable with practice and will increase therapist effectiveness.

STEPS FOR REFRAMING

1. Identify clients' frames of reference and world view.
2. Identify behaviors to be relabeled, important information to be attended to which is now being overlooked.
3. Identify specific features, facts, or details of the situation or behavior to be relabeled, including others' reactions to these facts or behaviors.
4. Set up a context for the acceptance of reframes (yes sets, confusions, highlighting details held in mutual agreement).
5. Define event in a different way, or place in a different or larger context where it will appear differently.
6. Pay attention to client feedback to see if reframe is accepted; if not, start again at 3 or 2, or go to task assignment.

IDENTIFYING CLIENT FRAMES

All interactions with clients will be mediated or filtered through the client's way of perceiving the therapist and the world at large, so it is important for the therapist to be aware of client frames of reference. The most basic precept for success in therapy is to accept what the patient offers, to respect the patient's starting position, and work within that frame to achieve change, as in the case of the paranoid patient described above. The difficult part, as pointed out by Fisch et al. (1983), is avoiding the temptation to reason with the family, to confront their way of seeing things with your own preferred way. Such attempts, if too discrepant from the client's point of view, will not lead to a new point of view, but rather rejection of the therapist by the family. Try not to jolt the family by challenging larger frames or being too different from their current way of seeing things. Keep the old goals, facts, something they can hold on to, even if using all their material as an indicator of success, cooperation, or some positive quality quite different from what they imagined it to indicate. Even if you never succeed in changing the family from viewpoint A to viewpoint B, they may reach a modified version of their own reality, A' which is more workable than A (de Shazer, 1982).

Rather than attempting to change larger frames of reference, it is best at first to limit oneself to repunctuating or relabeling data presented by the clients. One does this partially by listening carefully to the family and using their words and general language in presenting one's reframes. One does not try to impose one's own reality and language on the family as particular schools of therapy sometimes do. While the therapist may have favorite ways of presenting reality, standard labels, frames, and metaphors, which are of general benefit, it should be remembered that these will probably not have as much power for motivating change as those of the clients. One may on occasion need to teach clients new classifications for reality, but even these must fit into their larger world view.

It cannot be stressed enough that fitting the reframe to the clients' unique way of seeing the world is more important than the brilliance or elegance of the reframe. This is partially true because it is important for the clients to care about the opinion of the therapist. If that opinion is too discrepant, or if the therapist too quickly dismisses the family's way of seeing things, the family will not consider the therapist's view, or there will be a backlog of resentment likely to surface later (Bandler & Grinder, 1982).

Learning the clients' larger frames is presented by Fisch, Weakland, and Segal (1983) as simply a matter of "listening to what clients are saying." They suggest paying particular attention to what the clients' specific attitudes and opinions are about the presenting problem, the family's position on the matter, and then trying to reduce this to a basic statement of their position. They also suggest paying attention to some general characteristics such as whether family members are conforming versus independent, daring versus timid, pessimistic versus optimistic, caring and nurturing versus more cerebral and aloof. It is hoped the therapist can put this in a sentence or two; if not, it will be too complicated for use during the session unless working with a team.

In its entirety, one needs to attend to the concepts, premises, and assumptions relating to those aspects of family life which are being reframed. This may include the family's likely response styles (e.g., compliant, defiant, blaming, apologetic, protective); problem-solving styles; their sequence and process of constructing meaning (Bandler & Grinder, 1975); their understanding of the therapist-patient relationship and the role of the therapist; major premises about the world; hopes, fears, and expectations, and the labels which the family uses for thoughts, feelings, and actions. The latter are particularly important, and should be observed for their positive or negative emotional impact on the family since labels will frequently be in need of adjustment and will be potential motivators for the family.

One learns by listening to what the patients say, and observing what they do and how they respond. The best assumption is that the meaning of the communication in the family is the effect it has, regardless of one's own association to its meaning. Frames of reference will vary tremendously and one has to constantly remind oneself that the family's meaning may not be yours. Erickson and Rossi (1981) in their general discussion of indirect communication give a useful description of frames of reference:

> . . . you listen to what the patients say, and you use their words, and you can understand those words. You can place your own meaning on those words, but the real question is what is the meaning that a patient places on those words. You cannot know because you do not know the patient's frame of reference. . . . A young man says, "It's a nice day today." His frame of reference is a picnic with his sweetheart. A farmer says, "It's a nice day today." His frame of reference is that it is a good day to mow hay. The young man's frame of reference was his own subjective pleasure, the farmer's the work he did in relation to hard reality. (p. 255)

One also learns about clients' frames by attending to their occupations, leisure pursuits, stage in the life cycle, generation, and subcultures. These should give important clues to their frames of reference. For instance, knowing a client is on a weight-training program may help you draw parallels between weight training and therapy progress which will make sense to him because it connects to another aspect of his experience, and opens up a whole new range of labels and frames which may be helpful for viewing his experience. The stiffness and pain associated with the initial work is an expected sign of progress in weight training and may help a marital client who has always avoided anger and unpleasantness view initial disagreements and difficult discussions as progress towards a stronger relationship.

One should also learn to pay careful attention to client word choice, the tonality of expression, areas of flatness, animation, or extra emphasis, misuses of words, peculiar words or phrases, and grammatical constructions used frequently. Nonverbal behavior should be observed as well as it may qualify the clients' verbal messages, and indicate how they should be interpreted, as mentioned in Chapter 9 on sculpting. All of these help the therapist to adapt to and understand the clients' frames of reference, and use them to change those frames or labels which are targeted for change.

A final caution about evaluating client frames is to be aware that clients will be adjusting their frames to yours at the same time you are adjusting yours to theirs. The extent to which they fail to do this is an indication of their pathology or rigidity in treatment and should help you to create realistic treatment expectations and choices of interventions. They will present themselves in a frame which is consonant with the profession of the expert they have contacted, and they may have contacted several. If you are a doctor you will hear physical complaints; if you are a psychologist you will hear mental abnormalities; if a social worker or welfare worker, complaints relating to support and shelter. All of these complaints may be related to the same problem and may simply be the patients' way of varying their presentation to capture your attention and interest. In addition, a client's presentation of reality may be bimodal, with one set of labels and constructs to deal with healthy behavior and one to deal with problem or sick behavior. It is useful to have a brief, nonproblem-focused discussion at the initial interview so that you will hear both frames and know how to move linguistically and conceptually from the problem focus to the health focus. This is what some therapists accomplish by having the family define their optimal outcome and then ask the family to further define it by phrasing all their desired outcomes in terms of positive behaviors rather than in terms of what they don't want to have happen.

This section has been concerned so far with only one aspect of observing the family, that of appreciating and learning their frames of reference. One should also pay attention to the family style, which for example, may be playful, oriented to authority, laissez-faire, or democratic. Their style can then be used when presenting reframes to them, making the reframes appropriately concrete and specific or metaphorical and vague, serious or humorous, authoritarian and one up, or puzzled and one down.

Choice of Reframe Targets

Knowing which behaviors or sequences to target for reframing is difficult. There are common situations in therapy, discussed below, where one can profitably employ reframes. Other possibilities must be felt by intuition and experience, or selected by theory. While theory is no substitute for experience, neither is experience a substitute for theory. A good theory will guide the therapist in choosing where to look for problems and how to intervene.

Common intervention indicators may be (1) black and white thinking, or extremely limited world views, (2) families who see only negatives or, alternately, who never comment on positives, (3) families who frame everything in terms of linear causality and blame ("I was only reacting to his action."), placing unilateral responsibility on one person and failing to see the interconnectedness of their behavior, (4) and families who resist doing a task which the therapist believes will be helpful. One should also consider reframing when needing to focus attention on specific solutions or problems, to delegate responsibility for change to the family, or to focus the family's attention on skills and resources they have for creating change.

The therapist can and often should focus on those aspects of the family which are being overlooked. Families frequently have an exquisite terminology for negative events in their life, but very few labels for positive events. They can name many negative attributes of each other, but may be stuck when asked to come up with just one characteristic about each family member which they like. Barton and Alexander (1983) have experimentally confirmed this deficiency of positive acknowledgment in delinquent families. Alloy and Abramson (1979) have done similar work which suggests that people only use about half of their experience in constructing their views of the world, and that individuals who are "normal" tend to choose the more positive half. Minuchin, Montalvo, Guerney, Rosman, and Schummer (1967) have noted the tendency for families stuck in repetitive problem patterns to overlook novel changes when they do occur, and pointed out how important it is for the therapist to highlight such changes.

Collecting the Details

The main skill to be learned here is to work to elicit details which will help in fitting reframes to the family's reality. One still has to attend to the details which are important to the family, but it is helpful to generate some overlooked features to counterbalance these. Events occurring in the session can also be incorporated into the group of details the therapist will include. These are useful as they are open to influence by the therapist, who may create family activities in the room which will highlight different behaviors or interactional possibilities for use in strengthening the reframe. These "facts" are also less open to dispute by the family as they occurred in the presence of the therapist.

For example, a mother was seen with her three adoptive children, two teenage boys and a 12-year-old girl. The boys were presented in a totally negative manner by countless examples and comparisons to both their sister and the previous children of this mother who was recently widowed, in her late sixties, and feeling a good deal of stress in addition to her parental concerns. It was necessary for the therapist to interrupt the mother's problem litany to engage the boys in a conversation not focused on pathology. During the conversation it was discovered that the boys were slow learners, but worked hard at school (offering the possibility of a developmental delay reframe), liked to do woodwork, engaged in mechanical activities by taking their bikes apart for repair, were interested in cooking, and showed a touching tenderness to a turtle they had found and adopted. All of these "facts" were possible building blocks for a different image of the boys, but none had been validated by the therapist. More details were collected by asking the mother to remain silent while the children discussed the situation at home and how to respond to the problems identified. The oldest boy took a leadership role, and the three participated in a very reasonable problem discussion, complete with realistic solutions. At that point the "facts" for a different frame were present.*

Creating a Context for Acceptance

There are several things that the therapist can do to improve the likelihood that the clients will consider his reframe long enough for it to have an effect. These include using the family's own language and phrases, particularly abstract or vague nouns or verbs and unusual figures of speech; putting things into the family's frame of reference; and making small rather than major changes. One also can go over material which is commonly agreed on by the therapist and family, emphasizing facts, areas of concern, and so forth to create what hypnotists refer to as a "yes set." This is particularly true of the details to be used in the reframe, which should be highlighted for the family right before or during reframes. A yes set is simply the creation of a series of agreements with the family so that they begin to develop the habit of agreeing with the therapist. Even disagreements may be framed by the experienced therapist as indicators of therapist-patient cooperation. Disagreements may be interpreted as indicators of how well the family and therapist agree, with the agreement emphasizing and highlighting minor disagreements and allowing a very positive process of mutual exchange of feelings and ideas.

---

*Mother had still to be reckoned with. Her frame was quite discrepant from one of "responsible boys." In such instances it may be useful to shift levels, and at a higher level interpret the responsibility of the boys as an indication of mother's success in imparting the knowledge of how to act responsibly, even if such behavior was not frequent. This latter reframe moves from a context of a knowledge skill, or temperament deficit to a performance deficit, and changes the problem from one of genetic determination or teaching to one of encouraging proper behavior—a more manageable task.

It is also helpful for the family to care about the therapist's opinion. This is accomplished by good interpersonal skills, such as active listening, by the creation of yes sets, and by the use of the clients' language, which encourages the family to feel that the therapist thinks like them, making the family more likely to consider discrepant points of view rather than ignore them. The therapist should also be neutral with respect to siding with family members. Therapists only present their current view of the "facts," so resistance, if there is any, is to the ideas and not the person of the therapist, who is free then to make another reframe if the first is rejected (Jones, 1983). The therapist will make mostly positive interpretations, particularly of powerful family members. It does no good to side with weaker family members through negative labeling, no matter how morally correct the therapist believes his or her point to be. They will suffer for it at home away from the support of the therapist. In cases of negative connotation where the goal is to have the client oppose the therapist's opinion on a specific matter, the therapist may wish to create some dislike. Alternatively, the family may be motivated to disprove the negative connotation by a wish to earn the therapist's approval.

For more resistant families it can help to create a prior set of confusion or defeat. With defeat the therapist emphasizes how the family has tried everything in their power, an admirable effort which has failed, and now must look for ideas which are outside of their usual approach because the usual approach did not help. This facilitates the acceptance of different frames from the therapist. With confusion, the family is bombarded with so many different ways of seeing things, so many challenges to their usual linear causal descriptions, so many alternatives, that they become confused and at a loss for one way to approach their problem. This may be accomplished by therapist vagueness in response to family vagueness (deShazer, 1982), including technical jargon. The family, now seeking any concrete way to organize their thoughts, will be more willing to accept the therapist's way of organizing their experience. This technique has been borrowed from the hypnotic literature. Its use here is similarly based on changing frames of reference in such a way as to leave the clients confused and ready to accept any organizing frame of reference (Erickson, 1964).

There is a body of other techniques which has developed from methodologies concerned with influencing people—hypnosis, legal cross-examination, car sales, to name the most prominent. These techniques deal with tricks of suggestion which can be used to get clients to consider new viewpoints or believe in new facts. Loftus and Palmer's (1974) work shows that words can be used to cue certain aspects of reality for recall, to alter recall, and even to create memories of what was not present in the situation. The latter is particularly powerful for the family and has been suggested by Minuchin et al. (1967) as well. As an alternative to waiting for new behaviors to occur, he would take a neutral or minor event and reframe it as having been an instance of a positive new behavior.

Words and phrases which presuppose the existence of what you want clients to consider can be very effective. These include the illusion of alternatives

("Does your child listen only for a few seconds or for longer?"), simple questions ("How does father show his caring?"), requests ("Tell me about the hopes you have for your daughter."). The above examples presuppose listening, caring, and hope. Equally powerful sentences can be constructed using a number of words, including those related to time (after, during, while, continue, since, before) and duration or commencement (when, still, during, start, stop, end, begin, before, after). Examples include:

> How long will you continue to be sensitive to your mate's needs before you tune them out?
>
> After you have finished helping _____.
>
> The next time you notice yourself thinking about your wife at work, _____.

These kinds of suggestions are hard to oppose because of the presuppositions included in the form of the sentence. Further examples of this kind of suggestion may be found in Bandler and Grinder's (1975) work on the hypnotic patterns of Milton Erickson.

Other powerful techniques are to place a negative in a sentence to focus attention away from the novel or questionable material and onto the negative, for example, "Mother does not realize just how concerned she really is." The attention here is focused on how aware mother is, not on whether or not she is concerned. One can also use the word "the" rather than the word "a" in questions to get agreement or recall of either spurious or real events. "Was it the lack of love from your mother?" is a much more powerful question than "Was it a lack of love from your mother?" since the word "the" presupposes the reality of what follows.

Adverbs and adjectives can also be used to influence reality, as their implications for gradations of meaning will be picked up by clients. Asking how long something takes will get a longer estimate of time than asking how short a time it takes. Even if extreme adjectives are rejected by the family, they will be more likely to meet you somewhere in the middle of their estimation and yours than if the adjective had not been used. Your use of "very jealous" may be denied, but concern and interest will be easier to believe in after using these words than indifference. Carl Whitaker (1982) uses this to great effect in his therapy by postulating much that is extreme and even absurd, making other risks or novelty appear more normal and safe. Loftus's (1979) work gives experimental confirmation to the fact that mildly and indirectly challenging a person's sense of accurateness of recall or perception can change later memory for an event.

Other techniques involve introducing information early on which will later be used to build a new reality. This should be done in an offhanded way so it is not challenged at the time. This will give the client time to consider it, and takes advantage of the fact that memory of and inferences about the statement will last longer than the memory of the source or of the accurateness of the statement. Also, since the cognitive schemata suggested will be used to control perception, they are best presented right before events, or as soon afterwards as possible, before the events are locked into another cognitive schema in memory.

The use of encouragements to get people to agree with reframes—using their language, tricks from courtroom technique, yes sets, confusion techniques—may sound like gross manipulation* of the client and may indeed be. The question of importance is whether it is done skillfully and for the clients' benefit. The therapist must believe in either the reality of the reframe or its usefulness as a means to an end which will reward the family for believing the reframe and keeping it alive. If the family is merely tricked into seeing things as better momentarily because the therapist wanted them to feel good about themselves, the probable result will be a family more discouraged than ever at their normal life which is so different from the one the therapist seemed to offer. They will be angry at the therapist for fooling them, holding out the promise of something better and disappointing them. This is particularly true the more power, authority, and rapport the therapist has, and is worse for reframes of labels than for reframes of context. Positive connotation usually avoids this problem by prescribing the clients' problem behaviors. Other task assignments can also be used to reinforce reframes. These will be covered in the section on variations.

Those who are uncomfortable with an indirect approach to creating new frames may want to consider using the more collaborative approach suggested by Grunebaum and Chasin (1978) who suggest saying "if rather than looking at things that way, we were looking at them this way, what would be changed." From our perspective this may be too direct a challenge to the concept of a unitary, essentialist reality, as this asks the family to admit it is wrong or to see reality as constructed and provisional rather than as one single "true" reality. We don't need to make philosophers of our clients, simply more effective people in their chosen lives.

Creating the Reframe

How to create reframes will be further elaborated in a later section. In addition to this advice, there are two other guidelines for success at this stage: (1) know what you want and pick a frame which will help move clients in that direction; (2) construct several reframes in your head, then select from among them the one that best fits the family. In constructing reframes it will help to consider the level of the reframing (societal context, complex activity sequences, single behaviors), the persons to whom the reframe will be made (heard by one person only, by the whole family, etc.), the response style desired and expected (compliance or defiance), and whether the reframe is a basic strategy of change or only one tactic of another basic strategy, such as task prescription (Jones, 1983).

---

*Manipulation: (1) to handle with skill, (2) influence; manage, (3) adapt or change. *New American Webster's Handy College Dictionary* (New York: New American Library, 1961).

For success, it will be helpful to remember to (1) match the clients' frames of reference and personal needs, (2) to match clients' actual language, (3) to match client goals while giving them new ways to achieve these, and (4) to consider how different the reality presented is from the clients' reality. Clients can be given new goals if we move to the level of the outcomes ("What will it do for you if you accomplish that goal? Is there another way to get that?"). It is harder to directly oppose their reality, but their reality may be transposed by placing it in a new context. Goffman (1974) talks of such transposition as being similar to changing the key in music, keeping the notes otherwise the same. In the case of therapy, the sequence of events may be the same, but if seen as play rather than as serious, they will not have the same effect. Trying to impose new meaning on content is less likely to be successful.

In general, it should be remembered that with reframing the therapist is not trying to teach the family anything. This is not skill training. You are to block old ways of seeing things to make way for alternative viewpoints. Tasks and prescriptions are used to introduce new content. The reframes offered should not be superficial or simplistic. This will merely injure your credibility with the clients. Reframes should be related to agreed upon facts or concrete events. Above all, don't lie. If you don't believe in the potential of the reframe or the potential benefit to the client of such a method, don't use it. Clients will read your nonverbal behavior and may distrust you. On the other hand, reframes will be easier to make when you accept the fact that you are not trying to discover the truth, but simply introducing new options for clients.

Two very general models of reframing and relabeling are to either take an activity with a label which leads to negative consequences

"I don't like event A to happen because it always leads to _____or makes me feel _____."

and to relabel A so that the negative expectations no longer predominate (i.e., to relabel the content of A); or to take an activity with a negative value attached to it

"I don't like A; A is wrong, bad, immoral, etc."

and put it in a context in which it makes sense and discrimination may occur in people's thinking or reactions (i.e., to reframe A in a new context). That is, activity A may be seen as all right part of the time, in some contexts, but not in other contexts, and it is better to have it for some than not to have it at all.

An example of both types of reframes would be a mother who brings in her two sons, ages seven and nine, who are both presented as not minding enough and too frequently involved in arguments with each other. Questioning indicates that the boys seldom come to blows, solve their own disagreements, but make a lot of noise which makes mother feel she has done a bad job raising her children. She also feels it is disrespectful when they question information she gives them or her reasons for asking them to do something. For example, one is talking on the phone to his friend who invites him to spend the night. Mother says no because she feels the other boy's mother must be tired after the two boys have played over there all day. Her son answers that the friend's mother is on the phone and says it is OK. This leaves mother upset because the boys were not compliant. The therapist, not wishing to argue with mother over her feelings of parental authority, instead begins to point out all the instances in the session where the boys have shown independent judgment (content reframe) and asks mother how she was able to teach such a difficult to learn and valuable trait to her boys. If necessary, the therapist may follow up by pointing out how valuable it will be for the boys to be able to use such judgment when a stranger at the store asks the boys to come with them so they can go somewhere nice while waiting for their mother (context reframe).

Seen in the latter context, mother may feel differently about the behaviors. What was before an indication of her failure as a mother is now an indication of her success. What was an indication of a totally negative trait is now something to be valued in at least some contexts. If needed, the mother can be taught a different way to give commands when she expects them to be carried out without question, and the boys can be instructed to sort out their difficulties out of mother's hearing, learning valuable negotiation skills in the process which the mother could also be made aware of. Such reframings should also increase the boys' sense of self-esteem, competence, and responsibility, and lead to decreasing arguments with fewer cycles where mother pleads and reasons and the boys answer back thinking that mother is inviting them to have a discussion with her. Certainly the emotionality of the interchanges will be decreased, which should help all interact more productively; the whole situation will seem like less a tug-of-war between mother and the boys. Finally, if the boys are trying to get mother's attention by the fights, they will now have to find a new, hopefully more acceptable way to reach this goal as fights are now labeled as OK, and not needing mother's attention.

Another example is that of a busy professional woman and her daughter who was lying to her mother about school grades, telling tall tales at school to impress her classmates and gain friends, and had recently stolen some lunch money which she spent buying treats for her friends. The issue of lying was the primary issue for the family. Unfortunately the label was so emotionally laden, calling up images of ruined lives, that it obscured much important interaction and was intruding into other frames, such as misperception and forgetting, and causing these to be reacted to as lying as well. The therapist's task was to create new possibilities for mother and daughter without denying the importance of the daughter's lying. The therapist chose to congratulate the mother on having a daughter with such a creative imagination. This served to free the relationship enough for mother to find new value in her daughter, and arrange for her to take workshops in acting and art. Lying was still an issue, but a more circumscribed one, and one which did not leave daughter feeling unable to please her mother.

Responding to Client Feedback

An aspect frequently overlooked by novices at this method is client feedback. With much attention placed on preceding steps, and so much effort invested, it is easy to avoid noticing that the clients failed to respond to the reframe so painstakingly created. This is human nature, but not particularly efficient therapy. Accepting that the customer is always right, it becomes important to move slowly, checking on family agreement with each aspect of major reframes. If the clients resist one should back off immediately, agree with the clients, and try another tack (Fisch et al., 1983). If clients are hesitant one can add new images from their frames of reference or experience to convince them, or make sure one matches their cognitive processing style (concrete, abstract, visual imagery, kinesthetic imagery, etc.).

Look for nonverbal cues of agreement in addition to the usual verbal cues, although even verbal cues will be telling. Polite agreement or overly enthusiastic agreement are both negative signs. Overenthusiasm is particularly worrisome as it usually indicates your inadvertent agreement with one side in a family argument. Failure to understand followed by excessive questions and intellectualization are also negative indicators. Nonverbal cues to look for are minimal head nods (yes nods), eye contact and head allignment with the speaker, movements synchronized to the speaker's, or signs of physiological relaxation either preceded by slight excitation or not. Relaxation will be noted by a decrease in muscle tension and postural rigidity, slowed or deepened breathing, decreases in blood vessel constriction leading to slight flushing of the face and dilation of the pupils, and a decrease in restless activity. Signs of excitation, when displayed alone are taken to be signs of disagreement. These include negative head nods, increased restlessness or activity, increased muscle tension and postural rigidity, break of eye contact, constriction of the blood vessels leading to a slight whitening of the face, and constriction of the pupils of the eyes.

VARIATIONS

Changing the Label

Relabeling is the most common form of reframing, often engaged in without the practitioner's awareness that it is taking place, or awareness that he or she is offering new options rather than giving the client the correct or real way to view the situation. Relabelings keep the context the same but offer a new definition of the content—the behavior or problem to be redefined. The behavior is moved from one class of activities to another, thus highlighting different aspects of the situation and allowing different responses.

The effectiveness of this strategy is based on the predilection of humans to deal with concepts rather than raw experience. We don't actually respond to behavior or perceptions for the most part, but rather to what they mean to us, and it is this meaning which is open to change. The model may be thought of as:

$$\text{Event a} > \text{Label A} \begin{cases} \text{attributes} \\ \text{meaning} \\ \text{classification} \end{cases} > \text{Consequences} \begin{cases} \text{feeling states, action} \\ \text{patterns, responses of} \\ \text{others, etc.} \end{cases}$$

We are so used to thinking in such classifications that our natural inclination is to speak in terms of them instead of observations. We do just suffer some umpleasant occurrence in our lives such as having to do the dishes for a sick sibling before going out to the high school dance. We experience *unfairness* and *injustice,* which are much harder to live with despite the fact that they are abstractions and inferences, not real at all. When one reframes depression as perseverance in pursuit of ideals, what is changed is one label for another label with different consequences. The concrete basis of these labels may not be named, but we are so used to operating with language symbols that it seems as if we are talking about a direct experience of reality, which is exactly the trick our clients fall for which gets them into trouble. A more complete example is: lack of erection (concrete event) > lack of caring (interpretative label and win-lose frame, "he is doing this to me") > rejection (label-appropriate feeling response) > emotional distancing (emotion-appropriate behaviors).

Relabelings may also be grouped under common therapeutic varieties. *Role relabelings* are very effective as roles usually call forth a number of action patterns, resources, and relationship implications. In family therapy for example, when one wants to emphasize parental traits the couple may be addressed as Mom and Dad, while they may be referred to as husband and wife, your spouse, or by first names or affectionate names to emphasize marital roles. A father who is not using needed managerial skills at home may be made the "boss" on a particular family "project." A master sergeant who carries too much of his role home may be relabeled as caring rather than coercive or threatening, but needing the help of his family to learn new ways to father. This may entail a variety of prescriptions, as discussed in Chapter 5. Behavior prescriptions may also serve as role labels. The children may be asked to salute father when he makes a request, thus reminding him of an inappropriate role, or with a sensitive father, to thank him for his caring when he acts out his sergeant role at home.

The salute is an example of a *nonverbal reframe,* which can be a subtle and hard to resist reframe. In a family where a mother was discrediting her teenage children's responsibility and general competence, a therapist at the end of the session showed the video consent form only to the mother. The supervisor noted that this acknowledged mother's incompetence frame, which could have been subtly challenged by showing the consent form to all the children, treating them as competent. Restructurings of family behavior, enactments of behavior patterns in the room, and tasks may also serve as action reframes. In the same family it was suggested that the children have a children-only problem-solving session to develop a behavioral contract and present it to mother, through the daughter, for her approval. This both respected mother's frame of parental authority and competency in her daughter, but also allowed the boys to show competence and concern by participating in the discussion. In another family the husband objected not to his wife's specific spending and budget, but to his feeling of inequity in the family spending which left him feeling depressed, neglected, and dispossessed. His wife was instructed to place a copy of all expenditures on the refrigerator door for him to initial. While he did not sign them all, his mood lifted and he felt more in control, despite the fact that there had been no behavioral change in his wife's spending, only in his feeling of being in control of the expenditures.

Developmental relabelings are also effective (Coopersmith, 1981) and commonly employed. A child may be defined as younger than his or her chronological age on the authority of the therapist, with no rationale. The developmental delay may also be described as (1) due to illness or other specific circumstances which have interfered with development; (2) as a deliberate act of the child to help someone; or (3) as a result of choosing to pretend to be younger. In all cases new modes of interaction are called for. In the first the child's behavior is defined as involuntary and is taken out of the frame of deliberate action, usually relieving intense emotional reactions. In the latter two the behavior is defined as under voluntary control with implications for change. In general, these redefinitions usually motivate the labeled child to disprove them. They serve in the second case to diminish unnecessary emotional reactions from others and to focus parental activity in the third. They may also help to eliminate unnecessary overfocusing on symptoms so that the family can focus on change where it is needed; for example, a problem the child is trying to solve for the family with symptomatic behavior.

Relabelings may also be evaluative and change target behavior from positive to negative or negative to positive connotation. This can serve to neutralize emotions and promote work in sessions and at home, or can activate emotions to increase the motivation to work. Problems can be changed from bad to good, from big to small or small to big; too big to work on, too small to concern oneself with when one has more important work to do. A decrease in harmful emotional reactions is exemplified by the frequently used reframe to transform behaviors from indications of parental failure to indications of parental success. An example was given earlier where mother felt her children's age-appropriate independence was an indication of her failure, and this was interfering with problem solving by mother who was so interested in succeeding in a limited way that she became inflexible. There the reframe could have been even further advanced by telling mother her children were "precociously independent." This would be a second, indirect suggestion of good mothering for having such precocious children (assuming, of course, that this is a good label, and not one meaning headaches for mother, as it does to some).

Two large classes of evaluative relabelings are positive and negative reframes. Positive relabelings involve pointing out the positive side of the behavior, and have been called "seeing the good" by L'Abate (1975b). Landfield (1975) has offered several examples of positive reframings: rigidity as steadfast purpose; immaturity as aggressive exploration; hostility as involvement; confusion as a breakdown in preparation for new growth. Weeks (1977) has noted the positive relabeling benefits of an increased sense of personal control, a freeing of the individual to look at other, more meaningful problems, and an expectation of change in the future. He lists several more examples of positive reframing:

reclusive: exploring one's own consciousness
withdrawing: taking care of oneself
passive: ability to accept things as they are
asocial: carefully selecting one's acquaintances
submissive: seeking authority and direction in order to find oneself
insensitive: protecting oneself from hurt
seductive: wanting to attract other people and be liked
wandering: exploring all possibilities
oversensitive: tuned in to other people, aware and alive
controlling: structuring one's environment
impulsive: able to let go, be spontaneous
oppositional: searching for one's way of doing things
self-deprecating: admitting one's faults to oneself
crying: ability to express emotion, especially hurt

One example of a positive relabeling involved a young college student who had excessive concern over his test-taking ability. His grades, previously good, were now failing due to his inability to take tests. Once in the testing room and started, he did well, but had come to dread tests because of the anticipatory anxiety they generated. He took this as an indication that he would fail the test, despite his level of preparation. As a result, he did not enter the room to take the test. This science student was given a long, detailed description of the physiology involved in the situation, which culminated in a description of anxiety as excitement, a bodily energy which was generated for use in an appropriate situation, which would deteriorate into anxiety if not used. This gave an entirely new meaning to his experience, which was now seen as a sign of test preparation rather than a sign of impending failure.

It is possible to positively label what a behavior connotes rather than the behavior itself, which remains negative out of context. The Milan group (Palazzoli et al., 1978) noticed, as have many others, that compliments which placed behavior in a positive light were less frequently rejected than relabelings which were perceived as critical. They viewed symptoms as attempted solutions or working solutions which helped support the status quo of the family. As a result symptoms were seen as difficult to change unless the status quo was otherwise supported, or the symptoms were replaced with better solutions. *Positive con-*

notation was developed as a way of gaining rapport with the family, of letting them know the therapist appreciated their good intentions, and appreciated their needs for stability. It was a way to support the status quo so that the family was more free to experiment with new patterns of behavior. It set up a situation opposite that of normal therapy where the therapist pushes for change and the family resists, fearing change and qualifying for treatment by continuing to need the therapist's help.

Families stuck because of repetitive interaction around a symptom, with almost exclusive focus on the symptom ("Everything is just fine except for our daughter's not eating.") are also good choices for reframing. Positive reframes of the symptoms and family interaction can help the family get down to the business of focusing on family interactions which need changing (Andolfi, 1979; Grunebaum & Chasin, 1978; Palazzoli et al., 1978). Such positive reframes may block scapegoating, help the identified patient escape the patient role, and give the patient a sense of control over his or her behavior. More will be said about positive reframes below.

In practice, positive connotation involves reframing the intentions of those who are being asked to change in the family. Symptoms are seen as benevolent acts which help protect the family, or support it in the face of outside threats. Such reframings are usually accompanied by behavioral prescriptions which encourage the family not to change. It is important to reframe both family and symptom bearer behavior, as blame would be implied if only one or the other's behavior was positively connoted. The goal is to describe the situation so that no one is seen as benefitting unilaterally at the expense of another. Such reframes may be made by direct statements, or questions which concern the negative effects of the cessation of the problem behavior on the family, e.g., "who would have to change the most?", "who would be most disappointed?"

Positive connotation is not intended to tell patients with serious or troublesome problems, or their family, that they are doing things right and do not need to change. Rather, when it is used well, the family may have the question, "If this is so great, why do we have to suffer to achieve our goal?" At the individual level, even the symptom bearer may feel the "sting" of the reframe, feeling somehow that he is a "sucker" for his self-sacrifice (Todd, 1982). While the Milan group has not proposed a theory of how it works, it is clear that the positive connotations, with their inclusion of all family members, help the family to see the interconnectedness of their behavior, reducing blame and allowing for solutions where the whole family succeeds without the need for a scapegoat. In order for positive connotation to be effective, the presumption is that the description of the family must be correct at the system or relationship level, that is, correct in the supposed outcome which the family is achieving or attempting to achieve with the symptom.

This approach was used with a family which presented itself for therapy because the mother was not getting along well with her 9-year-old son. She had begun a graduate program the year before, following fourteen years as a housewife. Her complaints focused on the demands of her son and their effect of keeping her from her studies. Mother also revealed in a discussion of her study habits that she worked best under pressure, particularly if she was angry. Given this, her son's behavior was reframed as that of a sensitive and loving boy who cared enough about her to let her get angry enough at him to do some good studying. He was instructed to "bug" his mother at least once a week at a time when he thought she needed to study. The report from the family the next week was that the boy's behavior had improved.*

Another case involved a 12-year-old girl who was seen by a pediatrician with unexplainable somatic complaints which did not conform to the expected neural pathways for the localization of pain. An interview with her family revealed that her pains developed when her parents argued, and effectively stopped the arguments. The girl was encouraged to continue to fulfill this important function for the next week, her parents asked to have some pretend fights to test her compliance, and the siblings were told they should take over for her in case she forgot or refused. The parents reported feeling foolish when they thought of fighting and didn't; the girl's pains ceased and did not return; the siblings refused to take her place; and the parents asked for marital therapy to more effectively deal with their differences. This was in stark contrast to previous therapy where they had terminated when the therapist suggested the parents had marital problems which should be focused on.

Positive relabelings also avoid the possibility of alienating parents by seeming to place blame on them for the patient's symptoms. Criticism, even if believed to be correct by the therapist (who is operating in the frame of an unquestionable, unitary reality) usually leads to indignation, resistance to the therapist's other ideas, and missed treatment sessions. The family might also engage in angry depressive maneuver as noted by the Milan associates (Palazzoli et al., 1978) who comment on the "we have completely failed" stance of families which reduces the therapist to impotence. The therapist is given responsibility for change since the family has failed, and the family waits patiently for the therapist to show them that he can do no better. Viaro (1980) addresses such matters quite clearly in his article on context markers.

Negative framings also have considerable value, and may be more helpful than any positive reframe. They involve taking something usually considered good and reframing it as bad, with the general implication that the behavior is carried out to the extreme or inappropriately expressed. They may be particularly effective in stopping problem escalations created by the effort to change the patient in problem-maintaining situations. These cases are recognized by excessive efforts which amount to minimal positive outcome. Families may be trying to achieve unrealistic results, and in their efforts may be damaging their chances of achieving realistic goals. For example, students who try to achieve perfect manuscripts on their first draft rarely are able to get them completed. Those

*Case reported by therapist, Sadell Sloan, Ph.D.

who work for successive approximations to good copy do better and work more productively, as do those who aim for only better than adequate products. In these cases the "perfect" is said to be the enemy of the "good" and is negatively labeled (Watzlawick et al., 1974).

Negative labeling was used in the case of parents whose son had been struggling for several years in school but was nevertheless seen as a genius. The parents took his repeated failures and withdrawals from class as an indication of lack of effort on his part. In addition to other interventions in the family, the student was told that he was not a brilliant individual as he has been led to believe. In fact, reflection on the facts he had presented of his high school years indicated he was somewhat of a "grind" who succeeded due to his working harder than the other students and using his ability to the fullest. This effort prepared the way for him to relax his first year at college and still achieve good grades, but led him to wrongly believe he should be able to continue to do well without working hard. His pattern was to do "well" in classes up until the first midterm, a result he described as being due to test anxiety. He was told that now he was to begin to work as hard as he had in high school, with the understanding that he was not a genius doing poorly (a fact supported by his intelligence test results), but an average student who had achieved success in the past and could again achieve it through hard work. Negative connotation is also useful where one wants to reverse the patient's opening stance in therapy for paradoxical results. With patients who present a host of evidence that other therapists have tried to help them and failed, you may want to be wary of trying the same yourself. Keeping the context frame, you announce that you don't believe they can change. Although some of your colleagues might disagree, you aren't optimistic. Now the clients may shift to the stance that they can change while you maintain your skeptical stance. Under this guise you can do useful therapy by warning them about what will happen to cause a relapse, always in the form of a baleful prediction which the clients will have to disprove. The clients' continuing disproval of your predictions are the indicators that therapy should continue, rather than the usual failure to change.

In the above use of negative connotations, the therapist expects and wants the client to oppose him. These interventions are thus said to be "defiance based" and work through the client's efforts to disprove the therapist. They seem to work best with those struggling with issues of control and independence, and should be considered with teenagers and the elderly (Tennen, Rorhbaugh, Press, & White, 1981). Examples include telling a teenage boy that the problem behavior he is exhibiting to his parent's dismay is unchangeable, and a sign of latent homosexuality, and the already mentioned labeling of anorexia as a "girl's disease" to a young male client.

One family organized itself around its opposition to the former father and husband who was now divorced and extruded. While not living in the most comfortable circumstances, they prided themselves on living independently of the father, who had been a wife abuser. Unfortunately, the family still found itself exhibiting coercive patterns which recalled the verbal and physical fights with the father. When the idea of their changing was presented, they were all willing for the others to change and saw their own behavior as justified. Rather than argue with the family about who was right, or scold them, replicating the family pattern, the therapist complimented the family on showing such great loyalty to the father that they kept his image alive by their fights. The daughter immediately objected to this idea, and her mother asked if there was anything she herself might do differently.

Viewing supposedly positive behavior as negative definitely shakes up the family (Jackson & Weakland, 1971), and can function as an outcome reframe ("Your goal is OK, but you are going about it poorly."). In general, negative connotations don't need to be as accurate as positive ones. You don't need to point the direction for client change here, only to suggest what it is that needs to stop. The client is motivated to prove the image held of him or her is wrong, but it isn't necessary to indicate how he or she should go about doing that. The therapist does have to be believable enough, well-liked enough, of high status enough to be worth being disproved rather than just being ignored. Family cues can be used to help encourage the family to disagree by picking appropriately negative labels after an introduction which creates agreement with the therapist and interest in the coming reframe.

Changing the Context

We have seen how the context may be held constant and behavior relabeled in a way that leads to change. Alternatively, the larger context a behavior is embedded in can be changed with consequent effects upon the perception of problem behaviors without relabeling the behavior. Since contexts usually carry with them a set of rules for how to interpret messages or events which occur within the context, behaviors are assigned new interpretations when placed in new contexts. Contexts can be changed in a variety of ways, with these ways being subdivided into those which enlarge the context and those which substitute new contexts without enlarging the previous one.

One aspect of enlarged contexts is that the new perspective achieved often results in problems decreasing in significance, either because they have been replaced by greater concerns or because they have incorporated the problem behavior into the realm of acceptable fluctuations of behavior which don't merit any intervention. For example, in one family the parents were struggling to teach their daughter the manners and proper behavior she had not learned in her first seventeen years: they were each told to consider their daughter a guest in their home who would be leaving in the next year, and then asked to decide what were the most important impressions that they wanted to leave her with, and how they wanted to spend the remaining time with her. This helped them to place some petty interchanges in a different perspective and concentrate on appreciating the girl more. The guest frame also helped them to concentrate more on their own manners and behaviors than their daughter's, with consequent effects on her behavior.

In another family the father was long overdue to die from a fatal illness and had lived with increasing disability and periods of confusing recovery for seven years past the date his doctor had given him. The family had made no plans for his impending death, which they denied extensively, and were confused and conflicted about caretaking responsibilities and the degree to which each should help around the house. Much of this conflict about jobs served to help distract from father's condition, and was focused on the father-son dyad, with mother doing her best to groom the son to take his father's place. In sorting out instrumental roles and task assignment in the house, the father was asked to think about what he would like to teach his son before his death. This led to a shift in the relationship, with mother and father for the first time discussing finances, making a will, considering moving to a smaller house, and so forth. The therapist's question, innocent enough to be heard, but clear in its implications, refocused the family on the task of both preparing for father's leaving and savoring the time with him while he was still alive.

A second way to enlarge the family's field of vision is to ask about goals being sought rather than to focus on the unsuccessful and repetitive means being employed to reach these goals. This very simple outcome reframe, shifting from means to ends, may have powerful effects on identified problems. Problem behaviors may be seen as inefficient or inappropriate means to achieve goals or as applicable in only a limited range of circumstances. Placing the problem in a context where it makes sense should also offer relief to the identified patient and those who are concerned for him. Seeing behavior as goal oriented helps to normalize it so it seems less bizarre, or less destructive than if it is seen only as an attempt to irritate or anger those who are affected by the problem behavior.

Gregory Bateson (1979) has stressed the fact that people's frames, their appreciation of the context in which they are operating, are functionally equivalent to the rules of conduct for a particular group. Context defines appropriate roles and the roles define appropriate behavior, all of this usually happening outside of awareness of those involved, except to the extent that someone breaks the rules and is labeled as bad or mad. Depending on the particular context, there may be a wide or a narrow range of acceptable behaviors. A change in context may change a behavior's acceptability (e.g., what was unacceptable is now acceptable as it means something different), again outside the normal conscious awareness of those involved.

As a result of Bateson's theories, great attention is paid to the manipulation of context. As the rules for behavior exist largely in social frames, social markers of context become important. Frequently one set of behaviors may be very close to, or identical with those of another context, and can only be distinguished by context markers, which are needed to interpret concrete behavior. In wolves, for example, the same behaviors are exhibited in playing at fighting and real fighting, though in different intensities. In human interaction, we communicate at the level of context, according to Bateson, not at the level of concrete meaning.

The Milan group (Palazzoli et al., 1978), and observers of their work, like Viaro (1980), have used this idea in a sophisticated way in therapy. The Milan therapists will define problems in the family as nonpsychiatric and tell the family they may return when they have a psychiatric problem, inhibiting a medical context and implying to the family that they should take over responsibility for changing the situation. Or they may tell a family that therapy is over, but they would like to continue to see them for research purposes. In one case they told a family which had an anorexic daughter who was improving that the couple now had normal separation problems with their daughter, and would be seen for support and consolation concerning their grief, but would not be seen for therapy as it was no longer necessary. The bill, by the way, was the same in either case.

Goffman (1974) has written extensively of the power of frames, and noted that one can change the meaning of behavior in the way one changes the key of a song, keeping the sequence the same, but changing the impact entirely. He speaks of five major contexts of human behavior: play, contests, ceremonials, technical redoings, and regroundings. *Play* refers to a context where the inherent joy of the behavior itself is the reward rather than what is produced as the outcome. These contexts may be used to teach clients different goals and to be less disappointed or to focus less on outcomes. Madanes (1980), who plays out problem situations in the treatment room, uses this context to great effect.

Contests refer to highly organized struggles for dominance and are marked by prizes for the winner. Often therapists use this context with rigid, highly coercive and power-oriented families. For example, de Shazer (1982) reports the following use: "The weaker one will do something quite outside of his or her awareness to wreck their chances of success, but it is impossible to tell beforehand who is the weaker of the two of you." This was used to ensure task compliance and avoid the usual struggle with therapist control in task assignment.

Ceremonials refer to rites of passage (marriages, graduations, retirements) and may be usefully created for situations where none are available, such as divorce. Unusual behaviors during such transition states may be incorporated into such rites or defined as indicators of change.

Technical redoings refer to pieces of normal behavior exhibited in preparation for the normal context rather than in the normal context. Rehearsals are an example of this, as are experiments, dry runs, documentations, and others which may be used to great effect in treatment. One therapist* did retakes of interactions with a family, like a film director, and got different reactions in this new context. Another† asked a couple to make a tape of a normal marital interaction to prove to their daughter that they could get on without her. This allowed marital therapy to go on without calling it that and upsetting the couple by defining them as needing help. One can also get good task compliance by asking people to do things as practice they are otherwise unwilling to do. "Apply

---

*Case described by therapist, Marsha Weiss.
†The therapist in this example was Thomas Todd, Ph.D.

for a job, for example, but be sure not to pick one you think you will get." "I want you to ask three girls to go out with you this week, paying attention to your technique. Since this is only practice, be sure to pick ones who will not say yes."

Regroundings refer to performing normal actions for reasons other than those usually offered for their performance. Erickson (de Shazer, 1982, p. 97) for example, asked a suicidal patient to give him her last three months since she was going to kill herself anyway, and had her do a number of behaviors, (such as a "last fling") which she would not do and needed to do as a part of her daily life. The result was a reinitiation of normal development which led to her marrying and raising a family. The behaviors requested by Erickson—spending money on clothes, hairstyling, flirting, etc.—had all been seen as outside the realm of daily life, but were helpful in achieving normal progression in this woman's life.

Context changes can be particularly useful in helping clients comply with assigned tasks. Frames may be adjusted so that tasks are consistent with client goals and values, or interact with client goals and values, as in the case of contests or bets between therapists and clients ("I don't believe you can listen to your daughter for more than two minutes without interrupting her to offer her some advice"). When tasks and reframes are given together, the effect may be synergistic, each complementing the other. Tasks may prove the label or interpretation of behavior given by the therapist (the couple goes out to dinner and enjoys themselves without an argument). Frames and labels may allow couples to perform tasks which they would otherwise have been unmotivated to do because of skepticism or might have sabotaged due to anxiety or antici-patory anger from the expected reaction of their spouse.

COMMON USES IN THERAPY

There are several situations which arise predictably in therapy and are usefully dealt with by reframing. One occurs upon first meeting the family for treatment. They are almost assuredly feeling vulnerable, defeated, powerless, and somehow wrong for having to come for treatment. One can start by talking about normal or positive aspects of the family in the small talk preceding the discussion of problems. During this time the therapist can indicate by his behavior and interest that the family has its own strengths and competencies and is valuable in ways other than simply being an interesting case or problem to solve. L'Abate (1975b) suggests that one start off immediately by pointing out the positives in the situation, noting that

> Many people suffer, but not all care enough about each other or have the strength
> to want to do something about their problems. Most people who could benefit
> from therapy are afraid to acknowledge that need to themselves. This family has
> demonstrated its strength and caring by asking for help.

Such reframes change the mood of therapy considerably, and reduce blame and anger. The reversal of the family's initial feelings of failure and powerlessness has a major effect on the direction of therapy.

Not all the blame, anger, and disappointment will be relieved simply by noting the positives in treatment seeking. Families predictably come in with questions concerning how to assign blame in the family, or will already have assigned blame and want the therapist's opinion on what to do next. If the therapist accepts the role of judge or policeman and assigns blame, treatment may end precipitously with the family separating as they now know whom to blame and have no further use of the therapist. It is more valuable to move the family away from scapegoating, where one family member is presented as the cause of all the family's problems, and away from simplistic definitions of family problems. Alexander and Parsons (1982) have noted the tendency for problem families to explain problems on the basis of individual traits rather than more complex explanations involving more family members and external factors such as stress, life-cycle changes, and so forth. They advocate consistent efforts by the therapists to "nonblame" each family member. This means responding to family criticisms, negative labels, and instances of confusing, unpredictable, or inappropriate behavior, with a therapist label or frame which indicates that the family members are behaving rationally and adaptively in some context where their behavior is aimed at attaining a legitimate goal. If this is accomplished blame and defensiveness should be diminished and the focus shifted to cooperative problem solving and family goals rather than blame assignment. Family members will also be able to more easily see their effects on each other. Since the therapist wants the family to construct a more complex reality than one of simple one-directional causality and blame, the reframes should include reference to contextual factors.

Nonblaming can take place on both an individual and a familial level. On the individual level reframes involve the positing of positive, socially desirable qualities, a nonjudgmental approach, plausible explanations of behavior which are not based on inherent sickness or bad intentions, and avoidance of imperatives and commands concerning what family members must do or not do (Alexander & Parsons, 1982). Nonblaming is particularly dependent upon the therapist's manner as well as his words, and involves the characteristics of attentiveness, warmth, and respect for the individual.

At the family level nonblaming involves a focus on the positives, the family's strength and resources, on what works and what all can agree on and work toward. It is particularly useful to have the family phrase all their requests for change in a positive way, in terms of what they would like to see happen, as opposed to what they want to avoid or see stop. This seems to speed the progress of therapy and put the family in a different frame of mind about its potential to get what it wants. The therapist might also want to find ways to place blame for the family predicament on outside forces in a way which allows them to get down to the business of therapy and to bypass the issues of blame they came in with. Bypassing blame, or nonblaming, usually is best achieved by changing trait definitions of behavior (behavior is due to something permanent, inherent in the individual, and usually under the individual's choice or control) to state definitions (behavior is due to something outside impinging on the individual and creating a transient state which will pass). Blame can be ascribed to outside forces, family tradition and history, accident, or whatever is workable, and the family defined as engaged in a cooperative effort to improve their relating, which is being together — loving and valuing each other unconditionally. Problems may be attributed to external stress, to cultural patterns which were functional in the past but now are not appropriate, or to family interaction patterns which similarly were once functional but now aren't because of a change in family membership or the development of a family member to a stage requiring a renegotiation of roles in the family. When done properly the nonblaming frame will cast all family members equally as victims of their mutual but poorly coordinated efforts to help, of their past ways which no longer work, their ignorance, and legitimate individual needs which fit poorly with the family. No family member will be seen as a deliberate villain, willfully choosing the bad traits which the family attributes to him or her.

At this point one is ready to move to a higher level frame for the family, from a focus on the individual to a focus on the family interaction. This is the basic reframe of family therapy. There are several ways to do this, including nonblaming. Generally, families present models of one-directional or "linear" causality, where the treatment seeker is seen as the victim of someone else's behavior, helpless to change it, able only to react to it. The therapist may become involved in the role of judge or referee, or in the role of seer, telling the family that his linear causal way of describing reality is better than theirs. However, the best approach is to bypass the issue of blame, since blame is a linear construct which hinders the family from seeing the causal interconnectedness of their behavior. Frustrated despite their good intentions, they change the context from one of competition ("I'm trying harder than you are") to one of cooperation against outside forces ("We're trying but don't seem to be getting anywhere").

The inability to see behaviors as interconnected seems to be a sign of pathology in the family. Describing the nature of the teamwork involved in the marital situation may be difficult, but many couples can readily identify areas where the situation is set up so one must lose for the other to win, and many are interested in setting up situations where both may win. The outcome reframes mentioned earlier are useful at this stage. Once couples realize they must either hang together or hang separately, the situation improves, particularly with parenting problems where one parent is not helping the spouse, but is in competition with the other.

Another way to raise the frame to a relationship level is to talk of the fit between people rather than their inherent traits. The underlying assumption is that the pathology to be dealt with exists not in one person or the other, but in the way they interact with each other. When one focuses on the match between needs it is easier to reach relational solutions than when one focuses only on individual characteristics. Readers of "Dear Abbey" over the years will have noted that roughly half of the spouses identified as having sex problems were oversexed and half undersexed. Rather than ascribe internal traits of excessive or deficient libido, it is easier to talk about how one spouse has greater needs for sex than the other. The same may be said for needs for affection, conversation, and so forth. With this kind of frame there is now room for negotiation and less opportunity for blame and scapegoating.

Trait attributions, punctuations, and vicious cycles are three common characteristics of family interaction patterns and will frequently need to be dealt with by the therapist. In the marital or family situation the primary problem with attributions is that people will tend to ascribe those actions of others which are positive and desirable to outside factors, while attributing the negative actions of others to enduring personal qualities. Naturally, the pattern is usually reversed when viewing themselves, so that their own positive actions arise from enduring traits, while their negative actions are seen as due to outside states. (Those who always view their own positive actions as due to outside forces rather than personal agency need individual attention.) As noted above, trait attributions as used by the common person ignore the complexities of the situation, placing too much emphasis on the individual, leading to blame and punctuation problems. Punctuation problems arise when dyads or family factions forget that the family dance is a cooperative affair, not so much one leading and one following as an intermingled sequence of activity in response to an outside tune. It is more proper to speak of quality of the dance or ability of the couple than the ability of the individual dancers.

When couples or families insist on talking about who is in fact leading the family dance and who is following, using this discussion to assign blame and guilt, vicious cycles result. These are circular sequences where each person's behavior is taken as the cause and justification of the other's behavior. Each round of the cycle becomes more intense, with each person focusing more and more on the other's behavior and ignoring their own behavior's effect on their partner. Such cycles are recognized by the bitterness of the struggle, its coercive nature totally lacking in rewards or consideration of the other, and in the sense of righteousness each partner experiences. In a couple where the husband declares that his wife allows too little sex and hence he has become emotionally distant from her, she describes the situation as one where he is emotionally aloof and talks to her infrequently, only using touch as an invitation to sex. This leaves her uninterested because she does not want sex without preliminary intimacy.

Another common example is the wife who criticizes her husband for his treatment of their children, while he accuses her of undermining his relationship with the children and causing the children's behavior problems by always interfering when he is disciplining them. She states that she must interfere to protect them from him ("If you weren't so rough I wouldn't have to intervene." "If you would stop interfering they would be better behaved and I wouldn't have to get rough."). Each has described their partner's behavior as causal and their own as reactive, both describing the same set of behaviors. From this position it is hard to move anywhere positive, and useless to assign blame as that usually only serves to fix the interaction. One could nonblame, explaining to the couple with the intimacy problems how men are socialized to view sex as an appropriate path to intimacy, while women are socialized to view intimacy as an appropriate path to sex. One could also explain the form of the vicious cycle to the couple while nonblaming, using an outcome frame as well. The couple arguing over child-care could have their goal of good child-care pointed out to them, as well as the way each one's solutions call forth the very behavior they are trying to change in the other. A third method which can be used in more extreme situations is to repunctuate.

Repunctuations deal with intentionality and causality, and basically are used to affix the blame or causal responsibility in a way that undoes the logic which attempts to describe one or the other spouse as in control of the relationship. This approach involves changing the perceived direction of causality in a circular interaction, or in other words, a change in the identification of the initial step in a vicious cycle. Sluzki (1978) provides a very detailed description of the process and one worth reading in the original. Usually the process involves both positive and negative connotation, one type for each partner. The partner defined as the victim is redefined as benefitting from his or her partner's behavior. The partner defined as the victimizer is positively connoted. Sluzki cites the example of a nagging, pessimistic wife who was complimented for helping her husband look like the good spouse and for being willing to accept society's condemnation. This left the husband looking somewhat selfish. Combined with a behavioral prescription, the relabeling had a positive outcome for the couple.

In general, the expected effects of this approach are to create a sense of shared endeavor between the partners, shifting the frame from competition to cooperation, win-lose to win-win, and a sense of control over the symptom, as now it is a voluntary rather than an involuntary act. It is easier to acknowledge as voluntary since it is now seen as a benevolent symptom. Such reframes are frequently done in conjunction with behavioral prescriptions to continue to exhibit the symptom rather than change it. This usually introduces some new behavior for at least one person, helps the clients conceptualize their situation at the level of relationship rather than at the individual level of pathological behavior in one person, and allows the couple to blame escalations on the therapist who told them to continue the behavior (Sluzki, 1978). Blaming the therapist should limit escalations since anger and blame is turned towards the therapist rather than batted back and forth between family members. At a different level of analysis, Bateson and Reusch (1951) declare that people punctuate reality to verify their own beliefs. Reframes are needed so that they can see reality differently.

The change of people's frames of action from voluntary or deliberate to involuntary constitutes a frequent use of this method in family therapy. This may be done by keeping the label the same, but redefining the intent from negative to positive, as done above, or by changing labels to place actions within different frames. The latter is the basis of Minuchin's (1979) saying to the family of a girl diagnosed as anorexic that he doesn't know what anorexia is, that it is Greek to him, and proceeding to define the girl as stubborn. This shifts the responsibility for changing the girl from the medical expert to the family members, who presumably know how to deal with stubbornness. This type of reframe is frequently employed with the intent of not only changing the unchangeable, but of placing responsibility for change with the family while at the same time picking a label calculated to increase emotions around the symptom and motivation for change. The most common of these changes are from medical to moral frames, such as from "schizophrenic" to "sloppy" or "lazy." Such a relabeling highlights areas which can change and encourages the family to work at what before seemed a hopeless situation totally out of their hands and essentially unchangeable. In other cases, demedicalizing a symptom may move it from the class of those things about which something must be done to the class of those things which are accepted. Stuttering is an example. This condition is frequently very mild and only made worse by explicit focus and attempts at treatment. Some authorities believe the label itself creates the problem through the reactions from other people which the diagnosis sets off (Eisenberg, 1977).

The opposite type of reframe can also be useful. Reframing individual acts as involuntary and outside of the control of an individual can reduce blame and excess emotionality. Attributions of negative motivational intent associated with undesirable behaviors so defined become meaningless with such a reframe, deescalating vicious cycles. Reframes from moral to medical are the most frequent types in this category. When medical authority declares family change efforts to be useless, problems may improve precisely because the family has given up trying to create change in the wrong way (cf. Watzlawick et al., 1974, for extensive examples of problem-maintained solutions), leaving treatment decisions up to the therapist. In more simple cases, the family may stop trying to change the unchangeable and live with the imperfections or create more reasonable expectations for each other. The cessation of futile efforts may lead to considerable improvement even without change in the targeted problem behavior. Grunebaum and Chasin (1978) point out another benefit of medical labels. They feel that when used correctly these labels assist parents in avoiding unnecessary blame and having unrealistic expectations of themselves. Otherwise parents may be saddled with guilt which paralyzes them and prevents further change. In these cases labels of individual pathology and responsibility may be more appropriate to facilitate change.

There are many other situations where reframes may be consistently used, such as suicidal ideation (Bandler & Grinder, 1982, pp. 18–21). What will be standard reframe situations for any one therapist will depend upon the type of problems encountered in practice, the context in which he or she practices, the general therapeutic strategies employed, and level of experience and comfort with the approach. It would be impossible to present all of these situations here, but one final standard form will be presented because of its adaptability to practice and its inherent power.

End-of-Session Reframes

These are a set of interlocking reframes which are used to provide a powerful impetus for change to the family. They are typically delivered at the end of a session, generally to the whole family, and may be embodied in letters, as described in Chapter 6. The general form, described by Ganahl (1983) is:

nonblame
positively connote
give a sense of progress of evolution
give a sense of the whole
highlight problem area to be focused on
highlight the family strengths and resources available
tie to observed family interaction and related history, but not so closely that the family cannot participate in finishing the frame from its own imagery.

Avoiding blame has already been discussed, and while often difficult can usually be accomplished by either placing blame outside the family or by the positive connotation. Positive connotation is also described above. Reframing aspects of the problems as signs of incipient or impending growth is usually accurate and helps diminish the emotional pallor cast over the family by their feeling of stuckness or deadlock.

The first three reframes in this set create a yes set, or what de Shazer's group aptly calls the "compliment" (de Shazer, 1982). They facilitate family agreement with the therapist and closer attention to what will follow. The next two reframes create a focus for the family to use in their problem solving, while the next one indicates where or how to look for useful solutions. Taken together these three constitute what de Shazer's group calls the "clue." The final step is a general one related to the whole sequence and creates a final yes set. With this step the goal is to be ambiguous enough for the family to add their own meaning, facts, and constructions to yours to finish the reframe. This is based on experience with hypnotic subjects which indicates that they expand or add to the imagery offered by the hypnotist to create more useful images with a better personal fit. The goal, as with positive connotations, is to have an impact on the family system. Surprise and/or confusion are better indicators of success here than intellectual agreement and discussion.

LEARNING THE METHOD

Learning these methods is best done through experience. They can be practiced on an "as if" basis, creating reframes which will never be used. This can be done in response to clinical material or in response to experiments in one's personal life. The observational skills of determining someone's frames of reference can and should be practiced in all situations for good communication. Further examples of the clinical use of these materials may be found in Watzlawick et al. (1974), Minuchin (1974), Feynes (1976), L'Abate (1975), de Shazer (1982), Fisch et al. (1983), Coopersmith (1981), Haley (1963), Palazzoli et al. (1978), and Bandler and Grinder (1982). Meichenbaum's (1974) text on cognitive behavior modification is also useful. More theoretical material will be found in Goffman (1974), Grunebaum and Chasin (1978), Bateson (1979), Valins and Nisbett (1972), Bem (1972), and Cronen, Johnson, and Lannamann (1980). While practice will help considerably, more sophisticated use of these methods will only come with an understanding of their theoretical underpinnings.

As with any method, the best learning comes with experience. Fortunately, in this case students can gain as much practice as they wish by putting these methods into practice in their daily lives.

5

Prescriptions

Use Them if You Can

As discussed in the preceding chapter, positive reframing may be to family therapy what interpretation is to individual therapy. Once the symptom, the symptomatic behavior, or the reason for referral has been positively reframed, the therapist needs to decide whether positive reframing is enough. At least with families, positive reframing is not enough. It will take more than words to shake and change a family. It will take a strong reminder, one that the family takes home and cannot ignore. Positive reframing, no matter how valid or well delivered, is not enough because a family can and will distort, forget, deny, and discount anything that has been said to them, especially abstract verbal statements that are not specifically anchored in the behavior that takes place in the home.

The family needs, then, to take away from the therapist's office something—a piece of paper, a note, a letter, a set of written instructions—that allows them to apply at home what they have learned in the therapist's office. In a way, this approach is not too different from what we get when we go to a physician or take a pet to a veterinarian. For lack of a better word and despite the medical connotations, we call this set of instructions a prescription because it does prescribe; that is, it asks the family to do something as requested by the therapist (de Shazer, 1982).

WHAT IS A PRESCRIPTION?

A prescription is a set of instructions or injunctions that the family is to follow at the request of the therapist. It may be stated in general terms, such as "Every time Jimmy throws a temper tantrum, make sure that you praise him for bringing the whole family together." Or it may be stated in specific terms, such as "Every time Jimmy throws a temper tantrum, tell him to postpone it until Saturday morning at 11 A.M., when he will be able to have his temper tantrum for at least thirty minutes. Be sure to remind him at least once a day that Saturday morning at 11 A.M. will be his time to have his temper tantrum." Because the preceding prescriptions are not mutually exclusive, they may become Points 1 and 2 of a prescription that goes from the more general positive reframing about the function of the temper tantrum (Point 1) to more specific instructions on how to handle the temper tantrum (Point 2).

Prescriptions may fulfill a variety of functions for the therapist. They can serve as (1) commands about what the therapist wants the family to do (if the word *command* is too strong, substitute *request*); (2) reminders from the therapist about what the family is to do (the more specific the better and preferably in writing so that the prescription is not forgotten, displaced, distorted, or discounted); (3) a push for change, asking the family to do something they may not have done before, even though it may seem unusual, even "crazy"; (4) if written, a binding contract between the therapist and the family. The prescription becomes the symbol of how the therapist chooses to help the family in response to their request for help. If the prescription is not followed by the family, the family may not be as interested in the therapist's help as they claimed they were.

Prescriptions serve another important function in family therapy: to test the family's ability or willingness to do what the therapist tells them to do. Diagnostically, the ability to follow directions provides one key to the family's functionality. If the level of upset or crisis is too high, the family may not be able to follow instructions.

Thus, a prescription should be given with a full awareness of the historical and situational context of the family at a given moment. As an example, consider the M family, who asked for help with their son Jimmy's temper. Focusing on the symptom alone fails to relate it to the rest of the family. What function does the temper tantrum fulfill in the family? Furthermore, what does it represent? Does it illustrate the incompetence of the mother? Or does it represent the parents' inability to pull their resources together in dealing with their son? Is the temper tantrum a cry for help and attention, or is it behavior that the family has reinforced for many years? What if the mother makes a big deal of the temper tantrum while the father pooh-poohs it, saying, "I had temper tantrums when I was a kid"? What is the position of the well sibling (i.e., the sibling who is not symptomatic) in regard to the temper tantrums? Do the temper tantrums allow him or her to be the "good" child while the tantrums define Jimmy as the "bad" one? A prescription would thus take into account all the factors that surround the recurring symptom, including the contextual forces that created and reinforced it.

Why is it important to prescribe? As noted earlier, prescriptions fulfill many functions that serve as a rationale for their use. Why is it better to prescribe than not to prescribe? Because prescriptions allow the therapist to learn very quickly what a family will or can do. Without prescriptions, the therapist may never know whether the family is willing or able to change for the better.

In the literature, prescriptions have been called directives (Madanes, 1984) and tasks (Andolfi, 1979). The term *prescription* has been chosen here because it connotes injunction and command. In this sense, we will do well to heed the admonition of Nichols (1984):

> The use of directives has become one of the most widespread techniques (read *method* in this context) of family therapy. Experientialists use directives to promote affective experiences in therapy sessions; behaviorists use directives to teach parents new ways of disciplining their children; structural family therapist use directives in the form of tasks between sessions; Bowenian therapists use directives to advise patients how to improve relations with their parents; and strategic therapists use directives to outwit resistance and provoke change. There is no question that directives are a useful tool in family therapy. However, when directives are the main focus of treatment, therapists become overly central; they direct families in order to manipulate them to relate differently to problems. The therapist who relies primarily on directives takes over the responsibility for solving problems, instead of helping families improve their functioning so that they will learn how to solve their own problems. (p. 87)

As discussed at length in Chapter 1, any technique that is being used by a variety of schools has reached the level of being a method. Furthermore, it is important to stress, as does Nichols, that family therapy cannot consist only of prescriptions. Prescribing is but one step in helping families change in the direction of becoming more responsible for their lives.

THE FUNCTIONS OF PRESCRIPTIONS

In addition to the functions already discussed, we need to remember that prescriptions fulfill at least three additional ones. First, prescriptions help in generalization from the office to the home. To expect families to change as a result of what they learn in the therapist's office is rather unrealistic. Some families may, but most families will not. No matter how powerful the therapist's interventions may be, the interventions are unlikely to transfer to the home unless a concerted effort is made. That effort is best achieved through prescriptions. Second, prescriptions allow the therapist to assess the family's ability to carry out assigned tasks and responsibilities. Essentially, prescriptions should be relatively easy for the family to implement, so that if the family does not carry out a task, it will not be a matter of ability but a matter of willingness and motivation. That is, they did not carry out the prescription because they would not rather than because they could not. Here, of course, the therapist needs to be sensitive to realistic contextual obstacles that may have hindered the family's willingness to carry out a prescription.

REFRAMING VERSUS PRESCRIBING

As said earlier, positive reframing for families is not enough. Both positive reframing and prescriptions are necessary in helping families. How are they different? In the first place, reframing in and of itself makes no explicit demands on the family. It may, indeed, have built-in, implicit expectations. One can positively reframe symptomatic behavior without prescribing it. Unless, however, there are serious and relevant reasons to reframe only, positive reframing should usually be paired with a prescription that derives (logically or otherwise) from the positive reframing. A prescription is an explicit demand made of the family; positive reframing does not, in itself, possess demand characteristics. In the second place, the two methods differ on a dimension of action. Although positive reframing does not require action per se, most prescriptions (except those prescribing no change) do convey a more or less explicit call to action. In the third place, the two go together to the extent that, ideally, a prescription follows more or less logically from positive reframing.

For example, as discussed at the beginning of this chapter, Jimmy's temper tantrum was reframed as bringing the whole family together. The tantrum could, of course, have been reframed in a variety of other ways, depending on the degree of fit with the particular situation. If bringing the family together was the stated purpose of the symptom, the symptom should occur again: Without it, the family does not get together! Further, it may be important that the temper tantrum take place only when the family is assembled. A third point to be made in the original *prescription*, then, is to require the whole family to assemble on Saturday morning so that they can be present at the temper tantrum.

TO PRESCRIBE OR NOT TO PRESCRIBE?

Prescriptions depend a great deal on the therapist's theoretical position. Some therapists would not be caught dead prescribing anything! Others would feel lost if they could not use prescriptions. The inclusion of this chapter does of course indicate that we subscribe to the use of prescriptions. We do not, however, subscribe to the mechanical and acontextual application of prescriptions. Prescriptions are a serious matter, not one to be taken lightly. Consequently, we suggest that prescriptions are neither necessary nor required in all cases. They should be used cautiously and sensitively. One should never, for instance, prescribe acting-out, destructive, or suicidal behavior. By the same token, one can prescribe patterns—such as discounting of feelings, discounting of personal worth, or discounting of the importance of each member to the functioning of the family—that may defeat a member of the family. Some guidelines, then, may be necessary in administering prescriptions.

Delivery of Prescriptions

The delivery of prescriptions may be just as important as the prescriptions themselves. How a prescription is delivered depends a great deal on the context that the therapist provides. Often it may be helpful to deliver a prescription with hesitation and uncertainty: "I am not sure whether now is the best time to do this. What do you think?" "Perhaps what I am asking you to do is quite premature. I am not sure that you are ready for it." Another way of delivering a prescription is through disqualification, either of the therapist or of the prescription: "I know you will think I am crazy in the head. At this time, however, I really do not know what else to do." "I am aware that what I am asking you to do sounds absurd now. However, before criticizing it, let's try it to see whether or not it works." A third way of delivering a prescription is by directly challenging the family's ability, motivation, and interest in following directions: "I really do not know whether you can do what I am asking. However, I won't know whether you can unless you try it."

Just as indirection may be needed with some resistant, rigid families, a certain degree of authority and certainty may be necessary with disorganized, even chaotic, families: "What I am asking you to do next week has been tried with hundreds of families, and I want you to try it, too. Do not worry if you fall flat on your faces. That may mean that what I asked you to do was too hard or too early or both."

TYPES OF PRESCRIPTIONS

Andolfi (1979) classified prescriptions into three types: (1) restructuring, or linear; (2) paradoxical, or circular; and (3) metaphorical, or symbolic. The first type—restructuring—is represented by prescriptions that use available elements and energies to change entrenched patterns of family interaction. By restructuring these elements and energies, this type of prescription allows latent characteristics to emerge and develop. In other words, restructuring prescriptions attempt to change the organization and structure of the family, using whatever is available to the therapist.

Restructuring Prescriptions

Andolfi (1979) subdivided restructuring prescriptions into six categories: (1) countersystemic, (2) contextual, (3) displacing, (4) system restructuring, (5) reinforcing, and (6) symptom oriented.

Countersystemic Prescriptions. Countersystemic prescriptions involve direct contradictions and countermands; for instance, asking the family to do the opposite of what they have been doing. If they have spanked and punished a child for misbehavior, the parents are now to praise and reward the child for that same behavior. Perhaps the best example of a countersystemic prescription is the one used by L'Abate, Baggett, and Anderson (1984) in dealing with mothers who allow themselves to be used as servants, cooks, bottle-washers—factotums—with all the responsibilities of the household but no authority. In this case, the woman, to revert her strongly entrenched position, in which all the other family members have the authority but no responsibilities, is asked to go on strike. Such a suggestion is of course resisted, not only by everybody else in the family but also by the woman herself. The more the therapist talks about going on strike, the more the rest of the family resists the suggestion. Eventually, if the woman is able to go on strike, either the rest of the family is becoming more cooperative in sharing responsibilities with her, or the rest of the family may refuse to cooperate with the therapist, demonstrating their commitment to the status quo.

Contextual Prescriptions. Contextual prescriptions are designed to change the family in the therapist's office, in ways such as the following: (1) altering the seating arrangements (mother and father together, with the children seated according to seniority, or, if the mother and the father are always rigidly together, moving them to opposite sides of the children); (2) requesting silence of a particularly vocal member who interrupts frequently; (3) engaging in conversation a particularly nonverbal member; (4) dividing the family into subgroups by generational or gender lines or by other characteristics; (5) encouraging the enactment (Chapter 9) of specific patterns of conflict by replaying or "pretend-

CASE STUDY 1

This case study shows how prescriptions can be used diagnostically to assess motivation for therapy. Although this prescription may have been premature and poorly delivered, the HWA was useful in fleshing out the poor prognosis for the family. The problem in the marital relationship was that the symbiotic relationship between the wife and her mother precluded the very existence of a marital relationship. Indeed, the husband seemed to be acting the part of a temporary babysitter. In a session at which the husband, the wife, and the wife's mother were present, the wife was told not to see her mother for a month. The wife said that she could not do that. Later in the session, the prescription was reduced to not seeing her mother for a week. The wife still could not (would not) agree. When the mother was asked what it would be like for her if she did not see her daughter for a week, it became clear that although the mother talked about personal independence, she had no intention of relinquishing her hold on her daughter.

The following week the couple did not show up. When they were finally reached by telephone, the daughter said that they did not want to continue, that she knew what the problem was but that she just could not follow the prescription. She added that her mother did not want her to continue marital therapy.

ing" to replay them; (6) suggesting specific topics to focus on and, by the same token, avoiding topics that are irrelevant or too emotionally charged. All these prescriptions keep the therapist in charge, on the ball, and active.

Displacing Prescriptions.   Displacing prescriptions move the problem away from the scapegoated identified patient (IP) and transfer it to another member or to another relationship; for instance: (1) focusing more on the so-called well sibling to find out how much investment he or she may have in the IP's being the "bad" child, thus making the well sibling the "good" child. This focus illustrates the degree of the well sibling's investment in maintaining the status quo as the preferred condition; (2) displacing attention onto the uninvolved caretaker, often the father, treating him as if he was the patient; (3) moving the overinvolved (with the IP) caretaker away from the IP and letting a less involved caretaker assume that responsibility.

CASE STUDY 2

When this couple got into an argument at the end of the first session, the therapists commented that the partners were very protective of each other. The wife agreed, but the husband looked puzzled. They were asked to think during the week about how they were protecting each other in the sense of keeping each other from being hurt.

The next week, they were asked about the assignment. The wife denied being protective, and the husband listed a number of ways in which he protected his wife, one of which was to intervene in the children's problems so that they would not bother her. The wife commented that she did not believe he was trying to protect her but had other motives.

At that point, the therapists suggested that although her husband intended one thing, that was not how it felt to her. Asked whether that assessment was correct, she responded yes. She was asked to tell her husband how his protectiveness made her feel. She told him that she felt as if he had no confidence in her ability. She felt as though she were in a one-down position so that he could be one-up. The husband was asked to respond to what he had heard to ensure agreement that they were hearing the same thing. Then the wife was asked to tell her husband what she preferred that he do and the husband was asked to respond until the two reached agreement.

System-Restructuring Prescriptions.   In system-restructuring prescriptions, the therapist attempts to develop new patterns of interaction: (1) teaching negotiation skills between parents, between siblings, and between parents and siblings; (2) changing sleeping arrangements at home, such as using an alarm clock to wake everyone rather than having the caretaker routinely assume that responsibility (L'Abate, 1973); (3) demanding, with equivocation, that children, including the IP, sleep in their beds and not in their parents' bed, except for roughhousing, play, and affection (mostly on weekends); and (4) encouraging sudden leaving by the parents (L'Abate, et al., 1984) to help reinforce generational boundaries between the parents and the children. In other words, in this category belong any prescriptions designed to change the context of the symptom at home.

Reinforcing Prescriptions.   Reinforcing prescriptions consist of maneuvers designed to strengthen incipient or beginning actions through encouragement, praise, and other rewards from the therapist.

Symptom-Oriented Prescriptions.   There are two types of symptom-oriented prescriptions: those in which the therapist becomes an ally of the symptom and those in which the symptom is attacked and challenged directly. In the first instance, the therapist not only reframes the symptom positively, as described in the preceding chapter, but insists that the symptom be maintained because the disappearance of the symptom would be too dangerous for the family. For example, because depression is an extremely useful condition to be in (as the royal road to selfhood, as an indication of emotional sensitivity and of being in touch with one's feelings, as the most authentic state of being because we are honest and all-together when we are depressed), it is important that the family and the depressed IP keep the depression as a way of learning more about themselves and the whole family. The therapist, then, should ally with any symptom that upholds the status quo.

On the other hand, the therapist may attack and challenge a symptom, questioning its usefulness to the family and questioning the family's need to keep such behavior. In this approach, the therapist takes the position of unbeliever, and the family needs to demonstrate all the reasons why they should get rid of the symptom.

Circular Prescriptions

Circular prescriptions are designed to "go around" the family system when the system is too chaotic, disorganized, or upset to follow linear prescriptions. When a family cannot (or in some instances will not) follow linear directives, circular approaches may be useful. They divide into two categories: One category consists of what have been called paradoxical prescriptions; the second category consists of what have been called metaphorical prescriptions (Andolfi, 1979; Weeks & L'Abate, 1982).

Paradoxical Prescriptions.   In the category of paradoxical prescriptions are at least five different types of prescriptions: (1) prescription of no change, (2) prescription of the symptom, (3) prescription of the resistance, (4) prescription of the rules that guide most destructive family transactions, and (5) prescription of defeating patterns.

Prescription of no change. A prescription of no change is relatively easy to implement: The family asks for change; the therapist urges them not to change. This may be the first order of prescription to be implemented: "At this moment I feel too overwhelmed by this family to ask you to do anything. Between now and next time I see you, please keep on doing what you are doing. It would be too premature or dangerous to do anything else." Or "I know that all of you want to change. However, at this time, changing might be too much too soon. Therefore, it will be better if you do not try to change anything until we get more information."

Prescription of the symptom. Prescription of the symptom is probably the most common as well as the most controversial of all circular prescriptions. When the referring problem has been positively reframed (as described in Chapter 4), it can be prescribed—provided the therapist follows some very specific guidelines. The prescription should follow the general procedure of assigning the symptom to a specific place (e.g., dining room, bedroom, kitchen, basement) and time, including frequency and duration (e.g., Mondays, Wednesdays, and Fridays or Tuesdays, Thursdays, and Saturdays, from 7:00 P.M. to 7:30 P.M.). After all, how do we control ourselves? By being at a a certain place at a certain time (frequency and duration), we indicate that we are in charge of ourselves, that we are fulfilling our responsibilities.

The reason that this type of prescription is controversial lies in its potential dangers. We cannot and should not prescribe destructive, even potentially destructive, behaviors. No acting-out behaviors should ever be prescribed. One can prescribe states underlying certain potentially destructive patterns, such as anxiety or depression, but never (well, almost never) should one prescribe behavior that will represent a threat or harm to anyone. The patterns of prescribable behaviors are sufficiently wide that the therapist need not worry whether anything

CASE STUDY 3

Linda and Scott began therapy complaining that Scott's temper outbursts and Linda's anxiety about being a good mother to their 10-month-old were hurting their relationship. At this time, Scott was having one to two outbursts weekly (as many as four in some weeks). Linda was very fearful of these outbursts. Scott was assigned the task of blowing up; Linda, the task of experiencing anxiety about not doing a task well. During two-and-a-half months of therapy, Scott had only one outburst, and according to Linda, it did not measure up to his earlier ones. Linda remained relatively free of her intense anxiety states.

Furthermore, early in therapy, an alternating pattern of victim-persecutor/rescuer was discerned in their relationship. Linda played victim, setting up Scott to persecute or rescue her (or both). Their assignment was to play these roles and also to report how they experienced those roles before a fight. An awareness of these roles helped them control their arguments, making them constructive rather than destructive.

is left to be prescribed. As will be explained in this and the next two chapters, hosts of prescribable behaviors are available. Because the symptom happens to be the most available, prescribing it, under appropriate conditions, is relatively easy.

Prescription of resistance. For families that are too resistant or chaotic (i.e., unable to implement any earlier, linear suggestions), prescription of no change can be used. The therapist must be aware, however, of the possible consequences, depending on what kind of family is asking for help. For instance, a chaotic, unorganized family may overtly desire structure and may ask for it, directly or indirectly. By the same token, when the therapist provides structure in the form of clear and straightforward directives, the family may not be able (for whatever reason) to follow them. The therapist then needs to be alert to subtle and not so subtle attempts to discount directives and to sabotage therapy. A noncompliant family may need to be confronted directly about their desire for change and whether they are willing to work for it. Verbal assurances and agreements, however, may not be enough. Only through the assignment of prescriptions will the therapist learn whether the family is compliant. Prescriptions, then, are one of the best diagnostic tests of how a family functions or fails to function.

A resistant family may be asked to avoid following the prescription because it may lead to change. Because change is a very scary and threatening possibility, perhaps it will be better if the family does not follow the prescription given to

CASE STUDY 4

The Walshes were a fairly chaotic family, composed of a father (Fred) who drank heavily at times, a mother (Ruby) who overworked herself to the point of exhaustion, and twins (Frederick and Kathy) who helped their father's drinking and their mother's overworking. They were seen in therapy for several months with a variety of complaints. In their last session, they complained that they never did anything together—and everyone blamed everyone else for that state of affairs. The mother blamed the children for not helping her and the father for going off on his own. The father blamed the children for fighting with each other frequently and placated his wife by telling her he was sorry. And the twins willingly accepted some share of the blame—they just didn't appear concerned.

These complaints were reframed to point out their positive aspects. Then the therapist prescribed staying apart, which everyone was doing. Saying they were not ready to be a close family, the therapist told the twins that they could help their parents by continuing to pick on each other; the mother and father should overwork and withdraw until they were ready to be close.

Although this family had not been seen at the time of this writing since that prescription, telephone conversations had suggested that the family members were much closer. The father had stopped drinking and was helping his wife around the house, and they reported that they were more tolerant of their children's teasing. A termination session had been set up to check on the improvements.

them. Here, as indicated earlier, the delivery of the prescription becomes as important as the prescription itself.

Prescription of rules. When prescribing symptomatic behavior is impossible or unsafe because of its potential threat, it may be helpful to prescribe rules of interaction that the family may not even be aware of. For instance, in a family that includes adolescents, the rule may be that any time a teenager's request is denied by one parent, the other parent will accede to the request. In this case, prescribing such a rule will be helpful because it is so strong and so ingrained within the context of marital discounting: "This pattern is so strong with all of you that I doubt whether I can do anything about it. While I think about it, why don't you go on with it? Be sure that when one of you agrees with your child, the other parent disagrees."

It is important that the therapist look for, discover, and bring out some of these repetitive patterns (i.e., rules), *without commenting on them.* However, once a hurtful pattern of interaction is fleshed out, it can be prescribed so that the family can learn to deal with it.

Prescription of defeating patterns. When defeating family patterns have been positively reframed ("Defeats may be necessary for you; they are the glue that keeps this family together"), they may usually be prescribed, as long as the space and the time of their occurrence are specified: "You should have a fight (figuratively, not physically) in your bedroom at least twice a week (depending on how often the family fights), from 8:00 to 8:30 P.M. How about Mondays and Thursdays?" Some of the specifics can and should be arrived at through negotiation with the family. The prescription should approximate as closely as possible what is actually taking place at home.

One form of defeat that should be prescribed is discounting ("What you say and what you feel are not important. What I say [feel, do, think] is important"). The frequency (intensity and duration) of the discounting could be prescribed generally (e.g., "Every time your wife voices an opinion, be sure to point out what's wrong with it") or specifically (e.g., "I want each of you to find ways of discounting one another at least once a day. Please keep a written record of each time you discount the rest of the family. The one who discounts the most will get a prize!").

CASE STUDY 5

A family consisting of mother, father, and a 16-year-old daughter presented the problem of the father and the daughter's fighting about which television program to watch (there was another television set in the house). The mother would have to settle the fight by taking one side or the other. The symptom—fighting—was prescribed to the family. Anytime the mother's attention was wanted, the father and the daughter were to fight over the television. After one such fight, in which the mother went in to ask who needed her attention, that kind of fighting stopped.

CASE STUDY 6

The family in this case study had been split by divorce. The identified patient (IP) was the 21-year-old son, who had taken the role of the father in the family and tried, whether asked or not, to solve the problems of his mother and his sister, aged twelve. At the end of the session, the mother and the daughter were asked to go to the IP throughout the week whenever they had a problem and ask him to help them solve it; he was to try his best to solve the problem. At the next session, the prescription was checked: Both the mother and the daughter said that they had not had any problems that they needed help with; the IP commented that they didn't really need to come to him to get problems solved.

In a session six weeks later, with the mother and the son, the issue of helping the mother with her problems came up again. At this point, the son realized spontaneously that he was trying to help his mother, not because of her need, but because of his own.

Metaphorical Prescriptions

Metaphorical prescriptions are of a higher, symbolic order than those already considered here. They belong to an abstract level that requires a great deal of expertise and comfort with metaphorical, or symbolic, communication. For instance, a family may be fighting about finances (or whatever); however, the underlying issue may be one of power and control.

One aspect—perhaps the main ingredient—of prescribing the symptom that is rarely discussed is the appropriate framing of the prescription. Often, paradoxical prescriptions fail because the clients see no reason for doing them; they thus discount the procedure altogether and continue their usual behavior. Unless a legitimate reason (framing) is given for engaging in the behavior, the essence of the <u>double bind</u> is reduced or lost.

For example, a couple whose problem is verbal arguments may simply be told to keep fighting. Sometimes this procedure may work, but the couple may react to what they consider the therapist's obvious attempt at manipulation. The trust and rapport between therapist and clients may then decrease, perhaps inducing the clients to oppose the therapist by continuing their behavior. The system is thus reinforced with the client's behavior and the therapist's obvious failure.

If, however, the same prescription is framed in the client's language in a manner that conveys face validity, the chances of success increase. For instance, if the therapist discovered in the session that the partners did indeed care for each other, he or she could make an appropriate transition, such as "Obviously you two care very much about each other, and the expression of this caring, as in all relationships, is vital to your relationship. Therefore, because fighting is obviously your way of expressing caring at this time, I'd like the two of you to continue fighting this week, perhaps increasing it in order to reassure each other how much you care for each other during this crisis." Such a prescription, logical yet confusing, truly creates a bind for the couple. Because they are hooked on the concept of caring, there is very little way of escaping the paradox. The paradox itself is often obvious to the therapist. The real challenge lies not in dreaming up the task but in framing it so that the clients will do it. In an instance of sibling rivalry, the issue may be to point out the competitive relationship of the parents, who cannot get together to discipline the children or who cannot bring their considerable personal powers to bear on the partnership of their marriage. Again, the issue is one of power and control. Thus, a therapist needs to be attentive to the abstract dimensions that subsume many of the destructive transactions in a family. Usually, although not always, such issues relate to power and control, dependence-independence, boundaries, limits, and clarity of communication. In some instances, the therapist may use a metaphorical object to point out to the family the underlying nature of their conflicts, a nature that can and should be prescribed freely.

Andolfi, Angelo, Menghi, and Nicolo-Corigliano (1983), more than anyone else in the literature, except perhaps Erickson, have devoted the greatest amount of attention to this type of prescription. They see the symptom or the symptomatic behavior as symbolic of the basic conflict underlying the family's dysfunction. The symptom simultaneously affirms and denies the origin and the context of the basic conflict. For instance, in anorexia nervosa, the child's behavior may represent a basic parental conflict about taking and giving. The authors distinguished various kinds of metaphors: (1) literary, in which the therapist refers to a well-known figure who has the same kind of conflict; (2) contextual, in which the therapist presents a connecting pattern or link by which most of the family's problems are interrelated—a "curse" or family heritage, a family script, or allegiances otherwise unmentioned. Sometimes, these seemingly abstract metaphors find expression in concrete objects, such as the family crest, the family Bible, family heirlooms, family pictures or portraits. In these situations, it may be possible to prescribe increased interactions with such objects: "Because it controls the entire family without your awareness, you may as well allow it to control all of you knowingly. Therefore, you should look at it [stay with it] for such-and-such a time [frequency and duration to be prescribed; the space is already defined by the metaphorical object]."

Other Types of Prescriptions

In addition to the classifications already mentioned, there are other ways of classifying prescriptions. One way is according to the dimensions along which they vary: (1) variable-invariable, (2) general-specific, (3) ad hoc versus systematic, and (4) direct versus circular. (If every type has not been covered in this chapter, do not worry; additional examples will be given in the next two chapters.)

Madanes (1984) has presented eight strategies for prescriptions: (1) prescribe the presenting problem or the symbolic (metaphorical) representation of the presenting problem; (2) instead of prescribing the symptom (if the family cannot follow it), prescribe the pretending of the symptom; (3) if the family cannot pretend, prescribe the function that the symptom is fulfilling within the family; (4) prescribe a reversal of the family hierarchy (e.g., if the children have a great deal of control, which the parents may deny, allow the children to become parents—in some of their responsibilities—and allow the parents to become more irresponsible, more like children); (5) prescribe paradoxical contracts like those in the examples already given; (6) prescribe who will have the presenting problem, a strategy that takes the pressure off the symptomatic IP; (7) prescribe the presenting problem with a slight modification of the context; and finally, (8) if a pattern is too entrenched, too rigidly held, prescribe a logical, physical extension of it that turns the pattern into an ordeal (Haley, 1984).

The Dangers of Prescription

If the prescription fails for whatever reason, do not attribute the failure to the family. Make sure that you, the therapist, take responsibility for the failure: "Very likely, it was premature for me to ask you to do it"; "I must have missed the boat; it was probably not the appropriate thing to do."

A carelessly delivered prescription may well miss the boat. It may be inappropriately and poorly timed; it may be inaccurate and invalid. A therapist always needs to be aware of the possibility of his or her error. A variety of results may ensue: (1) The family apparently follows the prescription, but nothing happens; that is, no change occurs. (2) The family is thoroughly confused by the prescription and unable to follow it, a situation different from that of blatant resistance, in that the family is otherwise cooperative and involved in the therapy. (3) The family overreacts in directions opposite to those implied or indicated by the prescription. (4) The family appropriately indicates the ways in which a prescription is inappropriate and that a more appropriate prescription is called for. In other words, a family will react to an inappropriate prescription, and the therapist will find out soon enough!

WHEN NOT TO PRESCRIBE

Prescriptions may be contraindicated in at least five conditions: (1) in acute crisis states, such as paranoid, delusional, psychosomatic, or psychotic conditions; (2) in the aftermath of a devastating trauma, such as suicide; (3) in the face of apathy, lack of interest or involvement by the family, when the therapist needs to motivate the family before intervening in any way; (4) in the presence of extreme acting-out or criminal behavior; and (5) when the family's thinking is too concrete or limited to understand any instructions (strictly linear, literal prescriptions may work better). If you do not try, you may not know. However, when in doubt, don't!

CONCLUSION

Well-delivered, appropriately timed, and properly couched prescriptions can be a powerful tool of therapy with resistant and chaotic families. In a way, this chapter, like the preceding one, is but one stepping-stone in mastering effective methods of family therapy. Prescriptions follow positive reframings and are followed by homework assignments and written messages, which are presented in the next two chapters. Families are powerful systems. It takes powerful methods of intervention to help them change for the better.

6

Written Messages

Put it in Writing

Among the methods designed to increase generalization from the therapist's office to the client's home, we have found letters given to families useful, indeed powerful and change provoking. Written interpretations, at least as we use them, are based on circular models of information processing derived from general systems theory as applied to the families of autistic children by Selvini-Palazzoli and her co-workers (Selvini-Palazzoli, Boscolo, Cecchin, & Prata, 1978).

During therapy, a great deal of information about a family is gathered, some of which cannot be handled within the confines of a traditional approach. It is important, however, to use this additional information for the family's benefit. The diagnostic value of therapy can be seen in the surplus information gathered during intervention. It becomes necessary, therefore, to give a family therapeutic feedback on the information gathered during the initial interview stages. As will be shown, even when written messages were given to couples or families at a follow-up session, they seemed useful. It has been found even more useful to give feedback through these written messages at the earliest stage of therapy, thus ensuring help for the inevitable ripples and reactions within the family.

THE VALUE OF WRITTEN MESSAGES

Anything that is worth reporting and remembering should be worth putting in writing. First, verbal interpretations can be forgotten, ignored, repressed, confused, distorted, or otherwise belittled and sidetracked. The efficiency and effectiveness of therapeutic techniques may be increased by giving interpretations in writing. Second, written interpretations may clarify communication and avoid the distractions that may interfere with oral interpretation. Third, written communications, especially if given to all members of a family, become a record that can be looked at repeatedly. They remind the family of what they need to think about or do—thoughts and actions that may not otherwise occur. Fourth, perhaps an even larger issue, and one that is apart from therapeutic efficiency or effectiveness, written messages pertain to the professional conduct of business. Most adult enterprises (industry, business, bureaucracies) get things done through written communications. Oral commitments may be misunderstood and thus broken. Written communications, on the other hand, are much more difficult to misunderstand and to forget. They become part of a record that mirrors and reminds the couple or the family of changes that need to take place in the marriage or in the family. Especially in marriage, which has so much potential distortion and deflection, it is important to show marital partners how many of these emotional issues can be put on paper and looked at with a minimum of distortion. The written interpretations may serve as models of how to record issues as carefully, concisely, clearly, and helpfully as possible. Consequently, some thought needs to be given to how to write these interpretations and when to present them.

Other advantages of written interpretations are that they clarify the therapist's perceptions and descriptions of the observations made and the information gathered during therapy. They are a record of what has been communicated to the family (and at what point during intervention). A written message forces the family to look at themselves, bypassing denial and other defensive reactions to the threat of change that is brought about by therapy.

A final value lies in the training potential of written notes. Students need first to pay attention to the surplus dynamics that arise from intervention, including just interviewing or observing. They need to look at the repetitive features of these interactions, to think about their meaning, significance, and functionality (or lack of it) and to form, as synthetically and positively as possible, an interpretive statement to be given to the family. In this way, surplus information is not ignored or misused, and the students learn a great deal while they help the family.

Other functions of these notes are: (1) to break impasses or repetitive, destructive patterns that are not otherwise breakable; (2) to confront issues not otherwise confrontable, especially when externalization, denial, avoidance, and lack of awareness are present; (3) to specify and crystallize vague issues; and (4) to depersonalize through the written word the emotionality surrounding any issue that the couple or the family faces.

GUIDELINES FOR WRITTEN MESSAGES

The writing of messages must be done under expert supervision. The statements should not be too long (certainly not more than a page) and should consist of no more than, and preferably less than, two or three important points. Each point may consist of one asset accompanied by its liability, or the flip side of the asset. Or, if no connection between liability and asset can be made, most assets should be stated at the beginning of the note, followed by the therapist's concerns—what the therapist questions, muses about, wonders about—which are given as part of what the family needs to consider. Each member of the family should receive a copy of the note addressed as a personal letter. The copies should be handed to a couple or a family at a point in therapy when some follow-up can take place. The main requirements of these written interpretations are that they be (1) positively couched, to increase the likelihood of completely new and unfamiliar thinking (Chapter 3); and (2) positively worded, to avoid any possibility of put-down or lowering of self-esteem.

Other criteria or issues to be considered in composing the written notes are: (1) their cryptic nature, (2) the absence or the presence of prescriptions, (3) the different levels (smoke vs. fire) being dealt with, and (4) focus on specific genotypical issues (the fire level).

The notes should be cryptic in the sense that they raise more questions than they answer. If the notes were clear, direct, and familiar interpretations, they would lose their surprise (sometimes, shock) value. The second issue is whether the notes should contain prescriptive directions. In a way, they should be diagnostic and interpretive but not judgmental or evaluative. Third, the notes should discriminate levels of behavior, that is, the presentational (facade), the phenotypical (most frequent mode of interacting), and the genotypical (underlying, inferred) (L'Abate, 1976). In this view of levels, a great deal of behavior, such as anger, is smoke (presentational and phenotypical), a way of avoiding deeper issues (the fire level), such as hurt feelings, loneliness, fear of hurt. Fourth, some of the issues that seem relevant to the genotypical (fire) level seem fairly universal, such as emphasis on Doing to avoid Being; emphasis on externals to avoid internals; imbalance of responsibility and authority; emphasis on thinking to avoid feeling; digital (on-off, true-false, right-wrong distortions) rather than analogic (continuous) thinking. (A review of the messages presented in this chapter will help create a more adequate list of underlying issues.) Fifth, messages should be *ad* relationships, not *ad hominem*—not directed toward particular family members but toward the relationships among them. The exceptions to these guidelines will prove the rule!

Consider the requirements before writing the messages. By their very nature, written messages are bound to produce a cognitive reorganization in a couple or in a family. In the following, we describe the process as well as the qualitative outcome of a combination of methods (i.e., positive reframing, descriptive and prescriptive messages).

BACKGROUND

The use of written communication in therapy is not new. Burton (cited in Pearson, 1965) used diaries for couples; Ellis (cited in Pearson, 1965) made a serendipitous discovery—when he wrote his interpretations instead of saying them (because of laryngitis), his clients seemed to progress faster. He commented that in research, therapy in written form makes it easier to

> parcel out the personal influence of the therapist and to determine whether the ideas of the school he represents are themselves effective. It may also be shown in the future that the use of therapeutic material in printed and recorded form may speed up the therapeutic process and make it less expensive than it now tends to be. (p. 35)

Burton (cited in Pearson, 1965), in considering the pros and cons of written communications (especially from the client's point of view), noted the following negative aspects. Written interpretations (1) may be dissociative; (2) may emphasize intellectualization rather than feelings; (3) may be used uncreatively by the therapist or the client; (4) may provide a defense against direct confrontation; (5) may reach the level of absurdity (if writing is overdone and personal contact between therapist and client is not maintained); (6) may alter the tone and structure of the therapeutic relationship; and (7) may promote introspection rather than the sometimes needed externalization.

On the positive side, Burton believed that written communications in therapy (1) may be a creative act and a catharsis (if written by the client); (2) may provide content for further analysis; (3) may evoke a rehearsal of the therapeutic hours; (4) may integrate better some contextual factors not otherwise considered in therapy; (5) may reduce the time required for treatment (if judiciously used); and (6) may be used in special emergencies.

The lack of relevant materials in the literature, outside the contribution of Selvini-Palazzoli and her co-workers (Selvini-Palazzoli et al., 1978), indicates that therapists need to study the application of written communications with a nonclinical population before applying them to clinical couples or families.

TYPES OF LETTERS

Some of the typologies used in other chapters (4, 5, and especially 8) may be used to classify letters. Here, however, we have limited ourselves to showing the kinds of letters that can be used in different situations.

A Linear Letter

Dear
I have really enjoyed these sessions with you and am quite fond of you both. You have a good sense of humor and care a lot about how the other acts and feels. Both of you seem to be working on communicating effectively with each other.
I have the impression, though, that sometimes you focus on money problems to avoid confronting issues that are more sensitive for you both. When you blame or put each other down and fail to deal with issues directly, communication and growth in the relationship remain at a standstill. Just because one of you behaves

in a hurtful way, that does not justify the other in behaving similarly.

Although you do seem to have a lot of commitment to this relationship, you tend to use your friends to escape marital responsibilities. By making your friends more important than your marriage, your involvement with them detracts from your relationship with your partner. I think you have to decide whether you want to be married or whether you want to remain single.

A Paradoxical Letter

Dear

I am very impressed with your commitment to your marriage and how much you care for each other. Each of you is very considerate of the other's feelings, and you do not wish to hurt each other.

I think that it's very commendable that you care so much for each other that you try to be like your partner. Each of you can depend on the other to avoid confronting your differences. This has allowed you to achieve a harmonious relationship, one that it would be too risky to change right now. Why tamper with a good thing?

Dealing with Functional Couples

The examples here are nonclinical undergraduate couples who took enrichment (L'Abate, 1977; L'Abate & Rupp, 1981) to get course credit for a general psychology class (Weeks, Wagner, & L'Abate, 1980).

Couple 1.* John and Ann have been married for two-and-a-half years. It is the second marriage for both; they live in the suburbs with Ann's two children from her first marriage and their own infant son. John is thirty years old, works as a manager, and is taking management courses. Ann is twenty-seven years old and devotes full time to being a wife and mother.

Pretest rating scales indicated that both John and Ann felt that they needed to improve their communication. Ann revealed that she had been beaten by her first husband on several occasions and that in her second marriage she tends to withdraw rather than speak up for herself during an argument. John would like to be more open with Ann and to be better able to express himself when he is alone with her. Pretest results also indicated a large discrepancy between John's and Ann's satisfaction with their sex life: John was apparently quite satisfied; Ann indicated a good deal of dissatisfaction.

From the initial interview and test results, the couple was presented with a choice of three enrichment programs. They chose the negotiation program. Throughout the enrichment sessions, John and Ann invested much energy and worked hard to look at themselves and at their relationship.

John and Ann began to see how they were carrying behavior from previous relationships and experiences into their current relationship. John began to look at his bullying behavior toward Ann and the children and to see how this behavior was a carry-over from his relationship with his father and his successful

*Names in all cases have been changed to prevent identification.

use of this role in the military and on the job. Ann began to examine her avoidance behavior during arguments as a strong manipulative technique that she used to frustrate and anger John. She also began to differentiate her behavior toward her first husband and his reactions to her from John's reactions, which were different.

John and Ann began negotiating and opening up in areas about which it had been difficult to talk. Both found it difficult to express their feelings about their sexual relationship. Ann brought this up in one session, and although we did not delve into the dynamics of their sexual problems, it was very significant that she had the courage to bring the matter up. The groundwork appeared to have been laid for a more open and comfortable discussion of this issue between themselves.

During the enrichment sessions, the couple spoke of their dissatisfaction with their social activities. They felt that they did not spend enough time alone together and that they had not gone out very much since being married. They negotiated this issue successfully in the final enrichment session, working out a plan for a "night on the town" one weekend per month.

In the follow-up session, John and Ann reported that enrichment had been extremely meaningful and helpful to their relationship. They felt that they had just scratched the surface and wanted to do more work. Toward this end, they intended to participate in an enrichment group at their church during the summer and indicated that they would be interested in more enrichment at the university in the fall. In discussing the follow-up letter, included here, which focused on taking responsibility for the other's feelings, responding to their own past experiences rather than their current marital relationship, and their habit of avoiding, retreating, or blaming rather than facing issues head on, the couple reported that they felt that we had really gotten to know them during enrichment and that they had come to look more closely at things that had always been there but that they had never really examined.

Posttest results, particularly Ann's, showed an overall increase on the rating scales. Interestingly, their ratings of satisfaction with social activities decreased, probably a result of their having focused on this issue but not yet having acted out their desires.

The following letter was given to John and Ann at the follow-up session after enrichment:

Dear John and Ann,
    You seem to care very much for each other and for the children, and you seem to be genuinely concerned about each other's happiness. We can see that you are working hard to build a secure life for your family. It seems to us that you show your love in a number of ways. By taking responsibility for each other's feelings and placing the other's feelings above your own, it is possible that you sell yourselves short and that you do not ask for or receive what you want from the relationship. It is also possible that by placing the children's wishes ahead of your own, you are discounting the marriage, perhaps taking some strength and support away from the family.

We have noticed that you are quite sensitive to each other's feelings and really try to respond appropriately to your partner's needs and wants. You have built a verbal and nonverbal communication system. We have noticed in the sessions that sometimes you respond to your partner's cues before checking them out adequately. Perhaps you are responding not to what your partner has said but to some of your own past experiences with others.

Both of you seem to be making a real effort to open up and talk with each other about painful and difficult issues. We recognize that this is difficult, and we admire you for the strength and courage you displayed while working toward these goals. It seems to us that when dealing with pain or anger, one or the other of you often chooses to avoid, retreat, or blame rather than face the issue and negotiate. When you use your strength to prove that you are right or to win, you defeat yourself and your partner—and nobody wins.

We want to thank you for your hard work and your courage in facing the issues that emerged during the enrichment sessions.

Couple 2.   Richard was twenty-five years old; Mary was twenty-three. They had been married for approximately one year. Both considered communication the area of their relationship that needed work. Pretest rating scales (L'Abate, Wildman, O'Callaghan, Simon, Allison, Kahn, & Rainwater, 1975) also indicated that the couple was not satisfied with the way they communicated; in the initial interview, Richard told us that he had problems in listening. Although Mary rated herself higher than she rated Richard on communication-related items, she, too, indicated that this area needed work. Mary's test results also indicated dissatisfaction with the couple's social activities.

Given a choice of three programs that were relevant to their needs, the couple chose the reciprocity enrichment program. Throughout the sessions, Richard and Mary generally maintained a distance from the enrichers and avoided confronting the issues at hand. It became evident during the sessions that both were intellectualizers. It was extremely difficult to get them to talk about their feelings. Richard, in particular, frequently cited the results of studies or talked about "the situation in society" rather than the specifics of their relationship. Although Richard and Mary expressed the desire to show more affection toward each other, they found such behavior difficult. Both come from families who overtly show little affection, and Mary talked about an aunt who had had a good deal of difficulty as the result of seeing a psychologist and letting all her feelings out in the open.

Richard and Mary operated on a digital system (e.g., "You are either all feelings or all thought"; "The expression of feelings is either good or bad"). It was difficult for them to see a middle ground between these extremes. They explained to us, however, that their intellectualizing was a defense against the outside world but that in their own "nation of two," they were quite capable of expressing their emotions. Although their explanation is in part a truism, during the sessions they had difficulty revealing behavior that produced feelings of anger or hurt.

Richard and Mary had difficulty looking into themselves for the causes of their communication problems and attributed much of their difficulty to outside sources. This externalization was partly a reflection of their smug attitudes, which also carried over into social activities. They had few friends at the time. Although Mary enjoyed going out, she found that she had to motivate John, who was not particularly eager to join in social activities.

Although no great change was effected in the couple's overall relationship during enrichment, the posttest data indicated improvement in communication and increased satisfaction with social activities. The couple felt that it had been good to have outsiders look at their relationship. Although they did not agree entirely with our follow-up letter (which follows), they felt that it made some good points. We attempted in the follow-up session to point out how "either-or thinking" (emotionality or intellect) could lessen the potential depth of their relationship, how each protected the self and the partner from showing hurt and anger, and how their complementary relationship resulted in one of them having to be on top and the other on the bottom.

The following letter was given to Richard and Mary at the follow-up session after enrichment:

Dear Richard and Mary,

You seem to be a very happy couple, persons who care a great deal for each other. You have shown us in the sessions that you have the ability to compromise and to work out problems. It seems to us that you may care so much for your partner that you want to protect the partner from your own feelings of hurt; thus you compromise your anger rather than work through the issues.

You also seem to have a very complementary relationship. The skills and interests that one of you lacks, the other seems to possess, so you function quite well as a unit. By sticking to these complementary roles and relying upon each other, you may limit your development as individuals. It seems to us that at times you use each other as a foil: Your complementary relationship often leads to one of you playing top position while the other plays bottom position.

You are extremely bright and intelligent people who really appreciate each other's intellect. You express your affection toward each other in many ways. It is possible that by engaging in "either-or thinking" (i.e., one can be either overcontrolled or overemotional), you may overlook the emotional spectrum between these points. It is also possible that your emphasis on the intellect detracts from your sharing the depth of your feelings and expressing your affection for your partner as well as receiving the full extent of each other's love.

We appreciate your hard work and honesty while dealing with the issues that emerged during the enrichment program.

Couple 3. Bill and Janet had been living together for the past three years. Bill was twenty-nine years old and Janet was twenty-two. The couple told us in the initial interview that they felt good about their many common interests and goals. The area that they wanted to work on during enrichment was communication. For this reason (as well as the pretest rating scale results, which indicated relative weakness in certain areas of communication), an enrichment program on how to negotiate effectively was chosen.

Although Bill and Janet always cooperated with the enrichers, they lacked a strong investment in working during the sessions. During the sessions, they tended to avoid confronting themselves and to avoid dealing with issues head on. The avoidance in the sessions reflected the difficulties they were encountering in the outside world. Resolving their problems was made difficult by their shared sense of competition. Their competition often resulted in arguments over what they agreed were trivial matters.

Although Bill and Janet considered themselves relatively unconventional, their behavior was quite conventional. They were aiming for an open relationship in which both would be free to pursue their own interests, but here their relationship encountered its greatest strain. Neither was willing at this point in their relationship to make a total commitment to the other. Yet, both got hurt and upset about each other's flirting with members of the opposite sex.

As the issue of their social activities kept appearing during the sessions, it became quite apparent that rather than facing this issue, both of them were avoiding it to protect themselves and each other. The enrichers thus decided to pursue this avoidance from another angle. At the end of the third enrichment session, Bill and Janet were given copies of a letter designed to get them to look more closely at themselves and at their relationship.

> Dear Bill and Janet,
> We are very impressed with how caring and protective you are of each other and how conventional you are in your opposition to each other. You oppose each other as if you were married.

This letter focused on how similar their opposition and jealousies were to those of more conventional, married couples, how their inconsistencies resulted in the repetition of issues without resolution, and how, by avoiding and placing conditions on their intimacy, they were limiting their relationship. Two other letters (which follow) were given to Bill and Janet.

> (letter given at the end of the fifth enrichment session)
> Dear Bill and Janet,
> In working with you during the past weeks, we have observed some things about your relationship that we consider important. We have mixed feelings about presenting these to you because we don't know how you will react to them. But we really like you and feel that you are strong, sensitive, and intelligent enough for us to give you these observations. Also, we believe that we have a responsibility to point out difficulties that are hard for you to see. We are very impressed with how human you are—you have inconsistencies. These inconsistencies allow you to keep your relationship going on repetitively. You don't seem to get bored with each other and you want to bind each other in the relationship, but you don't seem to want to commit yourselves to it. You want to protect each other, but you hurt each other in spite of your best intentions. You seem afraid to break off the relationship and afraid to make it better. You want intimacy with each other but are afraid to work toward it. We feel that there is a tremendous cost to your relationship in being superman and superwoman, in denying your vulnerability and neediness.
> We believe that you care enough for each other to be intimate in your relationship if you are willing to work on some of these inconsistencies, using the skills that you have learned in these sessions.

(letter given at the follow-up session after enrichment)
Dear Bill and Janet,

We see you as very warm and loving people who care about each other's feelings. It is possible that you care so much for the other's feelings that the caring leads to doubt, mistrust, and misunderstanding. Both of you seem to want to work toward a more intimate relationship. Being intimate involves the capacity to communicate and to share your hurt as well as your joy. It may be that both of you put conditions on your intimacy so that you deny your own feelings and thus stop yourselves from becoming more intimate. You seem to have many common interests and goals and to support each other in these endeavors. We wonder if you limit the support that you offer your partner, giving no more than you feel you receive. Limiting the support can limit the growth of your relationship.

We consider you very bright people, and we believe that you have firm convictions and ideas. Could it be that the very strength of your convictions and ideas weakens your relationship because it allows no room for creative compromise on important issues?

We have sincerely enjoyed working with you, and we appreciate the willingness to work that you have shown during these six weeks.

At the conclusion of enrichment, Bill and Janet said that enrichment had been less fun and more serious than they had expected. Bill told us that he had not looked forward to the last several sessions and had found it painful to look at certain aspects of their relationship. The posttest results showed that both Bill and Janet decreased their scores on the rating scales, probably a result of their having looked more closely at some of the problems and inconsistencies in their relationship but not yet having successfully resolved them.

Couple 4. Sylvia and Ben had been married for seven years and were the parents of a boy and a girl, both preschoolers. According both to pretest rating scales and the couple's comments in the initial interview, they felt that communication of feelings in general, and their sexual relationship in particular, needed enrichment. Ben and Sylvia were offered a choice of three programs— negotiation, reciprocity, and clarification of sexual attitudes. After some indecision, they selected the sexual attitudes program.

Although both came from families in which sex was not discussed openly, Ben considered a tacit acceptance of sexual relations a part of marriage and saw himself as having no problems in sexual functioning. In contrast, both he and Sylvia felt that she had a definite problem in relaxing and enjoying sex. Sylvia explained her anxiety as stemming from a childhood incident in which her mother had spanked her for playing doctor.

A recurrent theme stressed by Ben and Sylvia was that external factors (e.g., parental disapproval of sex, job pressures) were preventing them from relaxing and enjoying each other sexually. The enrichers' impression that the couple was using external factors to maintain distance and avoid communicating feelings that might be upsetting was strengthened when the couple revealed that their children slept with them in their bed. Sylvia explained that this was a way for her and Ben to give the children the attention they could not give them during the day because of their heavy work schedules. The enrichers confronted the couple, expressing their belief that the sessions would be of doubtful value if this pattern continued. The enrichers suggested that Ben and Sylvia assure the children that they were loved but demand that they sleep in their own beds. The couple willingly followed this approach, and by the second week of sleeping without the children, they reported that they were more relaxed in bed because of a combination of privacy and Sylvia's having lost a stressful job.

Another theme that Ben and Sylvia emphasized was the importance of patience in making their sexual relationship more mutually fulfilling. Although the enrichers were impressed with their hard work to make some positive changes (e.g., in increasing frequency), they felt that the couple had an investment in maintaining some dissatisfaction with their sexual relationship. Although Ben and Sylvia considered each partner responsible for initiating sex, for example, neither was willing to propose a means of putting mutual responsibility into practice. Both stressed that "it takes time" to become more responsive to the other's needs and desires. They exhibited a pattern of mutual protection throughout the sessions—either by going off on a tangent or coming to the rescue when either of them had difficulty communicating a feeling. Indeed, it appeared that focusing on sexual difficulties enabled them to avoid expressing personal feelings that each believed the other would perceive as threatening or hurtful. At the end of the fourth session, Ben and Sylvia were given a message pointing out this pattern and suggesting that their caring for each other might be functioning counterproductively.

> Dear Sylvia and Ben,
>
> As we end our sessions with you, we want to share some feelings about your relationship as we have observed it during the past weeks.
>
> We are very impressed with how much you care for each other. In caring so much, each of you may be afraid to tell the other how you feel because you fear that you will hurt the other or be misunderstood or hurt yourself. Both of you have been very patient in working out problems in your sexual relationship. You seem to have accepted the problem, confronted it, and dealt with it. You have complimented each other well, but in the process, you have cast each other in the roles of "the patient, helping partner" and "the troubled partner who needs help." If your relationship is to continue to improve, you may need to realize that at different times, each of you will need to give and have the support of the other. We can see that you are hard workers, dedicated to achieving and getting ahead so that you can have security for yourselves and your children. But in throwing yourselves into your work, you may create conditions that will distance you from each other and make it physically and emotionally harder to communicate openly and directly with each other.
>
> We applaud your determination to get the children to sleep in their own beds and hope you will continue to create an open atmosphere that will permit you to grow closer.
>
> It has been a pleasure to work with you. If at any time you feel that the Family Studies Center can be of assistance to you, do not hesitate to get in touch with us.

In spite of this protection pattern, Ben and Sylvia did apparently want to improve their sex life to a certain extent, and they did loosen up and show affection physically.

As Sylvia seemed to become more open about her feelings and less tense, Ben became less comfortable. Ben's pre- and posttest scores did not differ very much, but Sylvia's posttest scores were considerably higher than her pretest scores. However, Ben's pre- and posttest scores were considerably higher than Sylvia's. Ben seemed to have an investment in maintaining the idea that he and Sylvia had a nearly perfect marriage, perhaps to avoid facing his own fears and self-doubts.

In the last session, the enrichers gave the couple copies of a paradoxical letter that raised the issue of their mutual protection pattern, the ways in which they created distance between them, and the importance of giving and receiving support. Ben initially reacted to the letter by crumpling it into a ball. He later admitted that he did have difficulty in expressing his feelings and that although he was threatened by doing so, it would be helpful for him to learn how to deal with his feelings. Both Sylvia and Ben agreed that the sessions had been helpful. Despite the remaining problems, the enrichers felt that the program had made Sylvia and Ben more aware of the dynamics of their relationship.

The following letter was given to Ben and Sylvia at the follow-up session after enrichment:

> Dear Sylvia and Ben,
>   We are impressed by how you seem to protect each other in order not to hurt each other. If you choose to remain this way, your relationship will probably not change in any way. We believe that you have the strength and flexibility to change if you wish to do so.

Dealing with Resistant Patterns

A Resistant Couple.   A paradoxical message was presented to a couple who had been seen in therapy for approximately one year with minimal results. The couple had been in therapy numerous times over the years with a variety of therapists in different towns.

> Dear Bill and Joy,
>   On the basis of our detailed and prolonged observation of your marriage and after a great deal of thought and deliberation, we have come to the conclusion that you love each other so deeply and so dearly that any change for the better in the other is interpreted as a sign of rejection and a demonstration of disloyalty. You are so loyal to each other that neither can change for fear of disappointing the other.
>   We can see and understand, then, how impossible it is for either of you to change for the better because changing for the better would be a sign of disloyalty and rejection. We really wonder whether either of you can change for the better without disappointing the other.
>   We would like each of you to read this note every day but not to talk about it too much. We will talk about it next time we meet.

*Resistant Parents.** Mr. and Mrs. Casey (both in their 30s) had been married for fifteen years and had two boys, aged eight and ten. Mrs. Casey had requested that her individual therapist refer her to the Family Studies Center. She was requesting help for her two children, who, in her opinion, were having difficulty expressing anger. Each child had a two-year history of school-related problems, which had been given various diagnostic labels, including learning disability and behavior disorder. Following interviews with the parents (together and separately), the children, and the school personnel, and a review of the children's school records, the therapists concluded that the presenting problems reflected the underlying problems in the marital subsystem, which in turn affected the Caseys' ability to parent effectively. During discussions, it became obvious that they were unwilling to face child rearing as a team. Mr. Casey, who worked and went to school full-time, was unwilling to come home and collaborate with his wife about the children. Instead, he left her to handle the boys but often criticized her efforts. Mrs. Casey, who worked part-time, was the primary care-taker but was unwilling to confront her husband about his absence from home or his lack of contact with her and the children.

Each, in his or her own way, exerted power in the marriage. Mr. Casey controlled the marriage and parenting with explosive directness, blaming, and, most powerful of all, keeping silent and withdrawing. Mrs. Casey controlled by being indirect, distracting, and extremely verbal. The bid for power had resulted in an impasse and a loss of communication about parenting and marital roles.

The letter intervention was selected in the hope that it would break the impasse. Both parents were highly resistant to any change. This resistance had been demonstrated by Mr. Casey's comments expressing his doubts about the effectiveness of therapy. He stated repeatedly that he wanted to hear something helpful, something he had never heard before. Mrs. Casey's resistance was demonstrated by her hit-and-run attitude. She brought the family into therapy but tried to remain a passive observer. Confronting them directly and verbally would have offered them further means of controlling the resistance, opening the door to debate, dispute, and intellectualizations and giving Mrs. Casey an opportunity to distract the entire purpose of the intervention. The letter circumvented their resistance, rallied their emotions, and got them both involved in helping their children and their own relationship.

The couple were given copies of the following letter, which was read to them during a session:

Dear Mr. and Mrs. Casey,
    We appreciate the concern you have shown in requesting professional help in dealing with your children. We realize that it takes much strength to ask for help. Although other couples would have collapsed under the stresses that have come your way, you have been strong and stayed the course. As individuals, you show much concern and support for the well-being of your children.

*This case was handled by Fred Stevens and Trudi B. Johnston under the supervision of Dr. L'Abate.

Although it is clear to us that you care very deeply for the children, it is also clear that each of you has your own ideas about what is best for them.

Our first and only concern is the family as a whole. We are limited in what we can do about the school system. We do not view this as a win-lose situation and do not choose to take sides at this time for the following reasons.

From all the evidence—individual and family interviews, discussions with school personnel, and review of school testing materials—we have reached a position with which you, very likely, will not agree. The children are protecting both of you by forcing you to spend all your valuable time being their parents, keeping you from being husband and wife as well as individuals in your own rights.

Both Wally and Joseph have shown incredible sensitivity and integrity in their efforts to protect and direct your energies as parents. The acting out and the poor school performance have forced you to focus your time and energy on their education rather than to deal with partnership and selfhood. In effect, the children have taken on the task of pulling the family together.

We recognize the tremendous tension between the family and the school. We are aware that getting directly involved with you and the school system might only feed the children's efforts. Our involvement would reinforce their acting-out behavior to protect you, which is in neither your best interest nor theirs, especially in view of how few weeks remain until the end of school.

Each of you has specific ideas about what is best for Wally and Joseph. The resolution of this disagreement cannot be immediate. In the meantime, we face the end of the school year, and we have no time to lose in improving the situation. We see the best plan as the quickest and the simplest one.

First, we recommend that you, Mr. Casey, continue to be in charge of all involvement with the school, including all communication directed to or from the school. Mrs. Casey, you are to direct any incoming communication from the shcool to Mr.Casey. Also, Mr. Casey, as the boys' father and as a student yourself, it is vital that you take charge of all homework and study activities with the boys. Your guidance and direction on how to study and complete homework will make a noticeable difference. You, Mrs. Casey, must support this work by not involving yourself with the homework or the school. Instead, we recommend that you focus on yourself and the nurturing of the family, which you do so well.

Second, should you decide to continue working with us, we recommend that both of you consider seriously the issues of parenting. Each of you is to list separately the issues you face as parents and the solutions you propose. You are not to discuss these issues with each other until the next session. These strategies for parenting are necessary for the future well-being of the boys.

Third, at this time, you are not ready to work as partners, and it would be premature for you to do so. We suggest that you work independently in order to minimize confrontation, tension, and conflict.

We were impressed by the way in which you divided your responsibilities involving the boys' asthma. Your involvement and collaboration demonstrated to us just how responsible and caring you are. Mr. Casey's recent action with the school is an opportunity for you to demonstrate once again your effectiveness.

Again, we wish to emphasize our concern and enthusiasm for your family and for the efforts thoughtfully suggested here. We want to do all that we can to increase your skills and strengths in parenting.

Upon presentation of the letter, there was a long period during which Mr. and Mrs. Casey wept but did not speak. Both acknowledged the impact of the letter. Mrs. Casey said that the letter had "zeroed in on what was going on."

Mr. Casey called the letter "a slap in the face." The therapists probed, asking the couple whether they had any questions about the content of the letter.

In the week that followed, Mr. Casey began to come home immediately after his evening classes to help the boys with their homework. He began to get involved with the teachers and other school personnel in order to support the recommendations from the school and the therapists concerning homework and discipline. Later, during a phone call to confirm appointment time, Mr. Casey told the therapists that he had "left the marriage" about three years ago. This self-disclosure, in addition to other changes in his behavior, indicated his greater willingness to come back into the marriage. In the sessions that followed, the couple explicitly requested help for their marital relationship. The child-school problems also showed detectable movement toward resolution.

Dealing with Oppositional Patterns

The following are examples of letters that may be used to deal with oppositional patterns within the family:

1. We appreciate the way you care for one another in this family by talking for one another but not for yourselves. It is very caring of each of you to give up your own self for the sake of the family.

2. We marvel at how each of you defines yourself by opposing somebody else in this family. It must be pretty hard for each of you to define yourself without talking about anybody else in the family. To speak for yourself, by yourself, and with yourself, without the help of anybody else in the family would mean being disloyal to the rest of the family.

3. I like the way you protect each other (the family). You are somebody as long as you oppose someone else. What would happen if you had no one to oppose? Could you still be yourself? It would be really hard.

4. We like the way you read each other's minds. It shows you really care for each other. It is also a very good way to lose your self and let someone else take over. If you do not want any changes in this marriage (family), you should continue reading your partner's (family's) mind(s). In this way, all your energy is directed toward your partner (family), not toward yourself. Therefore, any change has to take place in your partner (family), not in yourself. This is a good way of keeping the marriage (family) exactly as it is.

5. You care so much about each other that each of you talks about your partner, using "you" and avoiding "I." As caring as this habit is, it is also a good way of keeping the marriage exactly the same, without change.

Dealing with Defeating Patterns

What are the differences in resistant, oppositional, and defeating patterns? Because we do not have a clear answer to that question, we shall answer with examples (L'Abate & Farr, 1981).

The Functions of Defeats.   Defeats have two main classes of function: One relates to families and the other relates to therapists.

Families. As long as family members work—actively or passively—at defeating themselves, they are involved with one another; if they are involved, they are maintaining the status quo. Whatever these defeats may produce, they do keep the family together. Furthermore, we must remember that, from a dialectical as well as a human viewpoint, for every defeat there is a success, or at least success can be presumed. We need to discover the specific functional payoffs of defeating behaviors. Every family succeeds at defeating and may even enjoy the success of defeat! As paradoxical and farfetched as the enjoyment of defeat may seem, when defeats are recounted, someone in the family is usually smiling. Defeats should not be regarded negatively. They have many important functions that can be positively reframed: (1) protectiveness ("As long as you defeat each other, you are also protecting everybody in the family"); (2) caring ("As long as you continue bickering, you keep everybody in the family from having to take on further responsibility"); (3) keeping things the same; (4) producing excitement, even enjoyment ("You certainly don't want to get bored"), in an otherwise repetitive, dull routine; and (5) keeping the family close.

Therapists. Because we learn from failures, our defeats are more important than our successes. Yet, defeats need to be anticipated, although, as the Milan group has recognized (Selvini-Palazzoli et al., 1978), this same awareness may prevent our doing anything about them. Defeats have a way of keeping us humble—no matter how successful and effective we may be with some families, attrition and dropouts are part of doing therapy. In fact, most of us learn, after a few years of practice, to accept a certain percentage of defeats, usually rationalizing them by negative externalizations about families. Externalizations are an avoidance of coming to terms with ourselves. Instead of using defeats to sharpen our creativity, instead of using them to spur us toward a more differentiated practice, we submit to resignation and passive rationalization. Rather than externalize blame, we can begin to use ourselves to come up with more creative and interesting patterns of coping with defeat. *Coping* is a better term than *solving* because it is doubtful that we can ever solve patterns of defeat. We are vulnerable and fallible human beings, and we are therapists. Anyone who claims to be more than this is asking to be defeated.

Reframing Positively. The pattern of defeat needs to be positively reframed, tied to success, enjoyment, caring, protectiveness, closeness. When this positive reframing has been made, one can go to the next step.

Application to excessive fighting and bickering. Dealing with excessive fighting and bickering may be intensive and may last a long time, even though most bickering can be reduced to issues of power and control. Bickering occurs especially in families with teenagers, and it represents a deterioration that has intensified during the years, since both spouses started agreeing to disagree and essentially established a reactive marital relationship based on sameness–oppositeness (L'Abate, 1976).

One family entered counseling because of the extremely defiant attitude of their youngest daughter, aged fifteen. The mother and the father were in their early 40s and had three other children—one son, aged eighteen, who lived at home, and an older son and a daughter, both of whom were married and living away from home.

Excessive fighting and bickering occurred each time the daughter was expected to comply with the rules set by her parents. It seemed that mother and daughter were most intensely involved in the power struggle, which usually escalated until the father entered the picture. Because the father had had two coronaries, the mother and the daughter would temporarily stop fighting, which by this time had usually reached the proportions of a brawl. It seemed that the parents had agreed that the mother would assume the heavier, more responsible role; the father would be the nicer, more passive parent. Because this agreement placed the mother in the role of disciplinarian, she and the daughter continually struggled over all issues.

The family was given a letter, along with the following instructions:

1. Father will read to the family the following letter, which is addressed to the daughter.
2. The letter will be read after dinner on Monday, Wednesday, and Friday evenings.
3. Mother will remind father to read the letter.
4. Please do not discuss the content of this letter with anyone outside counseling.

> We appreciate your protecting us because as long as you act up, neither Mother nor I will need to look at ourselves and deal with our middle age. You will also help your brother to stay the way he is.
> Consequently, we will understand any time you blow up that it will be to protect us and your brother. We therefore hope that you will continue to protect us because we need it.

This descriptive letter was used to reframe positively the general patterns of relating observed in this family and to relabel the negative behavior as positive. The family's relationship is described dialectically, in other words, as passivity and aggressiveness.

Congratulating the Family.   The family should be congratulated for their involvement with one another: "As long as you defeat one another, you really care for one another." Hence, admiration for the family should be expressed repeatedly: "You are a really tough family."

Application to divide and conquer. This pattern is especially visible in families with teenagers, who are masters at separating the parents, taking advantage of whatever polarization may be present in the marriage (Stierlin, 1974).

A family of four came for family counseling because of the acting out of the oldest son, aged fifteen. The father was a truck driver and the mother a shampooer in a hair salon. There was one younger sibling, a brother, aged ten, who was in the fourth grade. The identified patient (IP) was a large, handsome youth, who towered over his father. He was neatly dressed and appropriately groomed. According to the family, the youth was doing things such as leaving home in the family car without permission but going only a few miles away. He also consistently lied about his behavior and took things that were conspicuous by their absence. He also placed beer and other undesirable items in his room where they would easily be found.

The father was the disciplinarian, sometimes using physical force to gain control of the older son; the mother's responsibility was to establish rules and report the son's behavior to the father. Because the father was away most of the week, the older son was responsible for taking care of his mother. Problems arose whenever the parents attempted to set limits and administer discipline on which they did not agree. The inconsistent, poorly identified expectations and limitations appeared to allow this youth to divide and conquer his parents. As a result, everyone felt confused and defeated.

The family was given the following letter:

> I am impressed with the ability you have developed to defeat one another. This keeps your family together and unchanged. Succeeding by defeating is hard to master, but when instructions are not clear and not negotiated, it is easier not to follow through.
>
> I admire you for wanting every family member to feel the power of defeat. You are assured of this power as long as everyone does not have an investment in the instructions that are given. One person can then use this power against another, thus keeping the family the same.
>
> I want to congratulate the family for knowing how to be happy by defeating and being defeated. Because defeating seems successful, I encourage you to continue doing what you are doing and by no means would I encourage Mother and Dad to share authority and responsibility with each other because this change could break up the family.

This circular letter not only gave this family a more positive description of their relationship but promoted an evaluation of their family system. In very resistant families, this is a way to begin establishing and strengthening parental boundaries.

Both the mother and the father decided that they did not need to feel the power of defeat so much. They noticed that when they agreed on clearly stated expectations, disciplines, and consequences, their two sons acted out less frequently. The family did not really understand what was happening, but all family members agreed that when the siblings did act out, it would be up to the parents, together, to show authority and responsibility.

Prescribing the Defeat. Because defeat is now a positive expression, it follows that the family should assist, continue, and even escalate whatever they are doing to defeat one another. To make sure that the reframing and the prescription will not be ignored or forgotten, the therapist puts them in writing and ritualizes them (e.g., "Read this letter after supper on alternating days, either Mondays, Wednesdays, and Fridays or Tuesdays, Thursdays, and Saturdays") (Selvini-Palazzoli et al., 1978).

Application to continuation of patterns despite all types of intervention. Some families rigidly resist any type of intervention. In cases of this kind, therapists may feel as if they are hitting their heads against a stone wall. The family will not budge.

In the following example, the identified patient was a 15-year-old boy whose violent, antisocial behavior brought the family into counseling. This was a blended family consisting of a mother, her two children, aged fifteen and sixteen, and a stepfather. Although the stepfather and the mother had been married for three-and-a-half years, the mother complained that the problem could not be altered because the stepfather would not discipline either the son or the daughter. When this family was first seen, they had been in therapy for one year but said that they saw no evidence of change.

This was a first marriage for the stepfather, who was so quiet that no one ever listened to his "mumbling." The stepfather explained that because he had never had children, he really did not know how to parent. When the stepfather did try to move closer to his stepchildren, the mother interpreted the closeness as an indication that they were independent and no longer needed her. The mother would thus become overly critical of the son for not assuming responsibility for his work at home, which would again break up the stepfather-son relationship. The son would then become furious with everyone, and the stepfather would again feel incompetent. The son and the daughter acted out their frustrations by destroying property at school and at home and by fighting with those in authority.

In spite of numerous interventions to strengthen generational boundaries so that mother and stepfather would support each other, the mother and the siblings remained bound in an enmeshed relationship.

The family continued the same patterns despite all interventions. A letter was given to the son to read, according to the following instructions, to his parents:

1.   To be read by son to other members of the family
2.   To be read on Mondays, Wednesdays, and Fridays, after dinner
3.   Mother to remind son to read letter; if she forgets, stepfather and daughter to remind her
4.   Contents of the letter not to be discussed outside counseling

> I am impressed with the way in which you show how much you care about this family, especially your mother. I feel you need to be congratulated for having violent temper tantrums because these tantrums serve as a safety valve for what your father and your mother cannot do. I admire you for the way in which you show your loyalty to your mother.
>
> If this is the way you want to protect your parents from each other and if you want to continue to keep them apart, you should continue to blow up, but do so on Monday, Wednesday, and Friday of each week. Be sure to break some inexpensive item in your home and continue these outbursts; if you stop, they might get back together.

After the behavior was prescribed and ritualized, the youth found that if he could control his outbursts part of the week, he could exhibit more control in general. No one really understood why the mother was now accepting responsibility in her relationship with the stepfather nor why the son was getting along so well with him. This was an opportunity to unhook the son from the mother and move him closer to his stepfather.

The following letters were given to a family who had been in therapy for one year with little or no change:

(to be read once a week after supper on Tuesdays and Thursdays)
Letter for Mr. T. to his wife and children:
I want to thank you, Sara, for expressing the feelings I find hard to express. You care for and protect me a great deal, and I love you for it.
I want to thank you, boys, for keeping us busy with you. As long as both of you are active, neither Mother nor I can spend time dealing with each other and our marriage.

Letter for Mrs. T. to read to her husband and children:
Thank you, Al, for working so hard and keeping such good control of your feelings. As long as you control them as well as you do, I don't have to. Along with Dad, I want to thank you boys for protecting our marriage with your many activities. As long as you keep us busy, we won't need to change.

Letter for John T. to read to his parents and his brother:
Thank you, Mother and Dad, for allowing me so much freedom to explore and to create. I want to thank you, Dave, for taking some of the heat off me: As long as Mother and Dad concentrate on you, I am free to do as I like.

Letter for Dave T. to read to his parents and his brother:
Thank you, Mother and Dad, for taking such good care, charge, and control of me. As long as you do it, I don't have to. Thank you, John, for being and doing all the things I wish to but cannot yet be and do.

Admission of Defeat and Helplessness.
The admission of defeat and helplessness is a favorite ploy of the Milano group (Selvini-Palazzoli et al., 1978). Such an admission seems to mobilize family members into trying to do the opposite, that is, to win. Even better, one should start therapy with every family with the full realization (Andolfi, 1980) that underneath the pleas for help is a hidden agenda that pulls for defeat. The hidden agenda is present from the outset of each therapy. Should a therapist lose sight of his or her vulnerability and the possibility of defeat, that therapist will be defeated.

Application to disqualification. Disqualification may appear as a subtle or as a very evident pattern. It can creep up on therapists, then hit them all of a sudden, or it can explode in their faces at the outset. It is an insidious and entrenched pattern in families who have extreme, long-standing pathology. Disqualification consists of telling others—intimates as well as nonintimates—that they do not count, that they are not important. One can argue that disqualification of others is essentially a disqualification of the self. One can then talk about low self-esteem and other intrapsychic concepts whose usefulness in dealing with self-defeating families is questionable. The ultimate disqualification (for the therapist, of course) is the family's suddenly dropping out of therapy.

In looking at this pattern, we see that the members who enjoy it are usually hypercritical and perfectionistic; that is, no one, including the therapist, can satisfy them. The therapist should be on the lookout for this pattern when a family shows up with a list of previously defeated therapists.

The family described here was first seen in counseling because of the extremely antisocial behavior of the 16-year-old daughter, who had been expelled from school for persistent drug use and disrespect to teachers. A younger daughter, aged fifteen, also lived at home; she engaged in equally destructive behavior but was never caught. The father held an administrative position and the mother was a housewife, who reported that her husband wanted her to find work away from home. She could not do so, however, because of the trouble with her older daughter. The mother reported that all of them felt very insecure and scared about being in counseling because they had been in counseling before and no one had ever helped. The mother, in particular, doubted from the very outset that they could continue in therapy.

The mother made excessively critical comments about her daughter's behavior and said that she received no support from the father. Although the father tended to be withdrawn and quiet, he was extremely critical of the way the mother handled problems with the older daughter. The father reprimanded the daugher during the counseling sessions—whenever the mother reported that she received no support from him. The daughter was extremely critical of her mother and other authority figures but was easier on her father and her younger sister.

In this family, the parents talked about what they needed to do, but it was quite evident that no action was being taken. For instance, they administered no consequences when rules were broken; the mother made no move to find work; and the parents never showed their daughters that they were supporting each other.

The following letter was given to the family:

> I am aware that, because of the power of this family, I am feeling a real sense of defeat and helplessness. I do know I have power that you cannot speak to, but yours is also special. You are a special family, one that I cannot fight with. I don't know where I could have found a better family than you to defeat me.

This message provided the family with an incentive for continuing their therapy. Not only did the therapist's admission of defeat ensure their continued participation in counseling (in order to win), but the parents learned something about the strength of their influence when they were united.

After the therapist sent the first letter, admitting helplessness, another letter was presented. This time, it was important to reframe the family's pattern as "high standards of performance":

> Your standards for living are so high that few persons, including me, can really live up to them. You should be congratulated for your search for perfection (and for equating perfection and goodness, imperfection and badness). In spite of all the pressures to lower your standards, we hope that you can keep them up; the world needs people like you, who can uphold standards against all pressures inside and outside the family. We doubt that we can live up to your standards and wonder whether we will ever be able to meet them. Keep up the good work!

In another instance, the following letter was given:

> We congratulate you on your clear, organized, and fixed perception of the world and of each other. You call a spade a spade, know black from white, and erase all the gray areas of the world, making your lives much less confusing, less conflictual, and more stimulating than are most people's.
>
> Similarly, you have learned to be perfect complements for each other. Where one of you is weak, the other is strong. When one is indecisive, the other knows "the way." It is clear that each of you has in the other your better half, and it becomes even more important to stay close and together. You would be in a state of confused excitement if each of you were to find yourself grappling alone with the problems of life.

These messages forced the family to reconsider their extremely destructive, critical behavior and to increase their acceptance of themselves and others.

Balancing Family Upset.   After the therapist gives the first letter changing the role of the family IP from that of victim or victimizer to rescuer and putting the responsibility back on the rest of the family (Selvini-Palazzoli et al., 1978), it is often important to follow up by helping the children praise their parents. Having given the children something to think about, the therapist should give a second letter. In the second letter, the children should thank their parents for giving up part of themselves and their marriage to raise the children and should express the hope that the parents will be able to make up for lost time in their own lives.

Unwillingness to cooperate and to complete assignments. These families are on the opposite end of the resistance continuum. Their resistance is more passive and subtler than overt fighting. They may comply verbally but defeat one another nonverbally. In fact, this pattern also may be traced to the marital dyad. The wife, more articulate and explosive, actively defeats her husband through her continual complaints and diatribes; the husband, on the other hand, defeats her nonverbally. Typically unable to articulate his feelings, he acts out (e.g., by drinking, watching television, leaving home). In this pattern, a common one in the families of rebellious teenagers, agreements are not honored and transactions are not completed because no one takes personal responsibility. This can be said of most self-defeating patterns.

This family came to counseling because of their 16-year-old son's nonverbal aggressive behavior. According to the family, the adolescent's aggressive behavior and unwillingness to comply were unbearable. When confronted with this or any other problem, he pretended to be sleepy. Because of a poor relationship with the parents, an older brother and a sister had left home before completing high school.

The parents came from very different backgrounds, which led to confusion about how they should discipline the children and what their expectations should be. The mother attempted to be the enforcer but felt she got no support until she exploded in rage. Although the father was concerned, he could not offer his wife much support because he either left town on business or avoided her (by not listening or by engaging in another activity) whenever his son's behavior required attention. Because the mother was the most verbal member of the family, she defeated both father and son by either exploding or completing statements for them. They, in turn, by not cooperating or talking with her, also refused to take personal responsibility for dealing with family issues.

The following instructions and letter were given to the mother:

1. The letter is to be read privately on Monday, Wednesday, and Friday.
2. Please read it after dinner, in the privacy of your room.
3. Please remember not to read this to the other members of your family.

> The job of raising two children without a father has been hard, but you are to be commended for the wonderful way in which you have sacrificed yourself to take care of your daughter and your son. You are to be congratulated for the work and the sacrifices that have gone into protecting your children. Because of the special way in which you care for your younger son, you are assured of raising him to be like his father. It is especially clear that you need to keep protecting your son from further involvement with men because that will ensure his being more like his father.
>
> I am so impressed by your commitment to keeping tight reins on your family; as long as you do this, the family will stay together and unchanged. I think you should continue this and should also give more of yourself by knowing what your sons and your daughter are doing at all times.

Depression.   Depression is another self-defeating pattern frequently seen in family therapy. Most approaches to the treatment of depression are linear; very little has appeared in the literature concerning a circular treatment approach. When depression surfaced (which often takes time because it is usually disguised by the depressed person as well as the other family members), it is important to reframe it positively in two different aspects: (1) as protection for the family (e.g., "As long as you are depressed, no one in the family has to change") and (2) as a blessing rather than a curse—those who cannot become depressed are the unfortunate ones (e.g., "You are lucky that you can feel and be whole"; "Depression is the royal road to selfhood"; "People who cannot become depressed do not ask for help: They can be found in cemeteries, morgues, and hospitals").

After the positive reframing, we have usually found it helpful to prescribe the depression in a ritualized fashion (Selvini-Palazzoli et al., 1978); for example, "I want you to get depressed on Mondays, Wednesdays, and Fridays from 9:00 P.M. to 9:30 P.M." It is important to link this prescription systematically by having the mate or a parent remind the person to get depressed and to set the kitchen timer for thirty minutes: "Get on with your depression so you can learn something about yourself. Make notes of everything that comes into your head as you feel depressed." The depressed person should do this alone, usually in the bedroom. If more than one intimate (usually a spouse) is involved in the depression, assign that person to remind the reminder about the time of the prescribed depression.

The Ultimate Defeat.   The ultimate defeat, of course, is the family's dropping out of therapy, usually with little warning or discussion. Here the therapist is left completely helpless: There is nothing that can be done about it. On one hand, the therapist is relieved that a difficult problem has been terminated. On the other hand, his or her therapeutic effectiveness has been brought into question by the family's dropping out. No matter what the therapist's reasons and rationalizations when a family drops out, it still hurts!

Undoubtedly, many other patterns of defeat could be outlined. We have not tried to list them systematically. Each family has its own unique and specific style of defeating. LeFave (1980) found correlates of dropping out of treatment that apparently went beyond any issue of therapeutic effectiveness: (1) age of the identified patient (the older the patient, the greater the chance of dropping out), (2) the greater the number of children, the greater the chance of dropping out, (3) the family's prior involvement with community agencies, (4) the presence or the absence of antisocial acting out, and (5) the father's attendance at the initial intake interview and early treatment sessions (L'Abate, 1975).

Avoidance of Intimacy

The following letter was given to couples who avoided intimacy by their patterns of bickering and fighting, put-downs and accusations, and lack of change after six to twelve months of therapy (L'Abate & Samples, 1983).

(Joe, please read this letter aloud to Mary each Monday, Wednesday, and Friday for the next 6 weeks.)

Dear Mary and Joe:

After working with you for so long, I am fairly convinced that you need to defeat each other to avoid getting too close. Intimacy can be a very scary and dangerous condition, and I can understand how it affects you in that way. For some people, intimacy means loss of control, loss of mind, loss of self, loss of strength, and in some cases, loss of life.

Therefore, I have no recourse but to recommend that you keep defeating each other as much as you can so that the defeats will allow a certain amount of distance between you. That distance will protect you, to some degree, from risking hurt, but if you are not willing to risk hurt, you can also protect your partner from the threat of closeness. Part of the way that you folks have managed this distance is by allowing your family's depression to continue on its current course. It may be that your current relationship is so comfortable that you will want to continue on this course for a while longer.

Dealing with Alcoholic Patterns

The next letter* was sent to an alcoholic who refused to come for therapy with his wife and children.

It is a privilege to be working with your family through your wife (and children), and I hope to have the opportunity of meeting you in the future (I appreciate your coming with them during the evaluation period). I can appreciate why you have thus far chosen not to enter (continue) therapy. The goal of therapy is change,

---

*This case was handled by Doris Hewitt, Ph.D., assisted by Dr. L'Abate.

and I assume that you like your family and your marriage so much the way they are that you do not want anything to change.

I commend you for the way you seem to care about your marriage. You seem to care so much for your wife that you protect her from having to assume any responsibility for changing. Of course, she does not need to change as long as you continue drinking. The drinking makes you look like the family member who has a problem. Your drinking allows your wife to look good to her friends and to get a lot of emotional support from them. That support means a great deal to her, of course, so this is a very unselfish act on your part. On the other hand, I wonder if you've properly considered your own needs. [At this point, the therapist may elaborate—but only briefly—on how the husband has not necessarily given himself proper consideration.]

I appreciate the protection you are affording your mate and your family by taking upon yourself the role of the scapegoat.

The letter, if it produces the intended effect, will anger the husband, but he will be puzzled about how to interpret it and will typically keep it to read and reread. It is assumed that if the letter has this effect, it will sooner or later make a difference in the person's thinking and behavior, whether or not he ever goes for therapy, and that it will help to break down his denial of addiction. The letter can, of course, be adapted for any kind of addiction.

A Letter for Linda*   *Background*. Linda (aged thirteen) is the daughter of Helen (aged forty-nine), who divorced her husband four years ago, after years of his alcoholism. For several months after the divorce, Linda visited her father regularly, but his drinking became a growing problem during the visits; she became frightened and quit going. Now the father sees her briefly when he comes each month to pay child support. She avoids being alone with him, although she says that he has never abused her.

Linda has an older brother who is married, lives in the Midwest, and has a child. Her older sister, who is married and has a baby, lives nearby. Another older brother (aged nineteen) is single and shares an apartment with two other single men. Linda was born six years after the next older sibling; the parents had not planned to have another child. In many ways, she has been an only child.

Linda insisted on sleeping with Helen after her father left home; the mother allowed this for two years, then forced Linda to sleep in her own room. Linda resisted this rule and insisted that both bedroom doors be open. Helen brought Linda for therapy because ever since the divorce Linda had refused to visit friends, stay overnight without her mother, or have friends visit her overnight.

The letter. By the third visit, no progress had been made toward Linda's spending more time with her friends or Helen's developing a social life of her own. The mother was instructed to read the following letter to her daughter two evenings each week, after dinner:

*This case study was supplied by Doris Hewitt, Ph.D.

Dear Linda:

I want you to know how very much I appreciate your protection and caring for me by never leaving me alone, especially at night. I know this calls for a lot of scarifices on your part, and I want you to know I appreciate it greatly.

Love,
Mom

The outcome. The mother read the letter as instructed for several weeks. The daughter was angry with the therapist about the letter; however, within a month she had a friend over to spend the night and visited some friends during the day. The letter helped the mother realize that Linda was largely responding to her mother's isolation; the mother began spending more time with friends, although Linda was always present.

Within five months (and several counseling sessions), Helen began to leave Linda with her sister and to go on weekend trips with friends from work—despite Linda's tears and protests. Linda came to accept these trips better. She agreed to babysit occasionally for her sister (she had refused to do so earlier). She became increasingly more expressive, looked happier, and developed some interests and activities of her own as she saw these same changes in her mother.

Dealing with Symptoms:
A Letter for Numbness*

Background. Both Lucy and Trey are twenty-six years old. A few months after they married at age twenty-one, both had religious experiences that affected their lives markedly. They gave up smoking marijuana regularly and using THC occasionally. Church-going suddenly became an important part of their lives. Initially, Trey experienced uncertainty and guilt about some oral-genital sexual activities the couple had enjoyed earlier, but as time passed, he was assured that these activities were harmless and appropriate as long as he and Lucy enjoyed them.

Trey's uncertainty made Lucy feel rejected and resentful, although she did not express these feelings. About this time Lucy developed extensive numbness throughout her body. She saw a number of physicians, who found no physical problem and recommended therapy. She did not seek counseling at that time because, as Trey overcame his uncertainty about specific sexual activities, the numbness faded away.

Lucy first went for therapy about four years later, when she again began to develop frequent numbness throughout her body and "felt like a zombie." Trey had decided to become a minister and had moved the family several hundred miles so that he could begin college. Lucy took care of their 3-year-old daughter and occasionally worked part-time as a clerk or a waitress. She missed her family and made visits home every few months. The numbness reappeared as she worried

*This case study was supplied by Doris Hewitt, Ph.D.

more and more about finances and experienced increasing stress and fatigue. She and the child returned home to stay with her parents while Trey completed the last few weeks of his sophomore year of college; when he returned, they moved in with his parents (who had a more spacious home) for the summer.

Living with Trey's parents would have been quite satisfactory except that Trey's mother disapproved of Lucy's not working outside the home. In subtle and not so subtle ways, she made it clear day after day that Lucy would look for a job if she were a responsible wife and mother. She seemed to overlook the facts that Lucy was having emotional difficulty and that both Trey and Lucy preferred that Lucy not work. Trey worked and contributed an ample portion of his income to his parents; Lucy did most of the housework and much of the meal preparation because her mother-in-law was gainfully employed. The mother-in-law kept searching the want ads for a job for Lucy, pointing out places that she might want to go for interviews. Lucy felt increasingly hurt and angry but kept these feelings inside; and of course, her numbness grew. Trey spoke with his mother and asked her to stop criticizing and badgering, but she stopped only when Trey was present and otherwise intensified her overall effort. Lucy continued to keep quiet and refused to confront her.

The letter. The following letter was written by the therapist for Trey to read aloud to Lucy every evening.

Dear Lucy,
   I want to thank you for the special effort you make to love my parents and to show that love. I know you love them deeply, especially my mom, by the way in which you don't respond to her subtle and not so subtle directives about what you should do about getting a job. Keeping your hurt and anger inside yourself and not offending her is very unselfish, even sacrificial.
   On the other hand, I want you to know that I don't *expect* you to be so sacrificial. It concerns me that you make this sacrifice at the expense of staying upset and bringing on episodes of numbness in your body.
                              Love,
                              Trey

The outcome. The long-term consequences remain to be seen, but the immediate response (when the therapist read the letter to Lucy and Trey) was very interesting. Trey snapped his fingers, his eyes lit up, and he exclaimed delightedly, "That's it! That's really it! I don't *expect* or even *want* Lucy to sacrifice for my mom! I want her to express how she feels and take better care of *herself*!" Lucy responded, "But I don't want to make your mom mad." He replied, "I don't care if you make her mad. If you do, she'll get over it. I don't want her to keep making *you* mad. She has no right!" Trey's words reassured Lucy. They agreed to talk with Trey's parents together and to confront Trey's mother in the presence of his father. Both expressed their intentions to be very open and honest about their feelings.

REACTIONS TO LETTERS

The best way to describe the reactions to written messages is that the reactions have thus far been paradoxical. Clearly, these letters do have an impact; that is, the couples and families we have studied have not been indifferent to them. On the contrary, the reactions have convinced us of the powerful effects that these messages have on relationships. According to our impressions (which would be predicted from knowledge in information feedback), any new information in the system will explode the use of this negative past loops (Selvini-Palazzoli et al., 1978). Reactions have included explosions of affect; strong verbal denials coupled, however, with behavioral changes; and verbal agreement and compliance that were not followed by any visible behavioral change. Verbal compliance without behavioral change is the worst result: If we get verbal compliance, we are not likely to see behavioral change.

ADVANTAGES
AND DISADVANTAGES

Experience with written messages has revealed several advantages as well as disadvantages in the method. One obvious advantage of a written message over an oral one is clearer communication. Often, the communicational disturbances of a couple or a family are very imposing, and interactions are influenced by continual contradictions and disqualifications. Writing avoids the pitfalls of oral communication.

The written message seems particularly helpful with chaotic families. As a structured exercise, the message can have a twofold intervention implication. The first implication is one of structured organization. In addition to the fact that the message itself reflects structured organization in its style and in the comments on the family's chaos, the task involves imposing some external structure and order. At the same time, the content of the letter may contain statements about how much the therapist likes the chaos in the family.

An advantage of written messages that is often overlooked is the effect that the process has on the therapist. According to cognitive dissonance theory, when one person does something for another person, the first person's fondness for the second increases. The response is based on the idea that if I do something for someone, I must like that person. Otherwise, why would I do it? Thus, after having agonized over creating a letter, the therapist can logically be presumed to have an increased investment.*

*We are indebted to Edgar Jessee, Ph.D., for sharing these observations with us.

The therapist can enjoy a couple or a family more after the letter. It often becomes easier to "see the good" in the family. However, this practice also may create a sense of protectiveness for the family. At this point, the therapist has to be careful not to get involved in rescuing the family or, more commonly, becoming emotionally enmeshed in the system.

CONCLUSION

Clearly, letters can have a powerful impact on those who receive them. Careful attention must be paid, however, to their style and content as well as to their timing.

7

Homework Assignments

*Give Families
Plenty to Do*

The line between prescriptions, either verbal (Chapter 5) or written (Chapter 6), and homework assignments (HWAs), or tasks, as they are commonly referred to in the literature (Nichols, 1984), is very thin indeed. Because distinguishing the two is difficult, if not impossible, it is safe to consider HWAs an extension, perhaps a bit more complex, perhaps a bit more elaborate, of prescriptions. They may vary along dimensions of specificity (i.e., HWAs may be a little more specific than prescriptions), and they may be a little more systematic than prescriptions, which in some ways may be more ad hoc than HWAs.

This chapter continues, in a more orderly fashion, the process started in the two preceding chapters. If we want families to change, we need methods powerful enough to produce change where it counts (i.e., in the dining room, the kitchen, the living room, the bedroom). We can perform all sorts of rituals, magical laying on of hands, tricks, and games. If, however, the family fails to change at home, all the work we do in the office signifies nothing. The family may report that they are feeling better or may compliment the therapist's astuteness and sensitivity, but if the family remains the same, how good they feel or how great they consider the therapist is irrelevant. If change is to occur, it must occur at home, not just in the therapist's office. To accomplish this transfer, the therapist needs to assign tasks, exercises, work that allows the family to learn new and more productive ways of dealing with each other. To meet this goal, the family needs to follow the HWAs given by the therapist.

PRESCRIPTIONS AND HWAs

In spite of the similarities betweeen prescriptions and HWAs (with some rewording, many prescriptions could become HWAs), the differences between the two methods warrant giving HWAs a chapter all to themselves.

First, HWAs make very specific demands that either may not be present or may not be explicit in prescriptions. In addition to the degree of explicitness, HWAs require a much greater degree of specificity than most prescriptions. For instance, most HWAs request that the family meet in a certain place (e.g., the dinner table), at a certain time (e.g., Friday evenings after supper), for a certain duration (e.g., one hour), and with a certain frequency (e.g., every Friday evening as long as therapy lasts or as long as the family needs the meetings).

Second, HWAs are geared toward encouraging instructions to family members about how to conduct themselves during these meetings, in which the interactions required of them are much more prolonged than any others in the family's experience. Most prescriptions are ad hoc, one-shot deals designed to work on past interactions; HWAs are more specifically directed toward helping families to acquire new skills that should help them in the future.

Third, prescriptions assume that the family already has certain skills (e.g., the ability to negotiate); HWAs do not make this assumption. HWAs assume that new, more positive skills need to be learned by all family members. By the same token, prescriptions are oriented toward the initial crisis or the referring symptom; HWAs are oriented more toward information and the practice of new skills that will, we hope, help the family in the long haul. Prescriptions are for the short-term goal of reducing tensions, conflicts, and symptoms immediately, or for the short haul, so to speak. The purpose of HWAs, on the other hand, is to enlarge the family's behavioral repertoire through the practice and establishment of new ways of interacting; HWAs are not appropriate until the initial crisis or the referring symptom has been successfully dealt with and the family is ready to learn new and more positive ways of dealing with one another.

HISTORICAL BACKGROUND

The use of HWAs goes back to the initial efforts of Mowrer (cited in Hunt, 1984), Kelly (cited in Shelton, 1979), Ellis (cited in Shelton, 1979), sex therapy, and eventually, the behavioral school (Kadzin & Mascitelli, 1982a, 1982b), mostly with individual patients. The use of HWAs in family therapy goes back to the early work of the Palo Alto Mental Research Institute. HWAs signify a different perspective on therapy from those advocated by the Rogerian or the psychoanalytic schools. This perspective indicates the need for the therapist to be much more active than had been thought. Especially in work with families, it is irrelevant just to reflect feelings or to offer deep interpretations of the family members' unconscious motives. Families want and need solutions to their problems, and at some level they realize that just talking about behavior is not enough. Behavior may need to be changed before it can be talked about!

In the family therapy literature, Rutledge (1962) was the first to recommend home conferences that included definite HWAs. He suggested that couples meet for two conferences a week for several weeks, at a set time (e.g., 8 P.M., Tuesdays and Fridays). In each conference the wife should talk for twenty minutes, uninterrupted by her husband. Then the husband should talk for twenty minutes without interruptions from his wife. The wife then has ten minutes for questions to clarify feelings. Afterward, the husband has ten minutes to clarify feelings. The conference ends at that point. At the next meeting, the husband goes first and the wife second, reversing the sequence. Rutledge also gave specific suggestions about how to express feelings (these suggestions have been incorporated in the instructions in Appendices A and B). Rutledge listed limitations and precautions for this approach but also listed as many advantages. A great many of the HWAs now in use were pioneered by Rutledge.

Maultsby (1971) is one of the few who researched the use of systematic, written HWAs in psychotherapy. He credited Albert Ellis (1963) with having started this practice, a practice that became standard operating procedure in sex therapy. Written HWAs were used with eighty-seven patients who were also receiving Rational Emotive Therapy. Obviously, it would have been difficult to parcel out the effects of one form of treatment (i.e., therapy) over the other form of treatment (i.e., HWA). Nonetheless, almost half of the sample of patients reported that written HWAs were helpful. HWAs reduced the length of time the therapist had to spend with the patient and allowed the therapist to see many more patients than could have be seen without using HWAs. In other words, HWAs may be considered a cost-effective method of treatment that supplements therapy.

FUNCTIONS OF HWAs

HWAs allow the assessment of the family's motivation for change (a primary value), and they allow the therapist to assess the level at which the family is functioning, either in their behavioral repertoire or in their motivation. HWAs also allow desirable behaviors to transfer (generalize) from the therapist's office to the family's home. HWAs should match, as much as possible, the stated or observed needs of the family.

TYPES OF HWAs

There are at least four different types of HWAs: (1) those that change the general climate of the family, (2) those that change general relationships (e.g., the family), (3) those that change specific relationships (e.g., parent-child or marital partners), and (4) those that change specific behaviors (e.g., communication, sexual behavior, assertiveness, depression). It may be difficult to guarantee a match between HWAs and any one of these four categories because very often, in working with families, we get unexpected changes or, oftentimes, no change. As we continue working with HWAs, we may eventually reach a greater degree of specificity than we now have. However, that level of specificity is attainable only to the extent that methods rather than techniques are used and evaluated.

HWAs AND BEHAVIOR THERAPY

HWAs have been widely used by therapists of the behavioral school. Kadzin and Mascitelli (1982a), for example, found that in regard to assertiveness, the clients who received homework practice and who engaged in overt rehearsal of assertive behavior made consistently greater improvements than the clients who did not use these procedures. Shelton and Levy (1981) found that HWAs had been used to work with alcoholism, anxiety, nonassertiveness, depression, insomnia, obsessions and compulsions, obesity, sex disorders and dysfunctions, stuttering, social skills, and smoking. More relevant here, behavioral therapists have used HWAs with couples. Stuart (1983), who has made the most extensive use of HWAs, has written a workbook containing practice lessons on increasing caring behaviors, improving communication, contracting for lasting interaction change, determining who should have the power to decide, and containing conflict. The program also comes with a self-evaluation component.

As Shelton (1979) noted, "Homework involves self-observation . . . to identify critical events antecedent to the appearance of the problem that may have caused the problem . . . and . . . [may] help maintain [it]" (p. 227). HWAs also involved "sound conceptualization" about what is most likely to be useful to the family. According to Shelton, HWAs should include one or more of the following five instructions (always given in writing). The instructions for HWAs should contain at least five different components: (1) a *Do* statement about what the family should do, such as "Meet in the dining room," "Read these instructions," "Talk in turns"; (2) a *Quantity* statement about the frequency of meetings, the length of meetings, where meetings are to take place (e.g., "three times a week from 7 P.M. to 9 P.M. in the living room"); (3) a *Record* statement about recording what happens and what is discussed (which allows the evaluation of compliance and efficacy); (4) a *Bring* statement about bringing the written notes to the next appointment; and (5) a *Contingency* statement about alternative plans or the consequences of not doing the HWA.

Lester, Beckman, and Baucom (1980) made HWAs an integral part of their treatment package. Couples rehearsed at home the skills learned in the therapist's office, writing down constructive and destructive communications. It is important that the therapist monitor the homework at the beginning of each therapy session, checking progress and correcting mistakes. If a couple or a family is unable or unwilling to work well on HWAs, the therapist should consider the possibility that HWAs may be premature and that the crisis or symptom that originally brought the couple or the family to therapy may not as yet have been resolved.

HWAs IN FAMILY THERAPY

Bross (1982) maintained that HWAs "extend the therapeutic process beyond the immediate [therapy] session. Tasks serve the treatment goal and are alternatives to existing behaviors. Additionally, homework tasks can intensify the relationship between the worker [therapist] and client" (p. 85). Bross quoted Reid and Epstein (1972), who insisted that HWAs be "feasible" (i.e., they can be accomplished) and "desirable" (i.e., the family considers them relevant and useful). Desirablilty was determined by assessing the positive or the negative consequences of HWAs. Bross also quoted Haley (1976), who emphasized how HWAs are to be delivered: They must be delivered clearly to ensure that the HWA will not remain undone because the family does not understand it adequately. Nichols (1984) used the term *tasks* to denote HWAs as used by strategic therapists:

> Tasks are assigned on the basis of a belief that change is born of action, not understanding. Tasks are carefully designed to fit the case; they are assigned to be done between sessions to insure that what is begun in therapy sessions is generalized to the family's environment. Since problems are considered to be maintained by family interactions, most tasks are designed to involve the whole family. Since change requires action, often action that appears illogical, tasks are generally assigned without explanation or comment. Tasks are tools used to change family systems so that they will be able to manage their own problems. (pp. 445–446)

De Shazer and Molnar (1984) reported on four routine HWAs, which are given to practically all families: (1) "Between now and the next time we meet, we (I) want you to observe, so that you can tell us (me) next time, what happens in your (life, marriage, family, or relationship) that you want to continue to have happen" (p. 299). Essentially, this is a routine prescription of no change, qualified, however, by stressing the importance of observations and a possibly heightened sensitivity to family transactions. (2) "Do something different" (p. 292). Although vague and general, this HWA widens a family's repertoire. (3) "Pay attention to what you do when you overcome the temptation or the urge to (perform the symptom or some behavior associated with the complaint)" (p. 292). This HWA induces some feeling of mastery and control over seemingly uncontrollable behavior. (4) "A lot of people in your situation would have . . . " (p. 293) (the therapist suggests ways that most people would react to a stressful situation, the reason for referral, or the symptom). Here, the reactions to the problem behavior are highlighted positively (Chapter 4), and the family is asked to continue behaving as they have in the past (i.e., no change); possible suggestions for change are offered as impossible ways of achieving the difficult goal of change.

Lange and van der Hart (1983) used a series of HWAs with families. All the HWAs included a list of the days, the place, and the times that the HWA was carried out. Other specific instructions follow: (1) Write down points of irritation; that is, make a "dirty laundry" list of whatever a family member does that irritates another. However, the person who records the source of irritation should neither comment on nor discuss it with the irritating member. It should be discussed in the therapy session to train families to voice complaints as adults rather than as children (or parents!). (2) Have discussion in rounds; that is, allow all family members to state their beefs without defensive interruptions or angry rebuttals. One subject should be treated at a time, and each family member should learn to listen to others respectfully, without interruptions (i.e., A talks, B listens; B responds to A, A listens; A responds to B, B listens). (3) Monitor by noting in writing each day the frequency of undesirable or irritating behaviors, but there should be no discussion at home—the discussion should be reserved for the therapy session. (4) Keep a mood meter, a chart, which is displayed prominently in the house and on which family members record their day-by-day moods, using pencils of different colors. When the graph has been filled, family members need to discuss the moods and the reasons that they occur, thus allowing the family to talk about feelings without becoming defensive. (5) Formulate wishes instead of accusations.

The methods suggested by de Shazer and Molnar are quite general and vague; thus, they can be used at the beginning stage of therapy, when the family is still in crisis. The methods suggested by Lange and van der Hart, on the other hand, are to be used after the crisis has subsided or decreased and the family is to learn new, positive, and more specific ways of interacting with one another. De Shazer and Molnar did not specify the conditions under which the HWAs are to occur. In fact, their intervention lies somewhere between prescriptions, as described in Chapter 5, and the HWAs described here. Their methods may, however, have an important function at the beginning of family therapy.

CASE STUDY 1

Robert and Helen, a couple who had been married for nine years, came for therapy after they had been separated for a few weeks. They had recently had their second child (who, in contrast to their first daughter, was not planned), had bought their first home, and Robert was about to finish his undergraduate degree after seven years of study. Helen maintained that Robert was irresponsible and left her with all the work of the house and the children while he went out with friends, both male and female. Robert complained that Helen tried to blame him for everything and did not take the initiative to do things on her own for herself but chose to play the martyr. Helen countered by saying that she would like to be able to get out on her own and develop interests and friends but that she could not because she was saddled with the responsibilities that arose from Robert's irresponsibility.

A number of different methods were used with this couple as therapy progressed.

Homework assignments. At the outset of therapy, the couple was given a series of assignments: (1) to write out a list of expectations about the ideal spouse (to help them clarify the specific behaviors that each wanted from the partner); (2) to list changes they wanted to make in themselves (as a means of changing focus from the partner to their own roles in keeping their system from changing); (3) (after having worked on themselves and having made some progress) to write contracts covering the responsibilities that each was willing to take in the marriage and, as the possibilities became clear, to set up new rules for the marriage.

In each assignment, the couple was asked to do the task separately, in writing, and to bring the written homework to the session to share with each other and with the therapists. The homework thus helped to establish continuity from one session to the next, to get each spouse to take personal responsibility for doing the assignment, and to clarify the issues. The HWAs were also the starting point for negotiation—learning to give and take, and to abandon the pattern of rigid charges and countercharges that they had exhibited at the beginning of therapy.

Outcome. The couple successfully renegotiated their marriage; Robert moved back in with Helen five months after they began therapy. The couple seemed more willing to share emotionally with each other during the sessions, and both seemed more aware of their responsibilities for themselves as well as to each other.

PROS AND CONS OF HWAs

Rutledge (1962) considered many of the values as well as the limitations of HWAs and the precautions to be taken when using HWAs. His list is still relevant and can be updated and elaborated to meet the needs of families rather than couples, who were Rutledge's original focus. On the positive side, planned and prolonged HWAs allow a further opportunity to deal with family matters and possibly to reduce the time and energy that are necessary to reach therapeutic goals. Repeating disturbing patterns of interaction under the control of the therapist affords further clarification, assimilation, acceptance, and reintegration in the family's changing. Change takes place where it should take place—in the home, not in the therapist's office. Well-planned HWAs may increase understanding and respect among family members because they are able to see one another under more propitious conditions than before. HWAs that are followed regularly prevent the accumulation of unexpressed feelings, which can lead to further distortions and greater conflict. Because all family members participate, HWAs ensure that change is occurring for the whole family, not just for selected individuals.

The advantages that we hope to see from the use of HWAs are increased honesty, trust, and communication skills, as well as the more positive individuation of family members, which may spread to other areas of family living. In fact, this very spread to other areas should be used as an indication of whether HWAs are helpful to the family. If families learn to transact their business on their own, without the therapist's help, they will be able to go it alone over the long haul. By focusing on resolving issues at home, where there are fewer irrelevant distractions, the family may learn to use therapy in a more selective and condensed fashion. HWAs allow families to take responsibility for their own lives without relying on therapy to surmount difficulties.

On the negative side, as mentioned earlier, planned and prolonged HWAs cannot be made in the critical, initial stages of therapy. The therapist should consider the intellectual, cognitive, and affective abilities of a family, tailoring

HWAs to a level that maximizes the family's strengths and assets rather than their liabilities. Oftentimes, HWAs cannot be given to severely disturbed families, in which paranoid, psychopathic, severe depressive, and possibly suicidal patterns may be present. The initial crisis must be resolved, at least in part, if the family is to reach a level of stability that will allow them to complete HWAs. An HWA that is not carried out is an indication that the HWA was premature, inappropriate, or ill-timed. Initially, some families may resist this direction in therapy, especially if patterns of helplessness, dependency, and apathy have not been dealt with. Some of the resistance should be positively reframed ("I can see how you may be afraid of change—'The devil I have is better than the devil I may get' "). Resistance is an expected reaction in most families, but it, like all therapeutic issues, should be treated as a friend, not an enemy. When a family persists in bringing up the past, they may not be able to work in the present. Past hurts and traumas, if they are pertinent to therapy, should also be handled through HWAs (e.g., "I want each of you to talk for at least one hour during the week about past issues"). Or better, encourage each family member to bring to the next therapy session a written list of past issues (family members should prepare their lists independently).

There is a great deal to commend and very little to fear when HWAs are administered carefully, diligently, and compassionately. In some ways, HWAs may be considered the sine qua non of treatment. If a family is not willing or able to change at home, how can we hope that they will change at all?

CASE STUDY 2

The W.'s were having problems keeping their two children from fighting. Michael, nine, and Brooke, five, were constantly picking on and teasing each other; Linda, their mother, was stuck in the role of figuring out who started the fight, who was right and who was wrong, how to punish justly. In short, she was playing detective, judge, defense attorney, and prosecutor for every fight her children had. To get her out of these roles, two homework assignments were given for two consecutive sessions.

First, the children were encouraged to keep fighting; Linda was told to continue her roles. She was also told to report to her husband, Larry, when she could no longer handle a particular fight. This assignment had the intended effect of reducing the fighting between Brooke and Michael. The second week, a more linear approach was used to teach the family a time-out method. Whenever Linda caught the children fighting, she was to ask them, "What is the rule about fighting?" Both were to respond, "The rule is no fighting." After responding, they were to go to their rooms for five minutes of quiet time. If the children fought in the car, Linda was told to pull off the road and go through the same procedure—not driving until the quiet period was over. This technique decreased the fighting even further and gave Linda some confidence in dealing with the children.

CONCLUSION

From this review of the literature, one can safely conclude that, except for the behavioral literature, (1) HWAs have been used in family therapy, although their central and important role has not been sufficiently acknowledged; (2) thus far, most HWAs have been ad hoc, one-shot, mostly improvised, and they have not been used to test theory; (3) as a whole, HWAs have not been derived from theory; and (4) the role and the importance of HWAs have not been evaluated as they should be. Because of these and other considerations, L'Abate and his associates (1986) developed a series of systematic HWAs designed to improve communication and negotiation skills, to increase intimacy in families, to lessen depression in the family, to improve problem solving and negotiation skills, and to increase intimacy.

8

Communication Training

Teaching Listening and Talking Skills

To understand himself man needs to be understood by another.
To be understood by another he needs
to understand the other.

Thomas Hora

Communication has been a frequently used word in professional and nonprofessional discussions for the last several decades. While many agree that the word has come to be overused, it is doubtful that communication is overemphasized. It may be defined for the purposes of this chapter as everything which one does to attempt to influence another's action and experience of the world, particularly to influence another to experience the world like oneself. It may also be defined more simply as the exchange of information. In that sense, the goal of communication training is to insure that the message sent is equivalent to the message received. The skills to achieve this end are simple, and a universal necessity, but they are not commonly exhibited or easily carried out. There are many traps to avoid and many inherent difficulties in such an undertaking. When these skills are successfully used they lead to increased family and marital satisfaction (Ganahl, 1982; Gottman, 1979; Murphy & Mendelson, 1973; Navran, 1967) and may be a major component of effective psychotherapy (Birchler, 1979; Gurman & Knistern, 1978; Jacobson, 1978).

Before undertaking a description of skill training, the reader may wish to bear in mind Wiio's laws (Goldhaber, 1979):

1. Communication usually fails, except by chance.
   1.1 If communication can fail, it will.
   1.2 If communication cannot fail, it, nevertheless, usually does fail.
   1.3 If communication seems to succeed in a way which was intended, it must be in a way which was not intended.
   1.4 If you are satisfied that your communication is bound to succeed, it is then bound to fail.

2. If a message can be understood in different ways, it will be understood in just that way which does the most harm.
3. There is always somebody who knows better than you what you meant by your message.
4. The more communication there is, the more difficult it is for communication to succeed.

These rules may seem flippant to the casual observer, but have an all too evident basis in human interaction. Wiio (Goldhaber, 1979) notes the wealth of research data which demonstrates the efficiency of the communication process to be very low, occasionally approaching statistical levels considered to be nonndiscriminable from randomness. If communicators take the process for granted, ignore the potential for misunderstanding, see it as simpler than it is, don't check on their results, design their communications to suit themselves rather than the listener, and overlook people's limited capacity for information processing, great misunderstandings may occur. They will probably occur even when care is taken.

The exercises and techniques presented here are a step towards eliminating the emotional and behavior problems which may follow from family communication. They are quite circumscribed, but will be sufficient given the desire of clients to communicate effectively and to eliminate destructive forms of communication. It is the latter which is most crucial for successful communication. In general, one is seeking to teach clients to give clear messages, to work actively to understand their partner's messages, and to convey respect and appreciation during the process of communicating. To be successful, clients will also need to seek feedback on how they were understood, and to respond to such feedback to complete the communication loop. Efforts will be complicated by the fact that people have been taught to suppress the expression of some feelings or thoughts, even though such expression is made nonverbally, confusing the listener with contradictory verbal and nonverbal messages. Complications also arise from people's ability to use content to talk indirectly about their relationship issues. Arguments about how to squeeze the toothpaste container may have little to do with content and everything to do with whose way should be adopted. To be accurate, communication must be clear about both content and relationship messages.

Completing the communication loop involves clear and direct speaking (what is being said, and to whom), active efforts to understand the speaker's point of view, paraphrased feedback to determine the degree of understanding, and confirmation or clarification of the original message by the speaker. Communication training can be useful in a variety of cases. The clarity introduced can help:

1. families where discussions about content are also covert discussions about their relationships;
2. families where the meaning of specific messages and communicational cues differ due to differences in interpretation carried over from grandparent generations

(Rabkin, 1967), for example, questions are questions in one family of origin, but requests in another: ("Would you like to go out to a movie tonight? . . . Not really . . . You never take me out.");

3. families where there are frequent incongruities between communication channels, (e.g., verbal and nonverbal messages do not agree because the speaker is attempting to mask emotions);

4. families where communication is vague and important features of the message— *I* am saying *this* to *you* in this *situation* —are left out;

5. families where people act as if there are contracts governing family behavior, but who fail to state their contractual expectations;

6. families with unreal expectations about communication {Satir's (1967) crystal ball and fragility syndromes: "If you loved me, you would understand everything I said" or "I am too weak to ask my spouse, father, or whoever what they mean, but I am powerful enough to guess without asking"};

7. families where members don't assert themselves and thus leave important wishes and preferences left unspoken, speaking only about their disappointments, often indirectly.

Communication training of the type to be described below will not necessarily help families such as those described by Laing (1965) or Hoffman (1976), where the intent is to obscure and hide with language, or where the cognitive skills to be more clearcut are not evident (Wynne & Singer, 1963), or where the "lethal processes" described by Luthman and Kirschenbaum (1974), which hinder communication, are in evidence.

SPEAKING SKILLS

The primary skill to be learned by speakers is to speak for themselves in a clear, direct, specific manner. Speaking for the self means just that—talking in phrases which begin with "I" and focus on the speaker's feelings, thoughts, intentions, wishes, perceptions, or actions. Likes, dislikes, preferences, and desires are particularly important to communicate. Sentences which begin with "you" or "it" are best avoided, as are sentences which have "they," "someone," "others," "people," etc., as their main referents. These sentences focus attention away from the speaker, make understanding more difficult, and undermine the communication process. Being clear means giving enough concrete detail so that the listener can understand the speaker's unique frame of reference. The use of specific instances and examples is very helpful and much easier to understand than abstract words which people may interpret differently. Indefinite terms (perhaps, maybe, possibly) are to be avoided as they increase vagueness and the ability to deny responsibility for one's statements. Directness means clearly indicating for whom messages are intended.

Other important skills are the ability to define important issues and stress them while ignoring other matters, and to stick to one topic at a time. The effort to convey one's experience is too great to waste on trivial matters, and the listener's ability to keep issues in mind is limited. Feelings should be accepted for what they are—highly personal responses which are not consciously chosen by the individual and which can't be depicted as either right or wrong. They should be conveyed with appropriate emotional intensity, rather than being denied or evaded. At best they will be conveyed nonverbally anyway, possibly confusing one's partner. At worst they will be misinterpreted in the worst possible way. This should not, however, be an excuse to ignore normal tact and courteousness. While feelings are not under the individuals's control, the manner of expressing them should be. Politeness will convey to the partner that they are valued and respected, and will allow them to concentrate on what is being said rather than on the speaker's feelings about them. Verbal habits such as saying "Please" or "I would appreciate it" should be encouraged. Using primarily positive comments is another form of respect which should be observed, though one may need to work to make this a habit for the family. Wahlroos (1974) recommends an 80-20 split between praise and criticism as the minimal level of praise for couples and families.

Families should also be encouraged to keep their relationship and content messages separate or congruent. Relationship aspects of messages are those which refer to definitions of what the relationship between speaker and receiver(s) is perceived to be or should be (who should be in charge, deferred to, etc.). Content aspects of messages are designed to convey the information immediately obvious and available from a written transcript of speech. When relationship messages become confused with content messages, arguments can remain unresolved for an indefinite period of time or until the relationship issues are addressed more directly. If the important issue is power or status in the family, the family will more profitably discuss who should set the family rules than which end of the tube the toothpaste should be squeezed at. Such problems can be partly avoided by speaking of wishes and preferences rather than needs or rights, by requesting rather than demanding, by seeking compromise and understanding rather than seeking to prove one's correctness.

A final skill involves seeking out feedback from the listener. Speakers should attend to the listener while talking, keeping eye contact and orienting their body towards them to allow the reception of important nonverbal feedback. Verbal feedback of the listener's understanding should be requested if it is not forthcoming. Feedback should focus on understanding rather than acceptance, approval, or agreement. It is particularly important for speakers to realize that events can be seen from multiple points of view, words can have multiple connotations, and partners cannot be expected to understand correctly just because one is trying to be clear. Communication should be tailored to the listener, not the speaker. The effect of the communication rather than the intent should be accepted as the meaning conveyed. Partners should not be allowed to say they understand without indicating what they understand. All assumptions should be tested verbally, particularly those of a contractual nature. All incongruous nonverbal reactions should be explored until understood.

LISTENING SKILLS

The listener's goal is to attend to the speaker, working towards understanding the speaker's feelings and unique point of view, and to indicate respect and esteem for the speaker while listening. The listening should not be done for the purposes of analyzing and interpreting the speaker's personality, advising or correcting, rebutting or proving wrong, agreeing or approving. Listening is a powerful act in its own right, raising the speakers level of self-awareness and self-exploration (Carkhuff, 1969a,b). Speakers often listen to themselves for the first time when they are closely listened to by another. In addition, the act of communicating to another seems to allow thoughts to flow differently from when they are confined to one person's consciousness. No less a thinker and speaker than Abraham Lincoln relied on this facilitative property of communicating. He once called upon a friend from his home state to attend him, rushed the friend to the White House, spoke to him for the entire night, and then dismissed him at dawn with thanks and gratitude for his assistance in spite of the fact that the friend had not uttered one word of advice.

Respect is shown by the careful attentiveness of the listener, the presence of a nonjudgmental attitude, and the attempt to understand from within the speaker's frame of reference rather than forcing the listener's frame upon the speaker. It is also shown by letting the speaker finish, and only interrupting when lost or overwhelmed by too much content. Attending to the speaker is as much physical as anything else. One can convey attention by maintaining eye contact with the speaker, orienting one's body toward them, maintaining a relaxed posture, slightly leaning toward the speaker, and leaving the limbs open rather than crossing them like barriers in front of the body. Minimal encouragements for speech can also be used, such as nodding the head, or using vocalizations such as "um-hmm."

Core messages and themes should be listened for and reflected back. This emphasis on important issues keeps the communication channel clear from irrelevant clutter and makes it more likely that what is important will be heard. One should not cry wolf with every little item, or include every single grievance in a fight, a mistake so frequent that it has a common name among family counselors, "kitchen sinking." When both content and relationship messages are offered, one should respond to the content unless the relationship message is direct ("Where the hell are my keys?" "They're on the table," with a neutral tone, not "Right where you left them," or "How should I know?"). Relationship discussions should be direct, and occur at a time when they are likely to do some good. The best times are those when all those involved are rested, fed, and free from other work or distractions. The time after someone has just arrived home from work or is in the kitchen preparing a meal are poor choices for discussion times. Small irritations like the key example above should be treated as temporary and natural fluctuations in a close relationship and ignored, or spoken about directly and specifically when they occur too frequently.

The speaker should be praised or rewarded in other ways for confiding in the listener and definitely not be punished by angry or insensitive responses. Maintaining confidentiality about significant interchanges rather than speaking about them to friends and relatives is another important ingredient for encouraging further discussions. The speaker will also be rewarded by the listener's attending to his or her own responses and sharing these with the speaker after understanding of the first communication is completed. The listener can pay close attention to the speaker's level of stress and immediate feelings, placing these above content in importance, and working to understand these before focusing on what has happened in the past, no matter how great the past's importance to the listener. Whether or not changes in the focus of the conversation are necessary, acknowledgments of the speaker's feelings are helpful ("This is difficult for you isn't it? I appreciate your making the effort to say it.").

THERAPEUTIC INTERVENTIONS

The best interventions are those which are the least intrusive but get the job done. With communication the therapist will monitor the family's communication, interrupt to stop destructive interchanges, unobtrusively model better techniques, and, if necessary, structure the situation with increasing restraints on the family and increasingly specific requests.

The basic requirement for correction of communication problems is that the therapist be able to observe the family speaking to each other. This allows the therapist to assess the family's skills and to provide immediate feedback or advice of a corrective nature. Pinsoff's (1983) general intervention strategy for destructive patterns is particularly useful. The therapist interrupts the first occurrence of the destructive pattern. If it occurs again, the therapist interrupts and labels it for the family. After that, occurences are interrupted and the family is asked to label it. This approach gradually increases the intrusiveness of the therapist while clearly expecting the family eventually to be responsible for their own communication. When communication is being focused on, the family should not be allowed to communicate through the therapist, since their normal communication patterns will be obscured by the participation of the therapist.

Minuchin (1974) and Sluzki (1978) give useful guidelines for encouraging family members to speak directly with one another. Family members can be asked "Have you told this to them before?" If they say "No, not until now." the therapist should request that it be said directly to the intended receiver ("Tell them now."), and that the speaker to turn to face and observe the listener if they do not do so spontaneously. If the one direction is not sufficient, the therapist can ask again, increasing the vocal intensity of the request, use hand signals to indicate whom to talk to, look to the intended listener rather than make eye contact with the speaker, refuse to talk with the speaker, move his or her chair behind the speaker, or leave the room.

Once communication does occur, the therapist can help improve it by asking that specific blank areas be filled in ("You still haven't said what you would like to be done."), that it be altered in its form ("Please repeat that, but this time turn your question into a statement."), or by modeling with the therapist or another family member speaking for the speaker ("I think what they are trying to say is that they feel neglected when you do that"). The speaker's not looking at the listener while speaking to them should be taken as a disqualification of the message and it should not be accepted. If this has occurred the message should be given again with the speaker looking at the listener, able to receive feedback from the listener through visual means. The therapist should pay particular attention to modeling the communication process while making such interventions, and make a deliberate attempt to keep his or her praise/criticism ratio at the 80/20 mark. At the very least the ratio should approximate a bank balance so that there are more positive deposits than withdrawals.

When communication cannot be sufficiently altered by the above approaches, more specific teaching exercises may be designed for the family. Family members may be given specific sentences to use in ritualized fashion (L'Abate, 1975a; Lange & van der Hart, 1983; Perls, 1973). These can be used both to highlight destructive processes and to elicit more useful processes. Perls (1973), for example, has couples play "resentment ping pong" where they take turns filling in the blanks using the format "I resent_____. You should_____." Couples can similarly be instructed to fill in the blanks in statements of their wants ("I would like you to_____"), their partner's wants ("You would like me to_____"), their hurt ("I feel hurt when_____") or any other topic the therapist feels is important and not adequately handled by current communication practices. L'Abate (1975a) carries this process one step further by having the listener initiate the sequence with a question ("What can you give me? What can I give you?"). Couples are instructed to ask these questions ten times consecutively, which adds power to the questions and helps the couple treat them seriously.

Content-free instructions can also be given in the form of specific communication rules (Bandler & Grinder, 1982; Wahlroos, 1974; Fagan & Shepherd, 1970), ideal structures for speech (Ivey, 1971), or speech usages to avoid (Bach & Wyden, 1970; Carter & Thomas, 1975; Lederer & Jackson, 1968; Wahlroos, 1974; Watzlawick, 1964). Speakers may be asked to convert questions to statements on the presumption that questions are ways to avoid making self statements and to speak indirectly ("Why did you leave the food out last night?" could be "You should have put the food away.") The use of "why" can be proscribed as it is unhelpful and merely serves to criticize. Instead, the effect on the self or the desired change should be stated, the emphasis switched from "why" to "how." Listeners can be taught to ignore "why" questions and respond with requests for alternative plans ("I don't know why it happened. What would you have liked to happen?" or "How would you like it to happen next time?"). The use of the past can be ruled out, and discussions centered on the "here and now." The use of the past to prove that the speaker is right is a particularly destructive process and should be curtailed by the therapist ("You're right. You're right too. What do the two of you have to give up to be right?").

With couples who have difficulty responding to therapist coaching and who do not respond adequately to some of the above suggestions, full-scale training can be initiated. Wells and Figurel (1968) present one model for such training. Usually this training takes place with two people, though several can be observing and taking turns in the speaker role. The pair is asked to take turns being the speaker and the listener for equal periods of time. The speaker is to express his or her feelings about a topic, avoiding blaming or attacking statements, and avoiding questions which would simply transfer the speaker role to the listener, while the original speaker still controlled the topic. Intense feelings may be expressed as long as they do not involve destructive modes of communication, as defined below. Statements are to be short, three to five sentences each. Following this the speaker pauses for a response. The listener responds to the speaker's feelings, keeping the response to one to two sentences. The response should be a concise statement of what is understood, not of agreement, advice, moral judgment, or any of the other substitutes for understanding. Questions are not allowed. The process can be summarized as follows:

SPEAKER: 3–5 sentences,
express feelings on any topic,
no questions, blaming, or attacking,
pause for response.
LISTENER: 1–2 sentences,
no questions,
respond to speaker's feelings,
statement of understanding, not agreement or advice.

The therapist will have to be very active in this process at first as couples will tend to fall into their normal communication patterns. To minimize the likelihood of this, couples can be asked to discuss problems of low to medium conflict rather than trying to learn a new communication process with highly conflictual material. It may also be useful to give the couple a more specific structure to use in their statements. If necessary they can be asked to make all of their statements in the form "I am feeling X about Y in situation Z" ("I feel left out when you read the paper at the breakfast table"), or "You feel X about Y in situation Z." The therapist will have to be particularly active in monitoring and preventing destructive or unproductive communication. This may mean simply asking a particular person to speak slower, louder, softer, or faster, or encouraging further statements, or fewer statements. Generally, however, more destructive patterns will arise, even after the couple has been asked to avoid them. In these cases Pinsoff's pattern of interrupting, interrupting and labeling, or asking the family to label will be helpful. Such communications may also be commented on neutrally, followed by instructions for how to use more positive, complete, or clearcut communications. The therapist can ask for statements of hurt behind destructive anger (L'Abate, 1975a), for inclusion of self needs with placators, for inclusion of the context with irrelevant discussion, for inclusion of one's own part in things with blamers.

There are a number of ineffective possibilities which should be watched for, most of which involve disqualifying the speaker or listener as a person or as a valid source of information. For the most part people will disqualify each other, but sometimes they will disqualify their own messages in order to say something without really saying it so they cannot be held accountable for it. Coercive and other manipulative tactics to force agreement or approval or retaliate for perceived injustices must also be monitored. Problematic features of communication to be corrected include:

Abusive talk: frequent or lengthy verbal criticisms, sarcasm, ridicule, blaming, judging, humiliating, exposing "dirty linen" in public, or belittling the other's ideas as dumb, crazy, wrong, silly, or unworthy of them.

Better than thou postures: preaching, lecturing, patronizing, condescending, explaining or using outside authority to prove the speaker wrong, analyzing the speaker's personality or interpreting his or her behavior.

Coercive behavior: bullying, nagging, yelling, whining, physical intimidation through threats or actions, emotional escalations, threatening with the "atom bomb" every time an argument begins ("If you can't change I will leave you").

Personal avoidance: sulking, pouting, ignoring, cold shoulder, speaking only through a third person and not directly to partner.

Topic avoidance: switching subjects, sidetracking, pretending not to hear or understand partner, silence, focusing on tangential elements of communications, denial, direct refusal to discuss a topic.

Excessive compliance: smoothing over, being nice, covering up, walking on eggs, excessive agreement, parroting the speaker, discounting the needs, wishes, and opinions of the self.

Guilt induction: comparing to one's self and own efforts, bragging about oneself, counting one's sacrifices, martyrdom ("It's OK, you do what you want and I'll struggle along the best I can").

Cross-complaining: "Yes, but" techniques; "My problem is more important than your problem."

Evasions: vagueness, incomplete statments, changing from past to present so frequently as to cause confusion, overgeneralizations, humor when seriousness is called for, use of clichés, failure to take a stand or state a clear opinion, using the paraphrasing process to never answer a legitimate question.

Interruptions: excessive questions, verbal obstructions: coughing, humming, crying, laughing.

Dogmatic generalizations: black-and-white thinking, use of always, never, should, shouldn't, lack of qualifications on assertions, categorical imperatives.

Mindreading: assuming one knows better than the speaker what is being said, failure to ask for confirmation of one's understanding of speaker.

Spokesmanship: speaking for someone else who can speak for him- or herself.

Super-reasonableness: avoiding one's feelings through the use of logic.

Straw man discussions: exaggerating partner's position, assuming other's requests are unreasonable, blaming partner for something which has been blown out of proportion or which cannot be controlled.

Talking past the point: continuing on one topic past useful discussion, repetitiousness, circumstantial or overelaborate speech.

Overinclusions: excessive emphasis on past history, making more than one criticism at a time, "kitchen sinking,"—throwing in all possible criticisms.

Acknowledgment deficit: failure to confirm other's correct statements and unique point of view.

Reinforcement deficit: failure to encourage, praise, or respond to the other in ways which signify appreciation for their effort to communicate.

When the approaches described earlier do not succeed in clearing up these communication difficulties, one should consider several hypotheses. The family may be too limited in its ego functions to tolerate too much closeness or differentiation and may be maintaining a comfortable distance through their disturbed communication. These families will not be helped through an educational or skill-training approach focused on communication. Families may also subscribe to a number of lethal assumptions about life and personal growth which hinder their interest in using these approaches. Luthman and Kirschenbaum's (1974) list of processes lethal to family growth includes:

1. Any comment from one family member to another is viewed as an attack.
2. Differences between family members are seen as threats.
3. Expression of anger is seen as an attack rather than as an attempt to make contact.
4. Expression of tenderness is seen as making one vulnerable to ridicule, attack, or disappointment.
5. Expression of sadness is seen as a weakness, lack of strength, and dependency.
6. Everyone must be reasonable all the time. Spontaneity means lack of control, as does expression of feelings.
7. Everyone must be nice and polite at all times.
8. Love is being dutiful and obedient. (Hence discussions should focus on commands.)
9. Intimacy is frightening.

Families may have trouble understanding the connotations of each other's behaviors and communications because of extremely different communication environments in their families of origin (Rabkin, 1967). These families may be helped by a discussion of family of origin differences ("In A's family closeness was expressed by engaging in activities together, but in B's activities were seen as distractions and closeness was expressed by sitting together doing nothing else.").

In other families, the conflict escalation routes are so well traveled, probably due in part to the predilection for interpreting all statements in the worst possible way (Gottman, 1979), or to exaggerated responsiveness to nonverbal cues and relationship aspects of messages, that the above communication training is premature. For these families preliminary exercises may be used which separate the process of communication over time and space (Wagner & L'Abate, 1977). Family members can be asked to write notes to each other or make tapes for each other, responding to the other's messages through the same medium. Such separation may aid the individual's ability to reflect and consider alternative interpretations of the other's messages and the impact of their own messages before uttering them.

Bandler and Grinder (1982, pp. 145–162) describe several methods for use with communication problems. They suggest checking on whether the response elicited was what the sender wanted, and attend to verbal, nonverbal, and action responses. They also ask the receiver if the message he or she receives is a familiar one and what the message is. If there is an inconsistency between the sender's stated intent and the received message, the sender is asked how important it is to get the message across and if they are willing to change their behavior to get the message across. The answer should be "yes" to both of these questions. Once they state they are committed to sending the message in a way that it will be heard, new communication approaches may be teachable. The receiver can be asked to tell the speaker how they need to sound and act for him or her to listen ("She would have to stop yelling, speak more softly and treat me with more respect for me to listen."). Both speaker and listener can recount instances in the past where messages were sent and received accurately, and how that was done differently ("When we talked about the arrangements for our vacation it was much better. We . . . "). The speaker can also be asked to imitate another speaker they feel is effective, or to begin by imagining themselves acting differently. They could also be asked to observe other people in order to discover communication models to imitate during the week.

PROBLEM-SOLVING SKILLS

Once the couple is successfully using speaking and listening skills, both must move beyond simply understanding the speaker's point of view and work toward reaching agreements and compromises, in short, to problem solving and conflict negotiation. There are many good models for problem solving or negotiation, most of them based on couples, but equally applicable to family discussions (D'Zurilla & Goldfried, 1971; Harrell, 1975; Epstein, Bishop, & Levine, 1978; Tsoi-Hommand, 1976). Our model (to be explained in Chapter 12) includes the following steps:

1. Identify issues or problems to work on. Choose one, specify and concretize its aspects and identify target behaviors to be changed.
2. Communicate the problem to the appropriate person.
3. Develop a list of at least three alternative behaviors or other solutions to the problem.
4. Evaluate solutions and select one.
5. Make a specific plan which includes who will be responsible for seeing the alternative

carried out, and who will do what, when, for whom, for how long, in what situations, with what rewards for compliance or consequences for noncompliance.

6. Evaluate how the solution worked.
7. Start over if necessary.

It must be recognized that the family skills necessary for problem solving will vary with the area being focused on (pragmatic issues versus emotional issues, for example) and that the therapist may not get a true representation of the family's abilities if he or she picks a topic area the family is too comfortable with. The therapist may see a telescoped problem-solving process, or one which runs more smoothly than those managed in conflicted areas. With regard to Step 1, the therapist should make sure that real problems are not being displaced onto other problem areas. With Step 2, the person with the resources to solve the problem should be involved in the process at an early stage, not simply told what to do at the time Step 5 is reached. The therapist should also ensure that one party to a conflict is not left out while another complains to outside persons about the problem. Step 3 is often shortened to acting on the first solution thought of, while Step 4 is often overlooked, bypassed as a result of too few alternatives. Step 6 is also overlooked, with families failing to identify which components of their plan were helpful, thus failing to learn from good experience. More unfortunate still are those situations where solutions do not work but no one monitors them and no new solution is proposed, leaving families to sink in depression or silent anger and frustration.

Gottman's (1979) work indicates that clinic couples often have difficultly with Step 1 because they cannot agree on a single issue and cross-complain instead. This involves each carrying on a discussion of an entirely different issue. During the middle stages clinic couples are marked by deficits in expression of respect, negative nonverbal behavior, and by long chains of statements about the meaning of their discussion (metacommunication) rather than the short metacommunication chains shown by normal couples. At Steps 4 and 5 counterproposals rather than agreements or compromises are presented.

Problem solving will be aided by family members paying attention to the suggested skills for listeners and speakers, and avoiding destructive or ineffective communication, as listed above. Speakers should pay particular attention to being specific; talking about wishes and preferences rather than needs, demands, or rights; identifying what they want rather than what they don't want (the former contains much more information and makes it more likely they will get what they want); giving alternative or preferred behaviors along with criticisms; making sure that there are more positive statements to the listener than critical statements; and talking about choices and changes rather than who is to blame, and about the future rather than the past.

Couples and families will most likely find it helpful to anticipate the need to talk over common problems and to set a daily or weekly problem-solving time. Problem solving should be limited to this time or to additional times mutually agreed upon by the family or couple. Problem solving should not be attempted at other times, and should not be mixed with other activities, for example, following lovemaking. Discussions should not be attempted if anyone is too tired, busy, upset, or angry, or if anyone is intoxicated, as this indicates they will not be able to adequately attend to the discussion or can disqualify their statements later on. The focus should be on understanding and agreement, with work proceeding to compromises where people meet in the middle or make trade-offs. (These points will be explained in Chapter 12.)

Anger is a particularly difficult issue, and one that must be dealt with differently. In general it is best to encourage others to let the family member spout off, to have an eruption which is given the same respect as a volcanic eruption. Members should watch and listen, but stay clear and not try to change the course of the process with logic or reasonableness. They may apologize if appropriate, but this may be premature if the other is not finished erupting and ready to hear them. The family should be taught not to expect rational behavior at all times and not to criticize people for having strong feelings. However, such feelings will not be treated as excuses for destructive communication. Counter-arguing should not be attempted at this time. Instead family members should make a date to discuss the matter later when the speaker gets below 7 on a 1 to 10 scale of anger, where 1 is no anger and 10 is completely angry.

To ensure that anger is not destructive, the speaker should talk about his or her feelings, not the faults of others; stick to one topic; allow a response from the receiver when the speaker is ready for it; aim for ventilation, not conquest; and balance criticism with a good deal of affection (McGinnis, 1979).

Families may also like to make a practice of "giving haircuts." This is an arranged period of five to ten minutes (which family members perceive as a very long time once started) in which one person may make any criticism he or she wants with the partner listening passively and not responding or counter-arguing after the time period is up. While this may seem to be encouraging something which is unnecessary, it often replaces days or weeks of more indirect and more destructive criticism.

With young children, problem solving is different due to the differences in status, responsibility, and experience between parents and children. The above rules of respectful communication are observed, but discussions are usually limited to attempts to understand the child's point of view rather than to convince the child to see the adult's point of view. In addition, commands may be given by parents to their children. To be as productive as possible, commands should be limited to important areas, be specific, be given only when the parent is ready to ensure compliance, and only to a child who is clearly attending to the parent. More than one command at a time, vague commands, question commands ("Would you like to . . . ?"), and plural requests ("Let's pick up your room.") should be avoided as they are poor communications, often setting the child up for undue punishment (Forehand & McMahon, 1981). For example, what should the parent do after receiving a negative reply to "Are you ready to go to bed now?" Parents should never ask unless they are willing to accept "no" for an answer. Commands followed by rationales should also be avoided, as discussion of the rationale often leads to forgetting or avoiding the command. If the rationale is to be given, it should be given first (Forehand & McMahon, 1981). As with adults, commands should be balanced by liberal amounts of praise and recognition, and it is better to specify what the child is being praised for ("It's great when you pick up your toys.") than to simply praise globally ("That's nice"). Recognition is also useful without praise ("You picked up your toys.") (Forehand & McMahon, 1981).

FURTHER STUDY

There are many self-help books on the market dealing with communication skills and assertiveness and problem solving. Some of them are quite good (Alberti & Emmons, 1975; Gottman, Gonso, Notarius, & Markman, 1976; Miller, Nunnaly, & Wackman, 1975; McGinnis, 1979; Smith, 1975; Wahlroos, 1974). These can be given to clients for bibliotherapy, and will be instructive to therapists who want to learn more about the process of communication training or to read more clinical examples before trying such interventions. There are also extensive professional works on the subject of communication training, with Guerney's book (1977) being one of the better volumes. Therapists might want to experience communication training firsthand by participating in one of the several training programs for relationship enrichment. The two best researched and clinically proven programs are the Minnesota Couple's Communication Program (Miller et al., 1975) and the Conjugal Relationship Enhancement Program (Guerney, 1977).

A final note of caution is that communication training will not overcome a lack of interest in or capacity for clear communicating. Its use can even be taken by some couples as a criticism of the way they relate. Further troubles will arise if the feedback process is taken as an end in itself, and used to delay decision making or to avoid taking a stand on an issue. Making the communication process too obvious, practiced, or mechanical can destroy some of the spontaneity and remarkable versatility of speech, as can too much talking about talking, instead of just talking (Gottman, 1979; Whitaker, 1982; Zeig, 1980). With these cautions in mind, communication training is a very valuable and versatile method for the treatment of families and couples, and in some cases will be the only treatment method needed.

9

Sculpting

Move Families Around

Family sculpting is a method in which family members are asked to arrange one another as a living statue or tableau. Drawing upon their creative instincts and using such nonverbal dimensions as distance, posture, visage, and gesture, the family members give concrete representation to their impressions of the family. Such a process is not new to the family. It occurs every day in such activities as seating arrangement, but is infrequently recognized or consciously controlled for an expressive effect. Do to its form this method achieves several purposes in therapy. In brief, it may actively involve inactive or nonvocal members; increase the clarity of communication within the family; enhance the expression of emotions; promote awareness of the internal and interactional experiences of the participants; allow new insights into family functioning for both the therapist and family; intensify the family's experience in therapy; objectify and defuse some aspects of their experience; help family members differentiate; and bring them to a fuller awareness of their own interconnectedness in a way which linear verbal representations are incapable of achieving.

Family sculpting is a potent process for concretizing and exploring relationships with the ability to condense meaning into an evocative, efficient image which is easier to store, retrieve, and relate to than equivalent verbal descriptions (Papp, 1976).

For example, in a student's representation of his parent's relationship at two points in time, the father was placed in a chair watching TV, his back to his wife whose outstretched arms reached towards him unseen and unheeded. Later, the husband turns three quarters toward his wife, having sensed a difference behind him, but now she is turned away, reaching for the phone. The scene is repeated several times and the pattern of mutual ignoring and missed invitations is firmly embedded in the observers' minds. While simple, these sculptings have an immediate and tangible impact that cannot be reduced to mere verbal description.

According to one of its advocates (Kates-Julius, 1978) sculpting is to verbalization as staging a drama is to reading it. Its active and novel nature demand more attention than family discussions, and it is ideally suited to counteract boredom and restlessness, inattention, and repetitive and deadening interchanges. As it is difficult to use a nonverbal behavior to obscure or intellectualize (Duhl, Kantor & Duhl, 1973; Simon, 1972), simple needs may be easier to identify and respond to, and more difficult to lose in the type of overelaboration available in speech. Incongruities are highlighted (Papp, 1976; Simon, 1972), and messages and feelings not attended to in the verbal channel may be seen more clearly (Papp, 1976). An inner life not expressed before may begin to reveal itself. Simply having made the covert overt and available for discussion can be very helpful. As the Islamic proverb aptly states, "If the darkness is great enough, one candle is plenty." Flexibility is increased by the newness of the medium as well, and family creativity heightened. Deprived of their predictable, repetitive interchanges families may listen to each in new ways and communicate in new ways.

The power of this medium to concretize difficult to grasp abstractions and make them real is tremendously valuable. Sculpting helps to make fantasies concrete, and concrete reality is usually easier to deal with than unspecified and unrealized fantasy. Conflicting realities may be presented which, when presented verbally, lead to confusion. Relationships can be looked at more objectively when placed before one in sculpted form for scrutiny, and families who avoid defining relationships will have a difficult time doing so with sculptings. They will find themselves up against the same limitations Merce Cunningham faced when he tried to create a totally abstract modern dance, devoid of any meaning, the effect only of content-free motion. His audience simply could not see the dancers on stage as unrelated to each other.

Depending upon how it is used, the process can give distance from one's experience, allowing perspective, or it can throw one more completely into it, awakening feelings and enhancing awareness. People may step back and see things as if for the first time, and in stepping back from the participant role to a more objective and critical stance they see what they have never seen from this inside before—their family as a whole. Feelings may be intensified to levels not reached before in therapy due to the involvement of the body and the potential for emotional evocativeness which most authors have recognized in this technique. Physical representations of longing and loneliness, for example, can be painfully simple and honest, and difficult to overlook or discount. A woman reaching out over a wall toward her husband, for example, or a father trying to hold his departing adolescent tightly to him, crushing her in the process, made vivid images for the family and therapist alike.

Having a concrete way to refer to something normally too abstract for words aids the process of treatment immeasurably. Change in the relationship can be charted by change in the concrete image, and can provide a useful stimulus for further change. For example, in one of Papp's groups (Papp, Silverstein, & Carter, 1973) the family depicted the father as the "rock of Gibraltar" upon which the whole family hung, stood, or fixed their gaze. The processing of the sculpture involved the father freeing himself of the encumbrance of his family to achieve a new, more satisfying position. This in turn led to other family members renegotiating their relative positions now that father had changed his. New possibilities were opened up and new problems emerged, with mother now having to deal with a clinging daughter. She decided the daughter could stand on her own and let go. Mother was still not on her feet and waited for her husband to pull her up, but he declined to return to his former position.

This example demonstrates how sculpting may serve as a useful go-between connecting reality with potentials for change, and how this mode of problem solving can serve to expedite solutions by allowing many more to be tried out in theory than would be allowed by the more lengthy process of in vitro trial and error.

Some of the most powerful benefits for family therapy occur due to the formal structure of sculpting. It emphasizes each person's uniqueness and importance by paying attention to each person in turn. Differentiation of family members and individuation is achieved by requiring each participant to portray, observe, and respond to their own personal experience (Papp, 1976). At the same time a sense of the family as a whole is achieved. Family members are not only united in the activity of sculpting, but also in images which emerge of the family as a whole. A dual vision of different levels of social reality, the familial and the individual, is achieved at one and the same time.

Sculpting demands activity of the family. Members who are easily interrupted, drowned out, or silenced can be included, as well as the well siblings of identified patients, who are often overlooked (Papp, 1976; Simon, 1972). Younger children who may be bored or restless at long discussions, and left out of the process due to a relative lack of facility with words, can also be activated. More importantly, this sets a useful model for therapy by involving the family in a collaborative process with the therapist. It is clear that they cannot lie back and let the therapist do the work for them, the Chinese laundry model of therapy where the dirty linen is dropped off one day and picked up later, cleaned up and pressed into shape. The family in sculpting will work toward discovering its own meanings and solutions. The family is the expert as far as its own experience goes, and the therapist is a fellow seeker, not a miracle worker. Together with the therapist the family constructs a more adequate or workable set of family rules through the sculpting representation of themselves. They learn not to expect the therapist to be an expert who will discover the one correct, preexisting reality of the family and tell them how to adjust while they listen passively for the verdict. While this may seem to be a radical point of view to some, it is useful to note that even such seemingly incontrovertible and real events as emotional reactions may be more constructed than "real" or discovered. Schacter's (1964) work shows that emotions may be determined by contextual and social processes as well as vice versa.

There are several benefits which derive from viewing reality from such an existential perspective. Views of reality can be valued not for their correctness, but their utility to the family and their effect on the family (Weakland, 1976). Assessment moves from the task of diagnosing the family type and telling the family the "truth" about itself to helping the family see ways in which they can be better. In this area the therapist needs their collaboration. Once the perspective shifts away from a bias toward identifying illness or failure and toward identifying what can be done with the family, there is ample freedom for the family to express their strengths as well as weaknesses. And it may be the strengths more than the weaknesses which determine the outcome of therapy. This collaborative perspective is not only respectful of the family's power to defeat the therapist and their latent abilities to help themselves, but also good therapy in that it teaches the family to acknowledge their latent abilities and take credit for the changes which occur in therapy. As a result, they are more likely to feel able to handle the inevitable next problem which comes along after therapy is terminated.

The total process is envisioned as being made up of five parts: (1) The family members begin ignorant of their own behavioral patterns and the sources of these patterns. (2) The patterns are made overt in sculpting. (3) At least one family member's awareness changes so they can see new options for behavior are possible. (4) The therapist encourages the family to think of new options, or makes suggestions for changes which can be made within the sculpting. (5) Through practice, in and out of therapy, the change becomes established. Of all these steps, the transition from 2 to 3 is considered to be the most difficult, as individuals are generally not adept at noticing their behavior patterns and thus miss the opportunity to change them (Jefferson, 1978).

Since sculpting's initial inception, many innovations have been created and have become useful additions to original techniques, and others continue to be created to fit therapeutic needs. It is a versatile technique which can be adapted quickly to serve many therapeutic goals and mesh well with a variety of therapeutic orientations. Structural theorists may use it to highlight family coalitions and boundaries, and to suggest changes in these. Experiential therapists may find appealing its ability to create new or enhanced awareness of the individual in the family, and a powerful, immediate, in-session experience of that context for the individual.

Family sculpting may be appropriate at any point in assessment or therapy, both with clients seeking help with a distressed relationship and clients seeking to enhance an already adequate relationship (L'Abate, 1975). The intellectual level of the clients is generally not of concern, though a minimum level is necessary. Sculpting has been used successfully with a chronic schizophrenic population (Kates-Julius, 1978) though with different goals and some constraints. Probably more realistic contraindications are related to social class and occupation with some groups being more conservative than others, and less willing to try anything creative, silly, or unmasculine. Sculpting does provide an active mode of expression for those who are action oriented, though frequently they will raise issues such as how is this going to help with our presenting problem. As a result, sculpting may be more beneficial with families who have an active interest in exploring their own process.

Indications for the use of sculpting include:

1. A language barrier exists between therapist and client. Families have difficulty using language or communicating to the therapist in their native language. Some members of the family are deaf or mute and the therapist is having difficulty including them. Members are tongue-tied, confused, or too young to be fully involved verbally.

2. The family uses language to obscure rather than to clarify. Language is used to deny, rationalize, overgeneralize, and the family is well defended verbally and adept at intellectualization in the verbal medium.

3. Therapy is blocked. The therapist feels at an impasse with the family, feels bored, or feels therapy is dragging or lacking in affective impact on the family.

4. Feelings are blocked, denied, ambiguous, seemingly not present.

5. There are unclear systemic issues. Verbal family material is highly sterile, confusing, unclear, conflicting. There are gray areas which need to be explored.

6. Families have reached a plateau in therapy, and may benefit from a new way of expressing themselves to reach issues at a deeper level or discover new patterns for relating or a new direction for therapy.

7. Conflict does not appear to be resolvable with verbal problem solving and families may use sculpting to map the system stuckness and to explore the effect of several possible alternatives on the system.

8. A transition has been achieved and the family would like to mark it in time by creating a sculpting which will condense the meaning of the event into a spatial image for saving.

Depending upon the type of family one is working with, how long they have been seen in therapy, and the intended use of the sculpture (e.g., assessment of family structure, emotional intensification), the presentation of this technique to the family will vary, with most sculptings probably following the general guidelines that follow. Introductions differ from professional to professional, but for the most part there is a great deal of overlap. In general, it seems that the power of this method will be present if the family understands the basic task and carries it out with the guidance of the therapist. Any set of instructions which gets the basic idea across to the sculptors and does not limit their imagination or predispose their choices will be sufficient. An inclusive list of steps in creating a sculpting is given here, though all the steps do not need to be included.

1. Warm up the family
2. Describe the process and give rationale
3. Select a sculptor
4. Choose the content of the sculpture (event, problem, or process)
5. Sculptor closes eyes, imagines alternatives, describes a scene or goes directly to work sculpting a scene
6. Elaborate or map family space
7. Determine role of participants
8. Sculpt individual members of the ensemble
9. Detail the sculpture
10. Sculptor adds self
11. Choice point:
    a. put in motion and ritualize
    b. give a descriptive title
    c. explore solutions to improve problem situation presented
    d. Sculpt other relevant situations until a pattern emerges
12. Derole and debrief sculptor and participants
13. Process and result, starting with sculptor's summary of his work
14. Begin again with a new sculptor

There are, as with any highly versatile technique, a variety of ideas about what should and should not be included. Constantine (1978) lists most steps in his direction, but feels one can still do a useful systems sculpture with only Steps 4, 8, 9, 10, 11, 12, and 13. He calls this a "minisculpture," and feels it to be more appropriate for rapid assessment than for more involved uses. Jefferson (1978) on the other hand, freely goes from sculptings into guided fantasy, psychodrama, and gestalt techniques.

PRIMING THE FAMILY FOR ACTIVITY

In any artistic endeavor, real sculpting, for example, the materials must be warmed up, made pliable to the sculptor's touch. Tools must be laid out for the work. The sculptor himself must work a while before his muscles come up to working temperature. As with many artistic endeavors, the process flows more smoothly once it is engaged, and the hard part is getting started. Once in the midst of work, ideas flow more easily, are added to, corrected, discarded, and replaced with much more fluidity than it would seem possible when merely surveying mentally the work ahead. So it is with family sculpting.

To begin with, we have found it facilitating to get everyone up out of their chairs and moving around before presenting the sculpting task. Often this is accomplished by moving furniture to clear an appropriately open space for the sculpting. This seems to minimize resistance and makes people uncomfortable enough that they would rather become involved in the task than stand around. Volunteers come forward much easier this way than when family members are comfortably ensconced in their chairs. If you are going to allow them to stay in their chairs, to start with it may be helpful to employ Simon's (1973) rule that everyone end up in a new chair by the time a sculpting is finished.

You may also want to use a more structured and less threatening nonverbal exercise to warm up reluctant families. This is particularly true with groups of families or individuals where there is reluctance to expose too much in front of strangers. Tasks can be used to help group members meet the other participants and make the situation seem more tolerable and friendly. This also is a good foot-in-the-door technique. Once people have said yes to a smaller task, they are more likely to say yes to a larger one. It lets family members know they can take a risk and benefit from it, or at least not be overwhelmed or ridiculed. This in itself is a valuable learning experience for some. Compendiums of such exercises for groups are readily available and translatable to family groups. Simple spatializations, as described below, can also serve as warm-up exercises. Some sculpting instructions, notably those of the Boston group (Constantine, 1978; Duhl et al., 1973; Jefferson, 1978) include as part of their routine procedure exercises which may be thought of as achieving this goal. Exploring the physical space of the room and creating an analogic mapping of the family space to the space in the room, for example, is less threatening at first than being asked to start right in with a sculpture of the family. L'Abate (1975a) has suggested a group discussion of what an actual sculptor does. This can be used as an ice-breaker.

In general, this period is not usually needed with families who are in treatment with the director of the sculpting, though it may be necessary in new groups and with an outside consultant. At most, you may need to make some comment to defuse the situation for highly intellectualized families who might fear looking silly, such as saying that the exercise they are about to do may seem silly to them, but it has been helpful to you in the past and they will appreciate it more as they get started. Or, the task may be reframed in such a way as to make it difficult for the participants to resist. With the intellectual family, we may stress the intelligence of a different variety which is required by the sculpting. With a rigidly unexpressive and impassive father, we may agree that he may not have the courage to undertake the task, since it is different from the usual type of courage he expresses.

CHOOSING A SCULPTOR

Once the family is on their feet and ready to participate, we ask for a volunteer unless we already have someone particular in mind, as we may if we want to investigate someone's family origin. Several practitioners suggest starting with particular family members, such as the children who may be more willing and expressive. We prefer to start with whoever is comfortable enough to volunteer. It is not our intention here to get caught up in family decision-making issues instead of doing sculptings. We might say for an opener:

In this exercise we will need help from one of you to start with. We are going to do something which will help us understand you a little differently. Most families think its fun.

There is some sense in avoiding fathers, who on the average are less game for expressive nonsense, but this is a stereotype which is too often false to be of value in clinical decisions. There is also some benefit in avoiding parents, at first, as they may set a destructive precedent with idealized, stereotypical images of family life which the kids may not feel free to challenge. However, the reality probably is that such parents are equally adept with silencing strategies of other sorts when their children do start. In the end, there is simply no substitute for rapport, respect, and timing. If you are forced to pick because no one comes forward and nonverbal cues of readiness, such as eye contact or forward tilt of the body in the seat, are unavailable, your best bet may be a child or adolescent. Simon (1973) suggests you look for the family poet or gossip, or adolescent since they will most likely present a unique view of the family.

DESCRIBING THE SCULPTING PROCESS

After choosing our sculptor, briefly describe the process and its usefulness, but avoid getting into a long discussion of its rationale or defense of its place in the therapy of this particular family. Generally these discussions are simply playing along with family reluctancies. The therapist's willingness to enter into such discussions may also signal a personal reluctance to enter into the sculpting process, making the situation even worse. On the other hand, glowing accounts of how valuable sculpting can be in eliciting unspoken feelings or enhanced expressiveness will most likely lead only to stereotypical and rigid sculptures with little detail or creativity.

A simple introduction would be as follows:

I'd like you to arrange your family and yourself as if you were a group of statues. You may do this any way you want to. Use the sculpture to show us how you see your family. You may place people around the room, in chairs or with props if you like, and can position arms, legs, hands, facial features, and overall posture. Any means of expression which occurs to you is acceptable. However, we would like you to do as much of this as possible without talking. You may need to give some verbal directions to aid people in assuming the postures you want. This is your sculpture and you don't need to explain to others why they are being placed as they are. You'll each have a chance to make your own sculpture, so you don't need to worry about this sculptor not positioning you the way you feel you should be.

A different and simpler opening is provided by Simon (1973, pp. 52–53):

"Now I want you to do something that may seem quite novel to you all, but it will help us understand what goes on in this family. Phillip, would you help me out, please? (What is it?). Well, I want you to make a sculpture. Right now. (What?

A sculpture?) Yes, a living one, made out of people, not clay. I want you to take the people in the family and arrange them right in this space here. Put them together in a way that shows how the family is with each other. Dad, Mom, you, and Roger. . . . Go ahead and start with anyone you like.

Introductions may be as simple as "We seem to be having trouble with words" followed by a quick description of sculpting, to more elaborate introductions, with all being acceptable if they get the family started on the task.

LIMITING THE FOCUS

While the above directions are sufficient for many families, for others they are too diffuse, and some authors recommend more specific instructions. Specificity may be helpful if the sculptor is having difficulty getting started, though one should not jump in too soon with help for fear of biasing the sculptor's freedom of expression. If it has not already been done and doesn't seem to be obvious, or if special sculptings are being done, the therapist will need to insure that the sculptor is limiting him- or herself to a specific situation, and that it is clear who will be included in the family sculpture. For those who wish to limit sculptures, one can choose specific times in the family history, specific family situations or problems, or specific places the family inhabits. Or one can sculpt specific abstract properties or family processes, such as power or boundaries, as will be discussed in the section on variations.

PRIMING THE IMAGINATION

In order to allow the creative process to work freely without interference from family feedback or from the sculptor's uncertainty and embarrassment, one can choose to have the sculptor imagine several scenes internally before putting them into real space. This has the benefit of allowing several alternatives, usually resulting in a richer sculpting, as well as teaching family members a useful problem-solving step—generating multiple alternatives.

SETTING THE SCENE

As the sculpting process begins, it is considered useful or facilitating by some (Duhl et al., 1973; Constantine, 1978) to have the sculptor relate the treatment room area he will be using to the family's physical or emotional space. The sculptor may mark off an area and refer to it as the family living room, or he may create an entire representation of their house in the area provided for them. Once this has been done, the sculptor can be guided through the space and aided in exploring it metaphorically. The sculptor may describe boundaries, quality of space, or their own sensory and kinesic experience to various portions of the space (Duhl et al., 1973). Others feel it is enough to have a dimensionless representation of the family in the same way that many sculptings are not set in any particular place but create an internal reality. In this case the family is represented as an abstract entity in which internal relationships are primary.

At a more formal level, particular correspondences may be made between aspects of space and intended meanings. Physical distance may be equated with emotional distance. One region of the family may be labeled as the cold region, another as the warm region, and family members placed accordingly.

SELECTING THE ACTORS

After the family space has been marked out and the sculpture has been conceived, the sculptor is ready to pick participants. Most often the sculptor will use family members to play themselves if they are present, and props for those who are to be included but are not there. Props are particularly useful if a co-therapist is not available and a family pet, relative, friend, or lover is to be included in the sculpting who is not present in the family session. Duhl et al. (1973) recommend the use of standard psychodramatic procedures for choosing who will play each family member. When the sculpting is done in a group, the sculptor will choose who will stand in for each family member based on his or her own internal associations to group members, and the members' willingness to be involved. While the two different situations, family and group, produce different results, they are both useful. With the family present there are often valuable emotional reactions for the whole group, and the opportunity to translate insights directly into action. With the group, stand-ins often produce valuable reactions to what the person they are playing must be experiencing. Props are the least beneficial alternative.

When using family members there is always the potential for family members to block and inhibit rather than to help. They may hinder the process of the sculptor, object to the view presented, or refuse to hold their physical position. An alternative that can be used in this case is to have family members represent someone other than themselves in the sculpting. This may lead to decreased resistance since they are no longer being asked to represent themselves in a way which they might experience as incorrect. It may also help them experience the family from someone else's point of view and aid them in seeing themselves more objectively as they are somewhere else in space and can see themselves, a view impossible if they are playing themselves.

SCULPTING THE FAMILY

The sculptor now adds family members to the sculpting, one person at a time. Each person's placement should be thoroughly explored, with the therapist encouraging trial and error to enable the sculptor to chose the positioning that suits them. Constantine (1978) believes that this trial and error process should be physical, rather than merely thinking about or talking about alternatives. He believes that this taps information or feelings which are stored in kinesic form and can only be retrieved by motoric activity. As the addition of each person will change the whole, the sculptor may need to go back and change persons already sculpted after a new person has been added. If the sculptor is leaving out important aspects of the sculpting, such as the interaction between family members, or details, the therapist should prompt by repeating relevant aspects of the directions or asking questions. Under no circumstances should the content of the sculpting be tampered with, as it is solely the sculptor's choice. The therapist will only encourage elaboration and detailing, not the development of a particular theme or content. The sculptor should be encouraged in his work regardless of content, with the therapist offering verbal encouragement for working at the sculpting ("That's good") rather than for the artistic quality of the production.

SHARPENING THE FOCUS

During the process of sculpting, after each person is put in place, or after its completion, the sculptor should be helped by the therapist to sharpen the detail of his or her work for increased expressiveness. This will come easier to therapists after they have completed several sculptings of their own and have begun to get a sense of what is missing, fuzzy, or incomplete. For example, if sculptings appear flat and uninteresting or unexpressive, the sculptor might give each family member a typical gesture or expression (Duhl et al., 1973), or might comment concretely on their perception of the sculpting as an indirect way of encouraging more detailing. You might say, for example, "Everyone has the same expression in this family" or "It looks like they've all been unplugged." Another approach would be to simply reiterate the guidelines for sculpting, saying that the sculptor should remember they are free to include gestures, sounds, movements, absent members, and so on. Or you can encourage the sculptor by teaching techniques to achieve more expressiveness while at the same time indicating an area to be detailed. Smith and Phillips (1971) suggest having the sculptors use their hands to silently sculpt their partner's face, drawing lines with their fingertips and arranging expression. They also suggest having sculptors use a hand mirror to show the person what they want, and to imitate the expression desired with their own face.

In general, your overall goals should be to give the least intrusive suggestions possible, leaving the sculptor as much freedom as possible with as few cues as possible from you. If these do not work, you can work up to more specific directions. There are ways to give directions which encourage expression without determining it, as well as to encourage concrete, metaphoric expression rather than representation of an already thought out abstract concept of the family. Later on the therapist may add his or her impression to that of the sculptor's, but at first they should learn to facilitate a simple sculpting by family members. In asking questions you should try to stay with the concrete and observable rather than making an interpretation. You should particularly avoid leading the sculptor back into verbal, abstract pathways, as you want to encourage a new process. The nonverbal, metaphoric, primary process, preconscious process, or whatever you choose to call it, is a very quick one which produces an instantaneous response. It is not the slow, logical, verbal process which slowly builds up an image to match an abstract concept. If the sculptor says "I want to convey intelligence and warmth in father," he is on the wrong track. You want the image to be primary, then to proceed to the interpretation. To do this you must encourage thinking in the concrete in all your questions. Thus, it is better to say that one hand is not detailed rather than ask "why did you leave that hand out?" The latter would simply lead back into verbal explanation which you are trying to avoid for now. Sample questions might include those of Papp (1976):

How were their feet planted on the ground?
What were their hands doing?
What was each hand saying?
How did they touch?
Where was each foot going?

Or you might ask:

Where are they looking?
Do their eyes meet?
What is the expression on his face?
Does he sit up straight or sink into the chair?

However, even some of these lead into interpretation if not understood clearly. The general form is to point out an area or body part which has not been detailed and to invite the sculptor to add detail in that region, and to show him how he might do that if that is needed; for example, "Now add mother's expression," or "Show mother with your hands how you would like her to hold her face," or "Give mother a characteristic expression," or "What does mother mean to convey with her expression?" (as an encouragement to add detail, not to talk about adding detail, e.g., "Show me with her face rather than tell me about it.").

So far two approaches to sharpening sculptings have been presented. One involves asking questions about specific features so that the sculptor can detail them when they are left vague. The other approach involves teaching the process of how to do sculpting and insuring that the sculptor stays with this process and does not become trapped into verbal processes. It is equally important that the therapist also insure that the sculpting is systemic; that it touches on the relationship of all members involved, and yields information about interaction. Sculpting is a powerful method for achieving these ends, but sometimes its potential is untapped until encouraged by the therapist. This is particularly true where the sculptor portrays everyone in relation to him- or herself but not to each other (Duhl et al., 1973). The family is presented as a series of dyadic relations to the sculptor. In these cases the above methods can be used to bring out the relationship between other individuals. You might ask, for example, "How does father touch mother?" "How do father and mother interact?" "Do they notice each other?" Another method for avoiding a systemic relationship is to be lazy and pattern every relationship on one general theme—all are holding hands, all are praying together, etc. In these cases it is helpful to encourage the necessary differentiation which the sculptor has left out.

THERAPIST FUNCTION

Throughout the sculpting process the therapist functions as the monitor of the process, as a sort of stage manager (Duhl et al., 1973) who follows the sculpting and keeps it on track. The therapist controls the process to keep it vital, but does not control the content. He or she may decide when to push, when to halt, when to ask for clarification or specification, or when to switch to a new situation, problem, or family interaction pattern. In this role, the therapist should keep in mind the need to conform to the creative process of the sculptor. Two common errors which Constantine (1978) points out in this respect are the therapist rushing the sculptor, presumably to fit the therapist's time schedule, and the therapist pushing for premature closure before the creative process has had ample time to emerge and unfold completely. As an example of the importance of time, Cosntantine (1978) reports that in couple sculptings he requires a full ten-minute period for each sculpting, no matter how soon the sculptors finish. Under these restraints, couples continue to find meaningful elements in the sculpting process beyond the initial aspects which were quickly identified, often in a one- to two-minute period after which couples felt they were done. Kates-Julius (1978) points out another danger of timing with psychotic populations. She felt that therapists may cause decompensation by pushing for too rapid exposure of psychic conflicts. Fred and Bunny Duhl (1982) generally address the latter problem both by working to create an atmosphere where one feels safe to experience and accept oneself and by working with metaphors, since they allow one to choose the degree of transparency of meaning.

Once the sculptor has set about the task, the therapist should insure that the sculptor is not being interfered with by the family. He or she should be given encouragement for the work they are doing and supported against the resistance of the other family members. Each sculptor's personal vision should be validated, and no one should be made to defend the way they made their sculpture. It is particularly destructive to allow family members to argue with the sculptor or challenge the veracity of his or her choices. The family may do this overtly by labeling the sculptor mad or bad, or less directly by discouraging their work, consoling them on how hard it is, offering help, and so forth. Or they may simply resist passively by not giving full cooperation to the sculptor in assuming the positions assigned to them, and forget their positions as soon as possible, or be too fatigued to hold them. The sculptor will need to be continually supported in his or her own view and the family silenced.

The above process is of great help in differentiating family members from each other, and since multiple points of view are an integral part of the sculpting process, the therapist need do very little to work toward differentiation. A lecture on the subject is definitely not called for, simply the reminder that each individual has his or her own point of view, and some appreciation of the merit of each individual point of view and the benefit of multiple points of view. This process of allowing and valuing points of view is important, and one of the common features of optimal family functioning.

Papp et al. (1973) also feel it is the therapist's responsibility to "abstract meaning" from the sculpture, and convey those meanings to the family. We feel this is at least half if not wholly the family's job, and that "meaning" should not be forced on the family. The family can be gently guided to see the therapist's interpretations, but not required to see his or her "truths." The one area which is crucial enough to force on the family is the perception of their wholeness and interconnectedness (Ganahl, 1983).

As a general rule, it is better for the therapist to approach this process with some humor rather than high seriousness and piety. The results of sculptings may be profound, but profundity comes much easier if it not expected and piously awaited. Humor also seems to be integrally related to the creative process (Koestler, 1978) and calls for the multiple points of view which allow for expansion of the family reality and tolerance for differences. The therapist should also be attuned to the potential power of touch. Touching is known to be of great impact in interpersonal interactions, so much so that we regard more highly those strangers who touch us, even by chance, than those who do not (Fisher, Rytting, & Heslin, 1976), and are more likely to respond to them helpfully. Touch can be encouraged by the therapist, and evaluated as family members respond to each others' touch and proximity. The therapist can also encourage this by touching the sculptor in offering guidance or gentle support.

Sculptor Adds Self

After everyone else is in place and has been detailed, the sculptor adds her- or himself to the ensemble. At this point the sculptor loses his objective view and becomes a participant. Things are likely to look or feel different from this new vantage point and additional changes may be made by the sculptor. The therapist may need to give the sculptor help in either sharpening the details of her- or himself, which is harder to appreciate since the sculptors cannot see themselves. It may also be difficult for the sculptor to become part of the whole, having so recently been an outside observer, and the therapist may need to once again insure that the sculpture is a total family sculpture and people are all meaningfully related to one another, with particular attention being paid to relations with the sculptor at this point.

Choice Point

Now there are several options open to the sculptor depending upon the time available, the goals of the therapist, and many other factors which will only be fully appreciated with experience. There are no hard and fast rules here, with different users of this technique presenting different suggestions. Some of these options involve choices concerning how to verbally process the sculpture. Others extend the use of analogic processes even further, delaying verbal processing for a later point. One simple method is to stop when the sculptor is done and ask him if he wants to change anything, giving him a chance to think about it (L'Abate, 1975a). If changes are made, one can process them verbally by asking how this sculpture is different and why the changes were made. If no change was made the sculptor can be asked to explain what he was doing and why. Simon (1972) favors this method. As with art therapy, the metaphor created by the sculptor with his work may not be fully recognized by him, and he may need the help of the therapist to "unpack the metaphor."

Another choice at this point can be to have the sculptor put the whole sculpting in motion before verbally processing what has been sculpted. Constantine (1978) feels that this allows access to musculoskeletal memory which otherwise is lost. Talking or thinking about movement and posture do not elicit this memory while actual physical activity will. The process of putting the sculpture in motion is also useful as it provides access to another dimension of the family's use of space. With static sculptures one gets a sense of the family boundaries and alliances, but not of the rules for traffic flow. With dynamic, or moving, sculptures one can see traffic flow and also have the chance to see action sequences repeated in time, producing a more dynamic representation of family stuckness and rigidity and family rules. As an added bonus, one may get additional information on alliances, triangles, boundaries, and on the shifting pattern of emotions as well as the connection between symptoms and family interaction (Papp, 1976). For example, Papp and her colleagues (1973) report the case of a 9-year-old boy who was brought in for a determination of the cause of his habit of walking around in circles. When asked to sculpt his family, the boy depicted his two sisters playing jacks in one corner of the room while his father and mother quarreled in another. Neither group paid attention to the boy who placed himself in the center of the room, alone. When asked to put the sculpture in motion to demonstrate how he reacted to the situation, the boy wandered from one group to the other, rebuffed by each. He described the problem situation as he walked around and around in circles. Both the description and the motion pattern were striking, particularly given the usual reticent nature of this child. The meaning was not lost on the family this time around.

Action patterns may be of several types. The sculptor alone can move through an action sequence, interacting individually with each static group in the sculpture, or the group as a whole can make a larger action pattern. The patterns are limited only by the therapist's and sculptor's creativity, but should remain concise to maintain their impact. That is because the image created will be at its most powerful to the extent that it condenses meaning, possibly several conflicting points of view or several levels of interpretation, into one image. In one larger family seen by the author, a sculpting was done in a group therapy situation with group members standing in for family members. The patient was a young adult who came from a highly complex family consisting of his natural father, deceased mother's parents, stepmother's parents, stepmother and new husband, natural father and new wife, and natural father's parents. He had few effective limits, leaving one group to live with the next when trouble arose. There was free communication between the group, but no one knew who was giving him money, clothes, shelter, and so on. He spent a good deal of money on drugs, was arrested several times, and went to the county prison the last time. One could not avoid being struck by the loyalty of this family and its liking of this young man, despite his ability to anger them. One could also not avoid noticing the conflict over his care and rearing which must inevitably arise in such a diverse and disconnected group. He was profiting in the short term by seemingly playing on one group's sympathy and dislike of another's child care methods. When a sculpting was done, he had put them all in different clusters as expected. But when it was put in motion, instead of seeing the usual pattern of kissing and talking and visiting which occurred before and after each therapy session, we now saw very isolated groups, with him going around to each in turn, the only connection between them, particularly between stepmother and father. His problem now began to look like it served an important function for the group.

If it is difficult to imagine how to create an action sequence, one can start with a dyad, making a sequence of action, reaction, and further action. Into this dyad one can ask the sculptor to introduce a third member, then a fourth, and so on, until the whole group is in motion. Or one can ask questions such as

"Who moves toward or away from whom?
How do they move?
What is the other person's reaction(s)?
What are the clues which regulate the relationship?

(Papp, 1976) and can construct an action sequence from the information gained. One can also use the actions implied by verbal metaphors such as "he holds me back" to construct action sequences. In general, it helps tremendously to have faith in the process of sculpting and faith in each family member's innate ability to use nonverbal processes to create meaning in this way. With encouragement, action patterns will emerge which put the sculptings in motion.

Having put the sculpture in motion, one can continue by then ritualizing the whole pattern. This is done by having the pattern repeated over again and again just as problems are replayed again and again in the real life of the family. Duhl et al. (1973) and Constantine (1978) suggest that the sequence be repeated at least three times. Their experience is that the repetition adds new meaning to the pattern and leads to additional insights and understandings. Certainly the pattern takes on a new meaning as it becomes repetitious and mimics real life (Papp, 1976). An additional benefit is that circular aspects may emerge which at first did not occur in the action-reaction sequence. In a role play situation a couple was portrayed in two stages of their life cycle. In one the husband was watching TV, the wife reaching out to him. In the next she was turned away, on the phone, with him looking back over his shoulder at her. By themselves they represent two different stages of an action-reaction pattern initiated by the husband. Put together and ritualized they create something quite different, a pattern of mutual avoidance or mistiming which leads to a fixed distance, with both partners cooperating in the distance. Now a more circular pattern emerges which creates a sense of the joint causality of the reaction which wasn't there before.

To increase the intensity of ritualized motion, Papp (1976) suggests running through the pattern in slow motion, or starting with a request to make a slow motion picture of how things happen at home. Duhl et al. (1973) suggest that no words be allowed, as these might dilute the experience. Jefferson (1978) on the other hand, lets these ritualizations and motion sequences lead into psychodrama with full use of words. Our feeling is that the slow motion silence may serve to accentuate emotions, just as they are exaggerated in silent motion pictures.

As motion tends to increase the power of a sculpting, one may wish to skip this step in order to decrease intensity with particular families. One could use stand-ins instead of family members to decrease emotional intensity and lead to a more objective understanding of patterned problem sequences. Or one could choose to leave the sequence metaphorical and not process it. To intensify a sculpting one would use motion, process the metaphor, and involve the family as participants.

Once the pattern of repetitive stuckness is firmly embedded in the family's awareness, one can work on changing it. One should do this before the process has a chance to dissipate into intellectualization, and hopefully before the return to verbal processing. Papp (1976) feels that verbal communication cannot change a scene. It can give understanding, but that only creates an opening for change. To fully utilize the potential of these techniques, Papp and Kates-Julius (1978) feel one should translate understandings into immediate action—a hug, a kiss, a new action sequence.

How one translates these into action, and why, are important questions. As a therapist you must be careful not to force your solutions on the family. Exploring new options does not constitute force. It merely gives the family alternatives to try. This is what is aimed for. Sculpting allows for the exploration of many new alternatives in a short period of time. More possibilities can be tried out in the concrete metaphors of space and time than can be tried in real time by the family. These are just potentials, however. Dramatic insights or changes in family pattern may fade outside the therapy room. One wants the family not only to understand or experience itself in a new or heightened way, for these are only preliminaries, but also to actively explore new possibilities for relating and interacting. On the other hand, one must consider the power of the family seeing itself in a new way, especially if the new viewpoint is spontaneous, not forced by the therapist.

Initially, the therapist can ask the sculptor, or another family member, to change things to improve the sculpting. An ideal sculpture could be made and the sculptor then asked to sculpt the family after it has completed the next smallest step toward its ideal. This will suggest new patterns or changes which the family feels may help (Duhl et al., 1973; Constantine, 1978). One interesting pattern which Prosky (1981) has tried is to ask several members to reach a more acceptable arrangement at the same time. This creates an action sequence which can lead into a ritualization highlighting unresolved conflicts and failed attempts attempts at resolution. If an actual solution occurs, that is the best possible outcome; but simply making the problem more obvious, concrete, and observable is a big step toward solution.

Once one is done with the sculpting it is often revealing to have the individual sculptor or family sum up what they have done in a verbal manner. If a simple sculpture has been done, one can ask the sculptor to give a title to his or her work. If one has gone through the more elaborate process of putting the sculpture in motion and ritualizing it, one can ask for a phrase. While using verbal pathways, this accesses a different process than the logical, sequential process. People thinking in logical, linear ways may have difficulty choosing a title, or may choose a very uninteresting one. They will need encouragement to just pick an image, trusting what pops into their head rather than picking specific characteristics and then picking a title to fit them using deductive processes. As much as anything else, the power of sculpting lies in teaching the family to use this different process of thinking.

Authors differ on when to ask for such a title. Smith and Phillips (1971) suggest it occur just after the sculpting is finished, as an additional means to gain awareness of the content covered. Duhl et al. (1973) use titles after the entire process has been completed and debriefed. They ask the sculptor of the family, sometimes with the therapist's help, to come up with a short, descriptive image which sums up the interaction and makes it easy to keep in mind. Their use is both expressive and mnemonic. One can also ask the family to select from various titles created by family members, or to create a synthetic family image out of those presented. This furthers individuation and the appreciation of multiple points of view. It also allows the therapist to observe family problem-solving patterns.

With one family, the image was of a "cage of tigers, with everyone pacing and alone" (Duhl et al., 1973). Another example was the "queen for a day family," an image which had meaning for everyone old enough to have seen that show. The family in this case was engaged in a contest to see who deserved the most sympathy.

A final possibility is to sculpt additional scenes which are related to the one just completed, before any processing. One would look here for consistent patterns running through several sculptings, for a common theme or interaction process, as is often evident in the work of a real sculptor. It is important to do this before processing or choosing a title since to do so may bias later sculptings and make them more likely to reveal the theme highlighted in the discussion of the first one.

A variation of this procedure advocated by Kates-Julius (1978) is to pick sculptures from several life situations or points in the family life cycle and to extract the common pattern of current importance from them and to ritualize and work on that pattern. When this fuller form of sculpting is being done then it is unlikely that one would have time for more than one member's sculpture in the single session. One must decide whether to work at eliciting each person's point of view and promoting differentiation, or to work more intensely with a given individual in any one session.

Processing the Result

How one processes the sculptings and makes interpretations depends upon the form of sculpting and the reason for its use. If one wants to differentiate family members, the processing may be different than if one wants to pull them closer together or to help them be more cooperative and less independent. If one is working with a group the process is different than when working with a single family. Therapist style also enters in here. Some work more collaboratively with families, while others are more removed and in a higher position of authority and understanding. Papp (1976) suggested that it is the therapist's job to abstract meaning and feed it back to the sculptor. Ruben (1978) also feels that the therapist should tell the family what he or she has learned, and then invite the family to comment. We tend to avoid interpretation and elicit the family's reaction first before biasing their meaning extraction process by imposing our own. This creates the proper implication that it is the family's job to do the work, and sets the stage for later collaboration with them where we might introduce our own ideas. Even if our and their ideas are the same, the process has more impact if they arrive at their own discoveries rather than have them handed to them. However, if we are worried about the family's ability to construct a positive interpretation of their reality or that they will miss significant aspects of it, we may offer our interpretation first as a means of reframing the family's reality or highlighting aspects of it which they have overlooked due to negative attributions about others in the family. Unless one can do this powerfully, and with some reference to previously observed interchanges in the family, it may be better to offer the reframe later. If done too weakly and too early it may not only be discounted by the family, but done so in such a way that it is harder rather than easier to see a more positive reality due to the effort the family puts forth in discounting unseccessful reframings. Simplistic, superficial reframes will also do more harm than good as they will rarely be accepted and will undermine the therapist's credibility with later efforts. More information on reframing is given in the chapter devoted to that technique.

In general, the sequence should be to derole, debrief the immediate and subjective experience, and then process it, though many variations are possible. The therapist will now move back to the more familiar verbal channels of communication for extensive discussion of the impact, experience, meaning, and implications or ramifications of the sculpture (Constantine, 1978). In doing this, Constantine suggests a specific pattern to follow in the return from the metaphorical to the present time. He debriefs the participants, audience, and sculptor in that order. Duhl et al. (1973), on the other hand, suggest starting with the sculptor. This group takes sculptors out of the sculpting and asks them to derole. They are no longer participants but are now in the role of the central observers. If the sculpting was in the past, they are brought back to the present and reminded that they are no longer as small as in the sculpture, as powerless, etc. After the sculptor talks, the actors or family members in the sculpting give their feedback, creating a multicentric point of view and providing rich enough data to create a systemic understanding rather than a more linear understanding of the family. All the points of view may be taken as essentially true, and woven into a rich and complex pattern, or some may be seen as erroneous interpretations and new, more workable realities can be negotiated. If observers are present, their nonparticipant points of view are processed next, followed by the therapist's comments or interpretations. In each case it is important to derole. This is often a useful therapeutic intervention in itself as it helps people who were acting as if they were still in past relationships or still their past size and age see possibilities for new ways of acting and for new power. This is particularly true when family members are playing themselves in the past, or as others see them. The family members need to appreciate, for example, not only that the potential of the father of the past is still available, but also that some of the menacing qualities are left behind in the past, or were never really present but an artifact of a particular situation in the past or a particular point of view such as that of a small child. If this is not done, family members may start interacting in the present on the basis of how they have seen each other in the past. Those readers who scoff at the power of dramatizations and imagination need only call to mind the power of dreams despite our recognition that they are only dreams. Having woken up from a nightmare in which a child is hurt, it is often necessary to go check on the child in bed, despite the conscious awareness that there is no connection between the dream and reality. The same is often true in sculptings and psychodrama, and deroling is necessary to bring one back to the current reality.

Another way to conduct the deroling and debriefing process is to have individuals debrief in place, which tends to intensify the experience and increase subjectivity. Then they are deroled, or they put off deroling, and asked to make changes in the sculpture while they are still in their roles. Rueben (1978) has still another way to proceed which includes elements of each of the above approaches. She photographs the sculptings and shows the pictures to the family for processing. This allows the family members to both derole and to retain some memory of the physical position they were holding. This method also gives the family a vision of itself as a whole, which is different than always seeing the family without oneself being in it. This is particularly true for the sculptor who is always to some degree outside of his own sculpting unless it is put in motion. Such usage of pictures also seems to encourage switching back to verbal discussion at the point when they are shown to the family.

How and when to begin the debrief process and interpret the sculpture is a matter of some disagreement. As mentioned earlier, some see it as the therapist's job to add richness to the sculptings by processing them before the family does. To our minds, this simply takes away the family's rightful role and may bias their own reactions to the experience. Similarly, if several sculptings are to be done in one session, say an evaluation session with each family member sculpting the family, it may not be useful to process any until all are done, again for fear of biasing the process or content of later sculptings. One of the more difficult decisions to make as a therapist is whether to add your own interpretations and insights or push for more from the family when their productions are empty, stereotypic, or they miss the obvious. The general rule to be followed is that the insight or experience is more powerful if achieved by the clients rather than if it is given to them by the therapist. If necessary, the therapist should try to lead the clients to process more and more of the available experience before intruding with a particular interpretation. Even in that case, as much reference to the clients' experiences already mentioned should be made, and the interpretation should be fit to the clients' language and way of seeing the world. There are cases where the therapist is interested in altering the family's reality with a specific reframing, and these may be given to the family in the form of an interpretation.

Several issues are obviously involved in the above decision, some of which relate to the larger structure of treatment. The one which has been mentioned extensively is the need to involve the family as the active component in their own treatment. One can convey this by asking them to reach their own conclusions rather than handing them the therapist's conclusions without their involvement. On the other hand, the therapist may feel that the family's reality needs to be challenged and that can best be done by presenting his interpretation of the sculpting. There is a middle position as well which emphasizes family-therapist collaboration in treatment and places high value on everyone's perspective, differentiating family members and seeking a final resolution in a multicentric point of view which supersedes that of any family member or the therapist. The latter perspective may emphasize the total family as the client, or emphasize individuals as the clients who need to have their individual realities validated and accepted by the rest of the family. As is obvious in the discussion, our bias is to proceed with minimum therapist influence and increase it as necessary.

Regardless of one's theoretical position, the means presented below for processing a sculpture can be useful. To increase the family's processing, one can ask questions which first ask the sculptor to elaborate on his production, and his or her experience in creating it. Questions which are useful here vary from open-ended ones such as "What have you created here?" to questions designed to get the sculptor to elaborate on specific experiences. One can ask:

> What is the hand saying?
> What do they say with their eyes?
> Why did you position the hands in that way?
> What is the meaning of the particular posture you used with father?
> Why did you place yourself the way you did?
> What expression were you trying to capture on your mother's face?

In doing this one should be sure to include the sculptor, and one may ask questions of him while still in position for added impact. These questions may include:

> How do you feel in this position?
> Can you think of a spot where you would rather be?
> What do you notice most from where you are?
> Does your position make sense to you? Is it consistent or are you saying different things with different parts?
> What would you need to feel more comfortable?

When other members of the sculpture are being debriefed, they may first be asked to comment in place. First, let them comment on their own experience, but avoid any comments about the incorrectness of the sculptor's vision of the family. Ask them to comment rather on what they have learned, what stands out, what their experience is in that position. Then you can ask more leading questions about particular aspects of their experience. "Do you feel like you need longer arms to reach out and touch your son?" "Are you uncomfortable with your back to your daughter?" "What can you see from where you are standing?" "What do you miss?" "How does the contact feel with your husband?" "Too much? Not enough?"

When self-selected positions are taken, such as when all are asked to find a comfortable position at the same time, the following questions taken from Constantine (1978) can be of use, again processing while people are in place.

How did you end up where you are? Were you surprised?
What did you feel while doing this?
Were you aware of how other people were placing themselves?
Who influenced you the most in your choice of position?
Are you satisfied where you are now? Would you want someone else to move?

After the debriefing process is complete and everyone involved has had a chance to speak, or sometimes during it to stimulate their reactions, the therapist may throw in his perceptions, comments, observations. Usually, this is best done in a manner which respects the concrete nature of the sculpting medium, rather than in a way which leads into abstract interpretations and intellectualizations. For example, in one sculpture with two individuals walking in place, waiting on a third to lead them, the therapist's comment was simply "That's a lot of energy to not go anywhere." This highlights a particular aspect of the sculpting, but leaves room for unique reactions from the participants.

Associations to other artistic mediums may also be useful, and verbalizing such associations may stimulate the family to also share their associations and thus begin to use a different process than the verbal, logical, linear one they are used to and have not been able to successfully apply to the problem they came in with. The therapist will need to insure that his associations fit the family's education and background. Families having a good liberal arts education will understand a reference to the similarity of mother and daughter to that of the painting of God and Adam on the Sistine Chapel ceiling, or to the fact that the kids are acting like flying buttresses, supporting the structure of their parents' marriage. The therapist will need to be careful here, however, as younger children or less educated members of the family may be lost by such references, resulting in a dialogue with just part of the family. In general though, the ability to get the family to share their associations is worth the risk, and is a process open to the younger children.

The therapist's contributions during the processing of the sculpting will work out best if they are thought of by the therapist as either elaborations of the family theme, or as alternate visions to be considered by the family. The contributions should be just that, not statements made from some superior position which should be given more weight than those of the family. It is true that the therapists, being in a position to see more than the family by being outside and observing more than any one family member can see, should have a superior vision. However, therapists may be wrong; they have their own families and family biases, myths, and blind spots. They also will find that it does no good to try to insist on their vision. If the family cannot be gently encouraged to see what the therapist wants them to see, it will do no good to insist on the basis of therapist authority. This kind of "yes, but"-ing by the therapist will just serve to discount what the family has achieved and alienate them from future cooperation. Even though a man may be smarter than an ox, he doesn't argue with an ox, and families, like oxen, are certainly more powerful than the therapist. Instead, the therapist gives clues and hypotheses. He points out pieces of the experience for consideration that have been overlooked—"It's most striking to me that no one seems to have noticed Bob with all the attention being paid to Mary," or wonders aloud what the meaning of an experience might be—"I wonder if mother is already starting to experience her husband as gone and pushing for her son to be more adult to take his place?" The therapist's reality is not "the reality" until accepted by the family. There are no immutable facts, just physical events and behaviors which may be given different interpretations.

In these cases it is best that the therapist operate like Agatha Christie's Miss Marple, asking questions here and there, introducing events to be considered, complimenting people on their insight, all in the service of stimulating others to see things the way she did, but by reaching their own conclusions. One must also remember that nonverbal experience need not be completely translated. This would be like pulling the wings off the butterfly to see how it flies.

This does not mean that the therapist does not try to organize and explain the sculpting experience for himself. He does. He also attempts to aid the family in seeing things differently if the family hasn't been able to break out of a limiting vision of their experience. It simply means there are respectful and effective ways to help stimulate the growth and development of others which do not include telling them what to do. There are times when a family-wide denial needs to be challenged due to a crisis situation which needs quick resolution; but direct confrontation is rarely the only approach, and it is better to help family members learn alternatives such as "how else could the family involve this boy?" before trying to get them to give up their old ways of doing things.

In interpreting the sculpting to himself, there are several dimensions which the therapist may want to consider, as well as certain types of information which may seem valuable. A structural therapist will be interested in coalitions and hierarchies, how boundaries around these are kept, and how rigid or changeable they are. An experiential therapist may feel such categorization is unnecessary and largely irrelevant, being more concerned with the family's own richness of experience promoted by the sculpting itself and the subsequent discussing of it. For those therapists who are interested in making interpretations, the organization of space and mass is a major interpretative dimension (Simon, 1973). How does the family use space? Does it fill it up or crowd into one small area and hover together in dependency on each other or fear of the outside? Who breaks free of the family mass and serves as a satellite or beacon, sending back information from the outside culture? Is the family firmly connected, tightly bound, or only tentatively connected by the lightest strings? Or are they all isolated and unconnected? Is there a center of mass? Does the family center itself around one individual, or two, or none? How does the family protect its space? Is it oriented only to the front, or multidirectional? Is the outward surface or the interior emphasized? How do outsiders enter the space? Is there room left open for others to attach themselves to the family, or is it self-enclosed?

Can one person leave without the whole structure collapsing? Are some family members more necessary for structural support than others? Are there holes from members who have left? Will the system evolve and heal, or is the hole permanent? Where are the structural deficits in terms of mass? Where is the sculpting likely to give way? In what direction will it move next? Is it expanding or contracting? Pulling against itself, organizing its mass cooperatively, or working separately in different directions? These and many other questions come to mind. Those which will be significant in any one family are those which will occur to experienced therapists who trust their internal processes. Other interpretive analyses of space are presented in Kantor and Lehr (1975).

For those looking for coalitional information, there are several cues. One would look for similarities in posture, orientation, and action to indicate coalitions. Are people looking at the same thing, engaged in a joint activity, connected by similar points of view, interests, or goals? Are both husband and son helping support mother? Are brother and sister pulling out of the family together? How people touch, or whether they touch can also be a good indicator. Loving, supportive touching, or touch to maintain contact can indicate alliances. Restraining or confrontive touching is a sign of opposition, though here parties in apparent opposition may be more connected than anyone else in the family, possibly engaged in a cooperative endeavor to shift attention away from someone else. Contiguity can also be a valuable indicator. Those closest emotionally may also be represented as having the greatest physical contact and proximity to one another. Again, one should be cautious, and not overlook the implied messages. A mother may be next to her daughter and a father next to his son, the parents separated by some distance, in physical contact with their children, but connected across space by their direct eye contact. Duhl et al. (1973) also caution would-be interpreters not to overlook the fact that closeness-distance continuums may represent independence rather than emotional intimacy, and as a result may be misleading to therapists who always interpret them in one manner.

Another useful clue to family functioning is the degree of variation within and between sculptings. Are they all the same and are all people in them similar? Do they address common themes and concerns in the same way? Do they present a multiplicity of views? Jackson (1965) found that clinic families showed fewer types of dyadic interaction than nonclinic families in interview situations. The latter exhibited more internal and intrasession variability. Others also have related family rigidity and impoverishment to lack of variability and pathological functioning (Andolfi, 1979; Palazzoli et al., 1978). The same conclusions may be drawn from impoverished, stereotypic sculptings.

Unexpressive sculptings are always difficult to interpret and challenge both the therapist's goals as well as his self-esteem. There can be several explanations, with those least likely to be entertained being those that include the therapist within the explanation. Since the therapist-family interaction is difficult if not impossible for the therapist to observe, and since self-esteem is involved, it is easier to blame the family for being resistive than to look at other explanations. It may indeed be that the family has a rule against talking to outsiders, or that their sculptings of ideal families are all limited and stiff because there is a family rule against wishing for something different in the family. On the other hand, the family may be using the sculpting to comment on the therapist-family relationship. People have exquisite ability to comment on relationships in indirect ways, and with the therapist not included in the sculpting, his relation to the family may be hard to perceive. Impoverished content or lack of responsiveness to content on the part of the family may simply mean that they don't yet trust the therapist. Generally what is needed here is better rapport, not gimmicks (Papp, 1976). The therapist may need to back up, establish his credentials or restate his concern for the family and respect for their strengths as well as weaknesses. The family may not believe the therapist is powerful enough to deal with their feelings, problems, whatever, and are fighting him with their non-compliance to test his strength. They may not be willing to move until offered some assurances that he will stick with them and can see some alternative solutions. The problem could also lie in the therapist's not tying the purpose or likely benefits of sculpting well enough to the family's treatment goals. Finally, it may mean the therapist does not believe in the sculpting process, but was stuck and decided to try it to see if it really worked. A response to this situation is to have the family sculpt the therapist-family interaction, and to consider making a therapist sculpting of the same interaction.

With children, the lack of content may indicate a fear of reprisals from their parents, to whom the children must answer after the therapists's protection has ended. Or they may be attempting to protect their parents, or be an active part of a process of denial and scapegoating taking place in the family (Papp, 1976).

Sculptings may also fail because the family is new at the process and is too overwhelmed at first. The sculptor may need to back up and better specify the scene to be presented in terms of problem or content, time period, or dimensions, such as caring or power (Constantine, 1978; Papp, 1976). Papp (1976) feels that sculptings may fail not only because the scene is too broad, but also because the material is too rich or overwhelming. Jefferson (1978), suggesting another possibility, feels that even though there may be no apparent or significant response to the sculpting process, sculpting may be causing a "softening up" process, making the family more open to future work. Papp (1976) would appear to feel similarly, and suggests some family's creative processes need more priming than others. One should keep trying, as it may take several attempts to get a meaningful sculpting. Another possibility is to try a "fake good" and "fake bad" sculpture before proceeding further. These often take away from the family the potential for using these sculptings as true representations of their family preempting the most stereotypic responses from occurring later.

Variations

In addition to the above-mentioned applications of sculptings, there is an array of other variations at the therapist's disposal. These include preplanned multiple sculptings, group censensus sculptings, and therapist-prescribed sculptings. This categorization was developed for descriptive purposes and is not a mutually exclusive one, nor does it attempt to include all possible technical uses of sculptings as new ones are being developed each day to suit the therapist's styles and needs.

Multiple Sculptings by One Person

Many forms of sculpting usage exist which are based upon comparisons of one sculpting with another. The most commonly used is that between the current family reality and the ideal or wished for reality. These two sometimes expose unrealistic family expectations in the form of overly ideal sculptings, allowing the therapist to explore how these wished for realities feel when portrayed concretely. "How does that feel to be so close?" "How long would you like to be in this position?" Ideal sculptings by different family members can also expose differences in goals and wishes which need to be acknowledged and possibly resolved. These sculptings also focus the family on change by asking the family to conceive of how it might improve, as well as how it should assign blame for the current problems. Once ideal family situations are portrayed, the individual can be asked to sculpt the first step toward achieving the ideal. Another variation is to use past, present, and future sculptings to determine patterns over time.

Kates-Julius (1978) recommended sculptings of the same scene or related scenes to help patients identify the feelings aroused and to intensify their experience of them. Another form of multiple sculptings which promotes integration is to stage the same sculpting over different treatment sessions (Jefferson, 1978). This not only creates a fix on a specific problem, but also highlights and reinforces behavioral change when it occurs.

Additional before-after sculptings are those which involve life cycle shifts and losses of family members. One can look at family sculptings before the departure of an older adolescent, the death of a child or parent, the divorce of a spouse. The "after" sculpture will often give information in these cases on how to fill the gaps left, and just where they are. Another possibility is to sculpt the family before the death or departure, particularly if it was unexpected, then to pull out the departed family member, leaving the rest of the sculpture unchanged. Often this helps the family see their loss more clearly and see more concretely the tasks ahead of them and the necessary roles which have to be refilled. This can also be done with impending or overdue changes, such as the departure of an older child. In order to take full advantage of such before-after sculptures, the family can be asked to adjust to the loss of the member by forming a new sculpting, possibly using the group consensus sculpting discussed below. These sculptings can also be used with life cycle shifts where someone is added, such as by a birth or remarriage, and where roles in the family are gained or lost. For example, when a stepfather is added, the family can be sculpted with the original father, then without the father, and finally with the stepfather. Then this position can be held and the stepfather asked to find a way to fit into the family, whether in the original father's way or a new way. Sculptings can also be done which start with the couple, then add each child to the family one at a time, sculpting just before and just after their arrival to see how the family has evolved to its current position.

A special class of multiple sculptings is that concerned with family of origin work. This work is primarily concerned with understanding three generational problems, the formation and passing on of family patterns and family problems, and extricating children from these patterns, whether they be middle or final generation children. The first benefit is that by seeing their parents sculpted when they were kids with their own family, or at earlier ages, the children see their parents differently, possibly for the first time. Parents are no longer just nagging, demanding, disciplining, but are also vulnerable, struggling, and so forth. They are seen as more human, more approachable, possibly more noble in intent as they try to avoid in their own family what they most feared or resented in their family of origin. The second benefit is that the youngest generation may see the family theme that is being acted out and choose to be different after having seen the results in the two preceding generations.

These benefits can be maximized with two particular sculptings. In one, the parents sculpt their family of origin when they were the same age as their problem child. Another useful sculpting suggested by Papp (1976) is to sculpt the family of origin and current family over time and at particular nodal life cycle events such as pregnancy, births, deaths, children leaving, and so forth to see the patterns which connect past and present. One looks here for who takes over whose roles, who takes over which tasks, how family traditions are followed by each generation, and what rules are consistent over time. The parents' marriage and the grandparents' marriage can be sculpted alone if time is not available for the whole development.

Group Consensus Sculptings

In this form, all members are asked to determine their own final position in a sculpture, usually that in which they are most satisfied. They may also be allowed to try to influence their entire family's final position. These sculptings can start from scratch, or from positions in previous sculptings. They are particularly useful with couples who present opposing ideal sculptings and a compromise or alternate solution is needed. The struggle to define relationships can be seen in these sculptings, often in dramatic form as couples wrestle each other in search of a satisfying position.

Prescribed Positions

In this style couples or families adopt prescribed positions and respond to this experience either verbally or nonverbally by further elaborating the sculpting using these positions as a starting point. This is an excellent use of sculpting in teaching applications and has benefits for therapy as well. The New York State substance abuse family services training for therapists includes similar teaching through physical metaphors of relationships (Pollack, 1981). Schismatic marital positions are represented with the couple back to back, arms interlocked, together, but with no shared vision. Similarly dominant-submissive (one up, one down in space), supportive (one leaning on the other to balance), and enmeshed (total, face-to-face contact, holding hands, eye to eye where one can see the space around them only through the spouse's eye) couples are also represented. These methods were developed for trainees, but they can also be adopted for use with spouses and in preventive groups for well families. Couples can be placed in a particular position and asked to comment on them and then change them if desired.

Proesky (1981) used a variation of the above approach in her clinical practice. Rather than start with a set number of potential patterns, she sculpts the family or couple into a pattern which seems intuitively correct to her. She may then ask one member to alter the sculpting to increase his or her comfort and follow this up by putting the whole sculpture in motion by asking each person to simultaneously work toward a more comfortable position.

Action scenarios can also be constructed. For example, the treatment process had stalled in sex therapy when a couple presenting with inhibited sexual desire could not adequately deal with the task of developing acceptable sexual invitations to use with the "inhibited" member. Attempts to deal with the problem verbally deteriorated into blame and counterblame among the spouses, leaving the therapist uncertain as to where their difficulties lay in the invitation-response process. The couple was asked to engage in a nonverbal game. One spouse was to imagine himself as a Chinese puzzle box, the kind that must be manipulated in a particular sequence to open and yield its contents. Triggers and levers are hidden imperceptibly in the apparently unbroken construction of these boxes, and must be discovered through trial and error. The other spouse was to work at opening the mimicked puzzle box. After some time for preparation the sculpting began. As it continued it became obvious that the spouse playing the box had chosen a very elaborate and complex sequence of manipulations necessary to open the box, leaving the partner frustrated and pessimistic about the chance of success. This was pointed out to the puzzle box actor. The couple discussed this "game" much more freely and lucidly than they did the analogous sexual situation.

Constantine (1978) warns the user of such sculptings to bear in mind that any time the therapist imposes a limited number of options or preselected dimensions within which to define the relationship, he runs the risk of limiting and distorting the results so that they may say more about the therapist's assumptions than the family's actuality. There are benefits as well, such as introducing new options for the family or in helping them to conceptualize themselves in a way which more readily leads to change. A family which studiously overlooks the recognition of power differences may be aided in constructing a more workable family hierarchy by being asked to map family power dimensions in a forced choice sculpture which assumes hierarchical differences in power.

More leeway is given to unique aspects of the family or individual experience in those sculptures which represent the family's own metaphors. Duhl et al. (1973) have clients make common metaphors which arise in treatment into action patterns, such as "he turns his back on me." Papp (1976) reports eliciting more extensive metaphors from the family members, which are then explored and put into action. She describes a family member picking the image of a racing train for his father who was always rushing out the door, a threatening sky for his mother with heart trouble, a field of bright flowers for his sister who would blissfully ignore the parents' problems. He described himself as a bridge with undiscovered cracks for the locomotive (Papp, 1976, p. 474).

Another example of therapist prescribed sculptures is given by Constantine (1978). The participant in this spatialization makes a different gesture to each family member in sequence until a rhythm or the lack of one emerges. At this point the sculptor can stop or alter the sequence or gestures, and then continue. One might also create a chain reaction sculpture where a gesture is received from one family member and passed on to a new member. The variations are endless, and as Constantine points out, they are limited only by the perception and creativity of the therapist, not by the catalogue of previously employed techniques. Smith and Phillips (1971), for example, have adapted them to provide a means of giving feedback from one spouse to another about their perception of their partner's nonverbal emotional messages. They have each spouse sculpt the other's face to show prescribed emotions such as anger, happiness, sadness, boredom, etc., and then check the agreement between spouses on the accuracy of the emotion conveyed.

Simple Spatializations

Constantine (1978) has developed a typology of three simple types of sculptings, called spatializations, to be used in exploring limited personal and interpersonal constructs. Space is used to map a simple concept, and the sculpting is converted into a living graph by people placing themselves in that space in relation to the concept. The three basic phases of these sculptings are: (1) defining the space, (2) placing members in the space, and (3) processing the results. People can either place themselves or one person can place all family members. Sculptings can revolve around a single point or a one-dimensional continuum, or they may involve two different concepts represented in right angle continuums.

In all three of these cases the therapist defines the space in reference to a single concept. In the point or polar spatialization it is a single idea, person, value, or process around which the others will arrange themselves or be arranged by one sculptor. The pole may be an actual family member, or the marital pair, or a parent-child pair. It can be a concept, such as open marriage, represented symbolically or written out on a blackboard, or a process, such as arguing, or the way things were in the father's family. In order to create vivid reactions, the poles can be physically labeled with newsprint, or given symbolic representations with objects. Constantine (1978) mentions the therapeutic usefulness of a "power" line, and its usefulness has also been demonstrated in groups. This works equally well with "caring." In both cases, the family reactions when trying to line up in order of increasing power or caring can be dramatic. In one family no family member would stay at the head of the line; they moved back away from the position of power. In other families they fight for the lead position.

In debriefing these sculptings, given their abstract and rather simple nature, it is not necessary to derole. It is most powerful if members stay in place to describe their experiences and respond to the therapist's questions. Questions similar to those recommended above for simultaneous sculptings can be asked, such as "How did you choose this spot?" Holding one's position helps one to take responsibility for their own feelings and point of view in the family. Seeing one's position as well as hearing it adds to the power of the method. If the sculpting was done by only one member placing the others, they may each be asked to choose a more likeable point at this time. Or the sculpting may be repeated using the same dimension, but a different "set" or context, such as lining up in order of the most liked or most cared for. All the comparison sculptings mentioned earlier can be done in this format. One may sculpt current then ideal positions; past, present, and future positions; one's own perception of where they fit and the perception of another family member. Laing, Phillipson, and Lee's (1966) Interpersonal Perception method could be used if desired to get not only a person's self-perception, but also their perception of how others see them (understanding) and how they see others' self-perceptions (agreement).

Boundary Sculptures

Boundary sculptures are used when one wants to clarify conflicting spatial or territorial rules between individuals within a system, whether it be the family system, family-therapist system, co-therapist system, or any other system (Duhl et al., 1973). They are also used to explore the personal boundaries of family members, both in the real world spatial sense of proxemics (Hall, 1959) and more importantly in a metaphorical sense which expresses one's experience of self (Constantine, 1978). In these approaches one looks at boundaries in detail, not just in general terms such as rigidity and permeability, but also at the experiences of closeness and distance, intrusion and inclusion, encroachment and encouragement, exclusion, and so forth. Boundaries are explored in themselves, their size, shape, variability, and permeability (Duhl et al., 1973). Passage across boundaries is also explored in terms of entrance and exit, invitations and prohibitions.

The permeability of boundaries can be explored actively by the approach of family members, or imagined or role-played individuals. Here one may translate action or metaphor into concrete language which has a colloquially accepted meaning. "You turned your back on him." "He can't get close to you." The sex, age, relationship, and other characteristics of the person approaching can be varied and differences observed. Does mother let her boundary collapse for a particular daughter? Is there a difference in mother's boundary for father and son, and who has the harder time getting in? Family rules may be elicited by having people not only approach and try to enter, but also to try to enter in various ways—seductive, assertive, aggressive, half-heartedly, sneakily, impatient or fast, more patiently, and so on (Constantine, 1978; Duhl et al., 1973). One can also ask the person involved to bring people into his space and look at how he or she invited them in, active, passive, direct, or indirect, and how much of a range or repertoire they have for doing this (Duhl et al., 1973).

FINAL SUGGESTIONS

By now the sculpting process should be clear, as well as ways to use this process. With simple sculptings one should count on at least ten minutes per family member. With more elaborate system sculptings, more time is needed and not everyone will be able to present a sculpting by the completion of the session. This is not necessarily bad. One should insure that ample time is available to process sculptings that are done in the sessions. The question of with whom sculptings should be done is still to be addressed. Among sculpting enthusiasts the question is how to adapt the methods of problematic groups, not whom to exclude. Simon (1972) feels sculpting works better with large families than with couples, and Constantine (1978) recommends the method for multiple family groups, but he also uses it with couples. Kates-Julius (1978) has shown that the methods can be useful with populations usually considered too psychotic, provided measures are taken to insure that the sculptings do not become too intense too quickly for the participants. To date, there is no good typology of families to use in deciding which types may benefit from these methods and which may not. It is not known if rigid types will take to them more or less readily than creative families, or benefit more or less than creative families. Nor is the impact of verbal intelligence on the ability to profit from these methods known. One can only try them and see, safe in the knowledge that the family can control how much it will expose by choice of metaphors, and that families are resilient systems, difficult to change and even more difficult to damage or destroy entirely. The therapeutic problem is usually not how to avoid too much impact, but how to have enough impact to make change possible (Papp, 1976).

General Guidelines

Those using these methods for the first time should use them with due consideration for potential results. Powerful emotions may arise (Papp et al., 1973) and the therapist should be ready, both by training and inclination, to deal with them when they do arise. These methods are not to be used as simple gimmicks to make people aware of feelings, and definitely should not be used as party games. While a sculpting can be done quickly and with minimal input from the therapist, the processing that follows may take more time and energy than expected. On these occasions, the therapist should be able to elicit the support of the family for its distressed members, or be able to take time for them himself. If the therapist is tired, or has left too little time to process the sculpture because it is late in the hour, a sculpting should not be started. It might be completed, but it would not be processed nor would resultant emotions be dealt with.

Kates-Julius (1978), in working with her day patient and largely schizophrenic population, felt it important not to expose conflicts too quickly. In more pathological families—those with less supports, few problem-solving options, and less individual ability to tolerate conflict—the work proceeds more slowly, with more emphasis on cognitive control and understanding, and a slow uncovering process. This can be achieved by using less intense approaches involving less motion and touch, stand-in actors instead of family members, limited use of psychodrama, maximum use of educative material and cognitive, verbal processing, more discussion during the sculpting itself, and processing the sculpting from an outside observer position rather than an inside participant position. One could of course argue that Kates-Julius' population was already involved in too much of the type of impressionistic, configurational type of process emphasized by sculpting, and that with such a population more verbal, linear, logical processes need to occur. In this respect it is interesting to consider Kates-Julius' (1978) observation that the patients in their roles as family members for the sculpting would drop their symptomatology while in role, and regain it after the sculpting was completed.

Duhl et al. (1973) emphasize the safety of sculpting metaphors since they can be used to express only what the client is able to tolerate and comprehend. Unskilled therapists may ignore this feature, however, and push clients to be aware of more than they wish, or are able to deal with, and therein lies the principal danger of the therapist acting according to his own insights and timetable. Healthier subjects will resist unwanted interpretations, less healthy individuals may only be able to do so with difficulty.

Potential users should also realize that the methods presented here as emphasized by Jefferson (1978) are examples, not final forms. They must be responsive to the family and the situation. If the therapist is too intent on applying the methods "correctly" he may miss opportunities to do something more therapeutic but less "proper." These methods, no matter how inclusive or complete they may seem are presented simply to identify a domain for the therapist to work in. They are not intended to fix the number or type of acceptable sculptings. At first the student will feel more comfortable following well-established paths, routine sculptings. As he or she gains experience, more variations can be tried and he or she can begin to develop his own approaches and variations, tailored to fit situations specifically.

Sculpting is a different process for sifting information and arriving at solutions. If the therapist does not value and use this process, it will be difficult to teach the family to do so or to obtain maximum benefit from sculptings. To improve one's capacity as a sculptor, one should work toward improving one's general nonverbal capacity. Therapists can benefit from practice at sculpting their own families or supervisory situations. They can practice speaking in spatial metaphors and analogies (Constantine, 1978), and they can also gain from participation in a variety of artistic endeavors, therapeutic or otherwise. Participation in dance and art therapy can be useful. So can mime and appreciation of actual sculpture, painting, and dance. The latter arts can increase one's awareness of the expressive use of space and motion as well as develop one's lexicon of expressive arrangements of posture, ensemble figure arrangement, and so forth. In the final analysis, however, the work still remains based on one's ability to work metaphorically in that process which has been called right brain, primary, analogic, nonverbal, intuitive, and other names, but which is difficult to grasp with logical, sequential, left-brain processes. In many ways the two processes are unknowable, each by the other, and their combination may result in additional potency of treatment.

10

Role Playing

Pretend, Enact, and Reenact

This chapter reviews the various methods used to move a family by involving its members actively in verbally and nonverbally expressive actions, most of which are based on pretending or playacting. The theoretical basis of role playing (RP) and its potential for growth goes back to three distinct and separate movements. The first movement, founded by Moreno (Wolberg, 1976), goes back to psychodrama and the psychodramatic methods of simulated playacting (Boles, 1972). The second movement, much more "scientifically legitimate," goes back to social psychology, a discipline that has used role playing experimentally for at least three decades (Friedman, 1972). A third movement, the behavioral one, has shown the usefulness of role playing in assertiveness training and role rehearsal (Green, Burkhart, & Harrison, 1979; Voss, Arrick, & Rimm, 1978). The humanistic school, as shown by parent training (Gordon, 1970) has of course used role playing as an active form of training that bypasses left-hemisphere intellectualization and relies instead on the active experimental involvement of the trainee. Role playing thus qualifies, by the criteria listed in Chapter 1, as a method rather than a technique. How a therapist applies a method is a matter of technique. However, the method is reproducible and relatively simple to implement (provided, of course, that the therapist is comfortable with and experienced in playacting, a skill that should be part and parcel of the training of all family therapists). In view of the solid and extensive record—empirical and experiential—of role playing, it is a wonder that it has not been used more extensively in family therapy. Role playing is an active, focused activity, one that allows the therapist to be in charge, to mold and teach a family at the level on which the family can work (Biddle, 1979; Calonico & Thomas, 1973; Corsini & Cardone, 1966).

Role playing is not for everybody. Most of the literature suggests that a minimum level of intellectual and emotional resources is required for role playing. Some (Rubin, 1978; Smye, 1978) have suggested that a minimum age of nine years may be necessary. On the other hand, a great deal depends on the therapist's ability to engage the family in role playing with a minimum of defensiveness and a maximum of playfulness. Role playing allows the bypassing of the intellectual aspects of family transactions by focusing more on the experiential and emotional aspects.

One of the primary functions of RP is diagnostic of what the therapist and the family members can learn about the family. Andrews (1972) advocated training family therapists in experiential RP so that they can attain three goals: (1) to develop empathy as a participant in family dysfunction when the practitioner plays a family role; (2) to develop sensitivity to the disturbed family as a system in distress; and (3) to develop interventive skills in altering family dysfunction through awareness of the use of self as a human encounter agent in behavior change.

HISTORICAL BACKGROUND

The historical roots of role playing, at least in this century, are found in the work of Moreno and his followers (Wolberg, 1976; Yablonsky, 1976).

Psychodrama

In psychodrama, participants assume roles that have either been assigned to them or taken voluntarily by them. It forces the individuals to act, play, pretend, and behave as if they were not themselves. This injunction seems to have the paradoxical effect of allowing them to be themselves. Psychodrama has been applied to family therapy by Madanes (1980, 1984).

Social Psychology

Research on the use of role playing in social psychological experimentation is so extensive that, all by itself, it could be the subject of a review. Suffice it to say that even though role playing in experimentation has been questioned (Spencer, 1978),* its use in social psychology has been extensive and shows no signs of abating.

Krupat (1977) reviewed the problems of laboratory deception research in the light of role playing. He concluded that although the legitimacy of RP data cannot be empirically determined, role playing and other nondeceptive methods can produce findings that complement other methods and that are capable of

---

*The critics of RP in social psychological experimentation have been Freedman (1969), Friedman (1972), and Kelman (1967). For theoretical background, see the writings of Piaget and those of Dabbs and Helmreich (1972).

standing alone. Hendrick (1977a,b) proposed an RP model with a matrix of five conceptually orthogonal dimensions: (1) role positions, for which subjects are type cast, (2) the kind of behavioral activity required, (3) stage setting, (4) script, and (5) the plot of the experiment. Alexander and Scriven (1977) maintained that RP methods are a valid procedure for gathering data of social psychological importance and that role playing may indeed be superior to traditional experimental approaches. Mohavedi (1977) questioned this conclusion and advocated a more differentiated use of RP and more research and theory on the concept "role." Mitchell, Kaul, and Pepinsky (1977) focused on the ethical and legal questions raised by RP research, especially in relationship to deception.*

Child Psychology

The developmental aspects of role playing have also been studied extensively, to the point of a definite relationship between age and the ability to role-play (Rubin, 1978). For instance, Quarton (1976) did find a marginal relationship between age and RP skills. Johnson (1977) found that age affected role-taking performance and communication tasks, and that a child's sex and IQ level affected referential communication performance.

Personality

The correlates of role-playing ability have been documented for (1) emotional maturity, (2) intellectual functioning, (3) empathy, (4) cognitive style, and (5) flexibility. As Thomas, Franks, and Calonico (1972) have shown, role-taking accuracy in the family relates inversely to power. Fathers were found to be less accurate role takers than mothers and mothers less accurate than children. Dominant mothers were perceived by children as poorer role takers than were less dominant mothers. Role playing has been found effective in modifying the feelings, attitudes, and behaviors associated with interpersonal conflict (Bohart, 1972). It was more effective than intellectual analysis or the discharge of anger and aggression. Role playing was also more effective with subjects who were open to their feeling life.

In a review of the literature on role playing, Boles (1972) described its current use as a technique of behavior change and evaluated a variety of cases of attitude change in the experimental literature. Assertive females playing hostile-dominant, friendly-dominant, friendly-submissive, and hostile-submissive roles better than nonassertive females (Atkinson, 1977). Underassertiveness seems related to a behavioral deficit rather than to behavioral rigidity. Greenberg (1967) found that the degree of involvement was an important personality variable in RP.

---

*For the relationship between RP and deception, see Cooper (1976), Greenberg (1967), Mitchell et al. (1977), Krupat (1977), and Spencer (1978).

From this all too cursory review, what can we conclude about the possible use of RP in family therapy?

1. Clearly, a family needs a certain degree of functionality if they are to role-play. Because role-playing ability is based on a degree of maturity, empathy, and articulateness, most functional and semifunctional families can participate in RP.

2. Families need to be rather flexible and action oriented. Very intellectualized and/or rigid families, who would benefit most from RP, find RP most difficult.

3. RP is not for actively chaotic, paranoid families or for families in crisis.

4. At this point, the specifics of RP with families can be found only by pushing the limits of its applications; that is, only through our successes and our failures can we learn how and when to use RP with families.

5. Rather than thinking of RP as a therapeutic technique, we should perhaps think of it as an educational tool for training families in skill learning, not changing.

6. RP is inappropriate with families in which there are very small children. To role-play, children should be of school age or older.

7. Sculpting can be the diagnostic base for deciding whether a family can participate in RP tasks.

ROLE PLAYING AND FAMILY THERAPY

Lange and van der Hart (1983) used terms such as *behavior rehearsal* and *behavior exercises* (p. 136) to refer to role playing, which they considered an important part of helping families to grow, not an end in itself. They regarded this process as consisting of several steps (p. 139): (1) Families relate experiences from the past, either immediate (the day before yesterday) or long gone (honeymoon, birth of first child), and of course experiences that were painful or conflictual. (2) The experiences are recounted in detail, but the affect relating to an experience is often missing. (3) To bring the affective into the experience, the therapist makes the family reenact the experience, reproducing it as accurately as they can. (4) The role playing of the experience and the affect surrounding it should allow the family to establish a feeling of control over a situation that they have seen as uncontrollable. (5) After the first reenactment (not more than five to fifteen minutes at most), the therapist asks for feedback from the family, then gives evaluation and feedback on the reenactment, making constructive suggestions about how the family can replay the situation better. (6) The situation is replayed; however, this time, the family incorporates more constructive ways of handling it. (7) Afterward, feedback from the family and from the therapist is used to assess whether the situation was handled to the family's satisfaction or whether it needs to be improved. (8) If the reenactment works well for the family, the therapist may assign it as homework to make sure that it is mastered. (9) If it does not seem to work well, the therapist and the family need to discuss the pros and cons; then the family may role-play another possible handling of the situation, which may work well for them.

Box 10-1   THE DISQUALIFICATION GAME

The disqualification game should be used with a family in which a great deal of disqualification occurs; that is, family members tend to discount either their own or others' communications (e.g., "You should not feel that way"; "What you feel is not important; only what you do is important"). Often, disqualification is subtle, and the family may deny it when they are confronted directly about it. The disqualification game may be helpful in such situations because the progression starts with relatively innocuous topics, which may seem inconsequential to the family, and moves to more serious and relevant topics. The purpose of the game is to show the ultimate consequences that result when parents do not set clear and firm limits and parents disqualify each other. The impact of this game, in the form given here, may be quite explosive. The therapist should thus be able to gauge whether the family can handle the game.

METHOD

Have the child ask three questions, one at a time, of the parents.

Example 1: May I go to an R-rated movie (depending, of course, on the age of the child)?
Example 2: May I take drugs?
Example 3: May I drive the car by myself?
Example 4: May I kill myself?

The parents are to give the same answers to all questions: One parent is adamantly opposed; the other either agrees or is wishy-washy about the issue.
To the first question, the responses may be as follows:

EXAMPLE

Father: Absolutely not!
Mother: Well, maybe just this once.

To the second question, the responses are reversed:

EXAMPLE

Father: Go ahead, but if you get arrested, don't expect me to get you out of jail.
Mother: I am against it. I do not want you to do it.

A FEW DEFINITIONS

Some of the terms used in this chapter are defined in the following list. A much more detailed discussion of roles and role playing in the family can be found in Spiegel (1971).

Role playing: a method of intervention that is based on simulated, hypothetical, and possibly playful interactions that are pretended.

Role assumption: implies a family member's willingness to take on a specific or a specified role, as a son's taking the role of the father (and vice versa) or the assumption of a more generic role, such as the martyr, the victim, or the rescuer (L'Abate, 1986).

Role rehearsal: the practicing of a role, usually new, in order to learn and master it to a level at which the person can play it comfortably or with a degree of ease.

Role reversal: implies the assumption of a role that is the opposite of the person's usual role. For instance, the person who usually plays the role of victim may find it useful to practice the roles of persecutor or rescuer (see Box 10–2). Johnson (1971) reviewed studies that used role reversal in interpersonal and intergroup bargaining situations. He found that three role-playing variables were important: (1) the authenticity of the person engaged in the role reversal, (2) the expression of an accurate understanding of the sender's message, and (3) the expression of warmth toward and acceptance of the sender. Accuracy emerged as the single most important variable in effective role playing.

A TYPOLOGY OF ROLES

A classification of roles may be helpful in understanding how this method approximates life, allowing the family to bring under control behaviors that would otherwise be beyond the therapist's reach. When the family reenacts these roles, whether real or hypothetical, the family is able to start new interactions that have not been in their repertoire. According to this classification, roles can vary along at least five different dimensions: (1) old versus new, (2) actual versus fictional, (3) assumed versus assigned, (4) same versus opposite, and (5) focused (specific) versus general (open-ended). Although other classifications are undoubtedly available (Spiegel, 1971), this classification should suffice for the purposes of this chapter.

Old versus New

In the old-versus-new category, the family may be asked to discard their old roles, whatever they may claim them to be, and assume completely new roles. For instance, if a family has been playing out the drama triangle of victim-persecutor-rescuer (see Box 10–2), they now have the choice of playing roles that will take them away from destructive transactions and that will be based instead on mutual trust, respect, and affirmation. They may be asked to play other roles—provider-leader, nurturer-arbiter, worker-follower. The assumption

Box 10–2   THE DRAMA TRIANGLE

In the destructive and vicious pattern of the drama triangle, each player can and does portray all three of the destructive positions described.

Victim: This is a universal position, often played as the oppressed, the martyr, and the butt of all jokes. The attitude of the victim is that all of the troubles in the world have been piled on him or her. More often than not, persons who play this game go out of their way to prove that they are, have been, and will be constantly victimized.

Rescuer: Every victim needs a rescuer, someone who will act as savior, who will spare the victim from suffering and offer protection from further trouble (i.e., the knight in shining armor). Variations on this theme are Daddy Warbucks, Tycoon, Superman, Gary Cooper, Clint Eastwood, John Wayne, Mandrake.

Persecutor: In this position, oftentimes the rescuer and the victim alternately assume the role of victimizer: "If it weren't for you, I would be . . . " In the most extreme cases, this role may drive others (usually professional victims) crazy or to suicide or homicide. The persecutor is oriented toward punishment and retribution; blood must be extracted from whoever is at fault—someone else is to pay the price.

By now, no doubt, you will see some similarities between the roles of the drama triangle and the incongruent stances in Box 10–3.

(Karpman, 1968; L'Abate, 1976; L'Abate, Weeks & Weeks, 1979)

of new roles also entails discussion about how difficult it is to assume new, constructive roles and to let go of the old, destructive ones ("The devil I have is better than the devil I may get!").

Actual versus Fictional

On the actual-versus-fictional dimension belong the roles that family members have been playing for years but that they may wish to give up because the roles are unproductive, counterproductive, even destructive, to the family's welfare. Rather than starting to play new roles right off the bat, which may be difficult for some families to do, it may be more helpful for the family to start by playing fictional roles, either of their own or the therapist's making: "Who is going to play the dictator? Any takers for playing a spy? We would like to volunteer to play an astronaut? What other role would anybody like to play? How about the millionaire? Daddy Warbucks, anyone?" It is important at this point to instill in the family an attitude of playfulness, a level of functioning that many families cannot assume immediately, certainly not during the beginning, critical phases of family therapy.

Assumed versus Assigned

The assumed roles are those that we automatically assume in the family (i.e., provider, cook, bottle-washer, buyer). How rigidly or flexible the parents play these roles will affect how rigidly or flexibly the children assume their roles. It is important to help families understand that no rules about assumed roles are carved in stone, no matter how strongly a family may protest. Some families are surprised that alternative roles can be played and that role playing is one way of learning these new roles. Some roles are assigned tacitly and assumed tacitly by family members. Family members need to understand that they have some responsibility in how each of them accepts a role. This understanding can be made more acute and immediate through the role playing of assigned roles — some pleasant, some unpleasant ("Who promised you a rose garden?"). The therapist can assume the responsibility of assigning roles, but only if the family is unwilling or unable to do it themselves: "Now I want you, Dad, to start playing the chief bottle-washer. You, Mother, will play the busy businessman. You, Jimmy, will play the distractor (see Box 10–3), and you, Helen, will play the nice, responsible girl."

Box 10–3 INCONGRUENT STANCES

In role-playing incongruent stances, there are four incongruent stances and one congruent stance. The four incongruent stances are easier to understand than the congruent stance. By the same token, it is more difficult to give up the incongruent stances and to learn the congruent stance. The four incongruent parts are as follows:

Intellectualizer, Computer, Know-It-All, I Know Better. The stance is assumed by keeping feet together, arms rigidly down by the sides, and the face smugly upward. In this stance, the person needs to repeat that to solve all family problems, everybody should be reasonable, using logic, facts, and scientific evidence to arrive at the solution. Some of the variations on this stance are Scientist, Encyclopedia, Ann Landers, Dr. Spock.

Blamer, Externalizer, Fault-Finder. In this stance, the blamer is perfect and blameless; everybody except the blamer is at fault. This stance is assumed non-verbally by spreading the legs apart, right arm outstretched rigidly toward a target, with the index finger pointing directly at the target. Verbally, the blamer needs to repeat *ad nauseam* (until she or he is tired of holding the arm up or the whole position becomes uncomfortable): "It's your fault!" Some of the variations on this stance are Judge, Patriot, Detective, Jury, Executioner.

Placator, Martyr, Peacemaker, Sufferer. In this stance, the person assumes all the faults and the blame of the family system. The basic stance (i.e., "please be nice to me") is assumed nonverbally by placing one knee on the floor while holding the other knee precariously and painfully halfway to but not touching the floor. Here, the person needs to practice by placing the palms together, as if in prayer, and repeating the refrain "Please be nice to me."

Distractor, Irrelevant, Impulsive, Hyperactive.   In this stance, the basic position is "I don't know, I don't want to know, and I don't care!" It is played by keeping the feet apart, knees together as much as possible, hands stretched upward and rotated while the person repeats, "I don't know, and I don't care!"

Congruent Stance.   In this stance, the verbal and the nonverbal messages go together (L'Abate, 1976, 1983). The stance begins with the person's taking responsibility for his or her own actions and using the pronoun "I," insisting on speaking for oneself rather than allowing others to speak on one's behalf. The congruent stance is a difficult one to teach unless the family is thoroughly fed up with their adoption of incongruent stances. It involves a minimum, if any, use of the incongruent positions listed, and it combines the verbal and the nonverbal channels of communication: "I mean what I say, and I say what I mean." The congruent stance also involves the use of personal, nonjudgmental statements about how the person is feeling, at that very moment, as a result of the behavior of others.

(L'Abate, 1976; suggested by Satir, 1972)

Same versus Opposite

In the same-versus-opposite category, which admittedly may overlap with some already listed, the therapist may ask the family to play the roles they usually play at home (if definite roles are indeed being played). After this role playing has been done so that everybody is clear about what role each member has been playing, each member is to play the opposite role; that is, one who has been overresponsible may play the irresponsible role, or one who has been playing the saint may now have to play the sinner. This role playing of course involves what has been defined as role reversal.

Focused versus General

It may be important at the beginning of role playing to allow the family to play general roles that may seem irrelevant to the roles in their family. Through this approach, the family may become comfortable with role playing, starting with general, open-ended roles and going toward more specific, and perhaps more threatening, roles: "Now that we have played the drama triangle in general, I wonder whether we can pinpoint which family member plays which role. Who plays victim most of the time? Who plays rescuer? Who plays persecutor?"

A library of role-playing exercises, covering a range of situations relevant to family life, is available in the structured enrichment manuals published by the senior author and his associates (L'Abate, 1977, L'Abate & Rupp, 1981).

The therapist can assign fictional, or imaginary, roles that can be assumed by various family members. The easiest form of role assignment is role reversal; that is, father becomes mother (and vice versa), or children become parents (and vice versa). Another way is to assign explicit roles that the family may have been playing implicitly. Role reversal may imply change from an expressive to an instrumental role. Roles may be accepted or rejected. If they are accepted, is the acceptance congruent or are there inconsistencies or contradictions in the role assumption? For instance, a father may assume the role of mother, but through his playing of the role may show his misunderstanding and distortion of it. Fictional roles can either be assigned or assumed voluntarily. Fictional roles may represent fantasy completely unrelated to family function (except as wishes), or they may be expressions of implicit roles that are played at a covert level in the family.

PROS AND CONS OF ROLE PLAYING

Role playing that is instituted during the initial, ciritical phases of family therapy will not work unless it is used episodically and *ad hoc,* as Madanes (1981, 1984) used it. Otherwise, role playing is much more appropriate after the critical, initial phase has been successfully surmounted, when it is important for the family to learn new, more constructive roles. Role playing that is used inappropriately, that is, at an inopportune or a premature time in the phases of family therapy or with a family that is unable or unwilling to role-play, may have various results. One possibility is that the family's resistance and defensiveness may increase to the point that they either drop out of treatment or stay in treatment without any visible changes. A second possibility is that an "explosion" may occur, in the form of one family member's acting out. A third possibility, depending on the rapport between the family and the therapist, is that the family may be able to tell the therapist about the inappropriateness of the role playing chosen for them and suggest a more appropriate and useful alternative.

WHAT DO WE ROLE-PLAY?

The variety of roles that can be played depends mostly on the inventiveness and ingenuity of the therapist. A host of topics, roles, and situations can be role-played. The therapist may find it helpful not only to experience role playing personally but also to become acquainted with some of the literature cited here. Spiegel (1971) elaborated on what can happen to family roles. They can be assumed, assigned, accepted, or denied. A variety of role conflicts may occur intraindividually when a discrepancy exists between the actual and the ideal family roles. Role dislocation, displacement, and repudiation may exist. In this chapter, we try to present the roles that family members can play easily.

Role Playing of the Symptom

Role playing of the symptom is probably the easiest and most easily implemented of role-playing situations, provided it is not based on acting out or physical attack. If the symptom obviously cannot be role-played because it would be too embarrassing (e.g., bed-wetting), the family can pretend that such behavior has just occurred. If the symptom cannot be role-played—for whatever legitimate reasons, not because of the family's manipulation—other alternatives are available.

Role Playing of Conflictual Situations

The circumstances surrounding the symptom—its antecedents or its consequences—can be role-played. If the conflict cannot be reproduced in role playing, introduce a metaphor symbolizing the conflict. For instance, if power seems to be an underlying issue, one family member might play the king, one the queen, and so on. Appropriate costume touches, made of paper or whatever and devised on the spur of the moment, might be used. Thus, another dimension of role playing that deserves attention concerns the *direct versus indirect* role playing of family conflicts and presenting problems.

THE USE OF ROLE PLAYING IN CLINICAL PRACTICE*

Role playing is an integral part of the methods in my clinical practice with families. I use role playing spontaneously during the therapy session as I guide families in assessing their interpersonal interactions with significant persons in their lives. For me, the use of role playing is both practical and effective, and it simplifies as well as enlivens the therapy hour. Also, it facilitates behavior change when interpretation and reflection prove ineffective.

Children and adolescents quickly pick up the idea of practicing productive communication patterns and naturally slip into role playing, either being themselves or taking on the role of parent, peer, or teacher. Some adults have to be encouraged and coaxed into role playing, but they rapidly learn that as they practice in the therapy session, they increase the possibility that they will achieve their goals of improving communication outside my office.

As I analyze my work and my style, I find that I use three primary kinds of role playing: (1) real-life role playing between two emotionally involved persons: that is, parent and child or husband and wife, who practice with each other in the therapy session while I coach; (2) hypothetical role playing between the client and me: I assume various roles—parent, child, friend, co-worker—and have the client respond as he or she does in everyday situations; (3) developmental-modeling role playing: I begin with a personal response and move step by step toward having the client develop his or her constructive scenario. Perhaps brief vignettes of these three kinds of role playing will help to explain.

*Peggy Mayfield, Ph.D.

Real-Life Role Playing

In my practice, I meet with parents and teenagers who commonly display acting-out behaviors and poor communication patterns. Many parents and adolescents want to spend the hour going down their respective lists of complaints rather than looking constructively at their own difficulties. To start some genuine communication, I stop this list of grievances by asking, "What do you really want from your child? What do you really want from your parent?"

Very often, the child says, "I want my parent to listen." I then direct the communication from me to the parent by saying, "Well, why don't you turn and tell your mother that you need her to listen?" If the child continues to respond to me or says that he or she has just said what is wanted, I continue to direct the communication to the parent by saying, "Ask your parent for what you want." If the parent refuses to listen, which is often the case, I begin to work with the parent on describing listening skills; then I begin to orchestrate the child's asking and the parent's responding until at least two constructive exchanges have been made. I then say, "Look! Listen! You did it! Let's try again."

Turning to the child, I say, "_____, what is something else that you want to say to your parent?" Usually the child responds to me first; again, I direct the questions to the parent by saying to the child, "Say to your parent what you are saying to me." Before the parent can respond defensively or critically, I intervene, saying, "You may want to give your child the idea that you are listening by saying, 'You sound angry. I understand that you want to have a date on Friday night.'" The parent usually wants to continue with a qualifying phrase, such as "but you did not come home on time before." Here I stop the parent and ask the parent to rephrase the statement into an "I want" statement directed to the child, who is to respond with appropriate listening skills.

Not all clients cooperate. The freedom to direct comes only after I have portrayed a caring, listening, and understanding attitude and after I have given some feedback indicating that I understand the specific feelings and problems of each person. Faced with humor, some tongue-in-cheek cajoling, and a little finesse, parents and children as well as couples cooperate. If one person refuses to follow the role-playing pattern, becomes hostile, argumentative, or defensive, I observe to the other participant: "It appears that Joe does not want to communicate with you and work this out, so I suggest that you and I work now on how to deal with a person who refuses to communicate." I never beg; I never coerce. I take as fact whatever the person gives and move on from that point. When the person who has withdrawn from the communication sees that my attention has turned to the other person, the withdrawn person often makes a gesture toward some constructive communication. Then I say, "Joe, do you want to try again?" At the end of the session, I request that the family try this pattern of talking at home and report how it has gone. At the following sessions, I return to the basic request statement and the basic listening and understanding statements as the underlying theme. In essence, I teach communication patterns through role playing. In later sessions, I reinforce the spontaneous, appropriate communication that fits this pattern and continue to emphasize the more subtle and discriminatory aspects of the communication patterns, always shaping and reinforcing, shaping and reinforcing.

Hypothetical Role Playing

In hypothetical role playing, I assume the role of persons who are important in the client's life. Usually, I do this after a client has described a difficult situation involving the client and a significant person. For example, the client may be having problems with his wife and may express anxiety, fear, or hostility. I may say, "Well, if your wife asks, 'Why did you come home late last night?' what do you say?" Sometimes the client continues to spill out the anxiety or the anger, but if something concrete must be done soon to change the situation and I judge that the client has expressed sufficient emotions, I interrupt again and ask the same question. I may have to do this as many as three or four times before the client gets the idea that I want an answer. The typical answer is defensive and filled with emotion. I say, "Let's look at your response. Do you think it helps you and your position?" Usually, the person recognizes the response as a negative one. Then I lead the client to brainstorm appropriate phrases. If the client cannot produce an answer, I give one. Usually the client personalizes my response by modifying it. Then I use the client's response and role-play the situation again. I start with a simple situation first, get a positive role-playing response from the client, then move to one or two more difficult scenes that encompass; second, an issue about which the client has serious apprehension; and, third, the situation or event about which the client has expressed the most fear or concern. The examples I choose always fit the context of the client's problems; they are not problems that I manufacture. I attempt always to convey through the role playing that I understand both feelings and problems and that I am attempting not to criticize the client.

As the client begins to understand the detrimental communication patterns, I role-play various ways in which a wife may relate to the client and have the client respond. When the client seems to hit on patterns that work for him and that seem appropriate, I review these patterns, often going spontaneously into the role of the wife immediately before the client leaves. Very often, the client gets my message and role-plays the chosen phrases that he has learned in the therapy session. Later we almost play a game with these patterns, a game in which I consciously reinforce the positive responses.

Developmental-Modeling Role Playing

At times, a family is very vulnerable and withdrawn or defensive and cannot interact in a role-playing scenario. I choose what can be called a developmental-modeling approach, in which I suggest what I would say in a situation that the family has described. When the family gives little information, I have to guess what the communication problems are and then assume the roles of one member and of another significant person, acting out what I think may be happening. For example, a child's mother may say, "Mary always argues with me and has to have a reason for every answer I give her. I'm so tired of the arguing and explaining. Mary's never satisfied!"

Using this sentence and my knowledge of the child and the family as a stepping-off point, I say, "Mary, is it like this? Maybe you say, 'Mother, can I stay in the pool another 30 minutes?' and Mother says no and then you say" . . . Here I pause to see whether the child will give me a statement. If the child doesn't respond, the parent often does. When I am working in the family group, a brother or a sister is certain to fill in the next sentence. I repeat the sentence and move on to the next statement, which I may have to fabricate but which is likely to be volunteered. I continue this process until I have built, if possible, a six- or eight-statement dialogue. I may have to return several times to the initial statement, modifying and creating statements until a clearly formed, pertinent pattern emerges. A typical pattern is as follows:

1. Child: Mother, I want to swim longer.
2. Mother: No. We have to go.
3. Child: Why?
4. Mother: Because you're turning blue.
5. Child: I'm not turning blue. I swam for 3 hours yesterday, and today I have been here only 2 hours; and you don't have to get my sister until 5:00, and it's only 3:30 now.
6. Mother: You swam 2 hours yesterday. I want to go to the store, and you have to get out.
7. Child: Why?
8. Mother: Because I said so!
9. Child: You're mean.
10. Mother: I'm going to spank you if you don't get out.

I point out that at least by Statement 5 in a dialogue, the tone of the communication has been set, and the outcome—positive or negative communication—has been decided. Holding up one hand, I point to my fingers, repeating the communication pattern through Statement 5. By Statement 5 in the example, the child has moved into the argumentative mode and put the mother on the defensive with her statements. By giving a reason in Statement 4, the mother sets herself up for Statement 5; by Statement 6, the mother has allowed the child to take charge. Either the child or the mother may be asked to work diligently to correct this faulty communication pattern, which leads to negative, hostile feelings, or they can negotiate together to change the pattern. When the child is struggling for or demanding control, I choose to work with the child first, focusing on the child's power to control by choosing words and influencing attitudes. Then the child and I construct a new communication pattern, which ends at least by Statement 5. Sometimes we leave all statements the same until Statement 5, then change that statement to "OK!" I then point out, "Notice the difference when you change one statement, repeat the original Statement 5, and then repeat the alternative Statement 5."

Frequently, when I role-play, I change my voice to that of the child, backing the mother out of the role and pulling the child into either the parent's or the child's role. As we can, the child and I work on the reasons that it is too hard to say OK. Sometimes, in identifying the positive communication patterns, the child and I draw a poster: The child draws pictures and writes as many words as possible; I add only a few words or a part of the picture. Then we share the poster with the parent. We keep the poster at the office but sometimes make a copy that the child can take home.

At each session for approximately six weeks, the child and I practice the communication patterns through role playing. First I am the parent, then the child; the child quickly catches on, mimicking the inflections in my voice and also playing the mother's role. By the end of the session, I have the child doing all of the role playing. I praise the child for every correct statement in #5, first with a touch and a positive word, then just with an excited expression of approval, and finally, with only a reasonable recognition that the correct pattern has been given. Last, I incorporate the parent into the praise and also into the role playing. My goal is for the parent to reinforce the child in everyday experiences and for the parent and the child to be able to construct positive communication patterns as well as to catch negative ones at home.

I use role playing with (1) couples, to attempt to reduce tension immediately if past arguments have ended in physical abuse; (2) individuals, to help them see their own actions and to perceive how they appear to husband, wife, or parent; (3) significantly withdrawn persons, to teach them how to carry on basic conversations about everyday events; (4) persons who need to overcome phobias and high anxiety; (5) persons who are chronically depressed, to change negative, self-defeating thought patterns; (6) persons diagnosed as having a personality disorder, to help them understand their behavior and develop constructive behavioral patterns. For persons who have a thought disorder, I use role playing to provide structure and encourage organized thinking. I have even used role playing successfully to negotiate a contract with an adolescent: He agreed that if he became suicidal, he would not hurt himself but would role-play what he would say to his parent.

Discussion

Role playing is an essential method of social skills training, and social skills training is an essential element in constructive, effective psychotherapy. If role playing is to be effective, it must be naturally and spontaneously interwoven in the fabric of the therapy hour, just as a good musician improvises melodies and modulates from key to key, as needed. Role playing is a tool that can effect behavior change or increase awareness and insight. As an end unto itself, role playing can be cold rhetoric and simplistic surface manipulation. But combined with a caring and understanding attitude, knowledge of personality factors and human interaction, and a sound philosophy of human development, role playing can be a significant and potent method of effective change and growth in families.

Feedback from clients has been favorable. Clients have consistently said that when a situation arises that is similar to one they have role-played, they think and respond quickly, with positive results. I have seen fearful, anxious, inhibited persons become persons who can telephone, purchase, and make conversation, who can ask for what they want and express feelings both of caring and of anger. I have seen specific negative behaviors change because of the use of social skills training in the psychotherapy session. Children have stopped stealing; parent and child have stopped arguing; couples have expressed feelings of love and caring; employees have held jobs that had been in jeopardy; and young adults have learned to respond to their parents in constructive ways. I have also used role playing with persons who suffer from mental retardation, cerebral palsy, epilepsy, or schizophrenia. I have found role playing especially helpful for gifted students who have difficulty relating to peers, to teachers, and to parents.

CONCLUSION

Role playing is a powerful method of effecting growth and change in families. Used carefully and compassionately, it should be part of the therapeutic armamentarium of every family therapist. Experience and training in role playing will pay handsome dividends to the student of family therapy.

Miscellaneous Methods

Confrontation, Contracts, and Group Composition

We have been able to classify the many promising family therapy methods into three categories: (1) confrontational; (2) contractual; and (3) compositional. Each of these characteristics can be present with the others, even though, it is interesting to note, whoever uses one method usually does not use one of the others. A fourth category of methods not otherwise classifiable in these three categories concludes this chapter.

CONFRONTATIONAL METHODS

In this category we recognize two major classes of methods: (1) methods using audio- or video-play feedback; (2) methods using expressive artistic productions either in the therapist's hands (or mouth) or in the family's past to encourage maximum impact; and (3) forced holding.

Audio-Visual Tapes

Daitzman (1977) reviewed the research and clinical applications and effects of audio and video tape confrontation techniques in family therapy. A variety of new applications, such as cross-confrontation and interpersonal process recall, were integrated into the process of family therapy. Thirteen specific audio-visual self-confrontational methods were reviewed along with positive and negative effects on the user. Alger (1976) uses immediate video playback in family therapy. Another reference to audio and video tape as used in marital problems is Paul and Paul (1975). Photographs, movie films, sound recordings, and videotape are the major forms of confrontational and audio-visual techniques.

As the most novel additions to a therapist's bag of tricks, self-confrontation methods have been abused, applied randomly and unsystematically. For that reason, Daitzman (1977) felt that there was an urgent need for well-designed and relevant research in the area. He warned about the adverse effects of videotaping using a study that reported negative personality changes as a result of videotape playback. These experiments used self-concept measures in which patients came to view themselves less positively following the playback experience. On the basis of these results, Daitzman suggested that it is important to gauge the possible results of videotape feedback on the self-esteem of the family members. He also cited another study in which there were changes in self-concept rather than in self-esteem after the presentation of a variety of subconfrontation techniques. As Daitzman concluded:

> With the advent of audiotape and more recently videotape, a potentially useful adjunct to the psychotherapy process in general—and in the family therapy process in particular—has been introduced. By viewing himself on playback, the family member has access to the most convenient and objective self-image confrontation ever available, and he can immediately and repeatedly view himself and the family system as others would. However, many therapists are failing to utilize the full potential and variety of techniques available when using self-confrontation methods in family therapy. Most novel additions to therapy, subconfrontation techniques are being employed randomly and unsystematically. *A continuum of methods, as well as techniques, should exist for each therapist.* (p. 8)

Guerin (1976) described how movies can be used in family therapy beginning with the film "I Never Sang for My Father" to "Double Solitaire," Bergman's "Scenes from a Marriage" or Cassavettes' "Woman under the Influence." Alger (1976) listed two especially significant values of video playback which need to be emphasized: (1) the possibility of obtaining objective behavioral data and having these data immediately available for integration into an ongoing transaction, making a truly significant development in the therapeutic art and the combining of modalities; (2) the shift of old positions which may occur when the therapist and the family step back from their usual hierarchical positions to that of cooperative interdependence in a common task marks another significant move in making therapy a more truly human and mutual adventure. Many of the advocates of video playback are enthusiastic about its use, but the fact still remains that a complete analysis of videotape interaction reduced to kinetic behavior would cost thousands of dollars.

Anderson and Malloy (1976) used family photographs to facilitate reminiscences of past individual roles, interpersonal relationships, and family dynamics.

Artistic Productions

Among artistic productions we distinguish among (1) drawings, (2) family art therapy, (3) play, (4) puppetry, and (5) storytelling.

Drawings. Geddes and Medway (1977) suggested that there are a variety of several innovative techniques developed in the last ten years for facilitating meaningful communication and interaction among family members. These techniques serve the purpose of highlighting relatively stable patterns of verbal and nonverbal communication among family members and bring to the surface various aspects of family structures, thereby eliminating focal points for intervention. Geddes and Medway presented the symbolic drawing of the family life space. They compared this technique with other techniques for facilitating communication and interaction among family members, illustrating the clinical use of this technique with a case example. In reviewing the literature, the authors extracted two types of symbolic interactive procedures which may be conveniently divided into those that tend to be task centered and those that tend to be expressive modalities. Task-centered procedures have been developed by Minuchin (1974) to facilitate family assessment. Completion of a task, such as replicating a model with a construction blockette or deciding together which family member comes closest to being the most "bossy," the biggest "cry-baby," or the biggest "troublemaker." The same kind of tasks have been used by Watzlawick and his associates (1964, 1970, 1974, 1976). In addition to task-centered procedures, Geddes and Medway (1977) reviewed expressive modalities like symbolic expressive modalities, family sculpting, family art therapy, which eventually led to the symbolic drawing of the family life space which was developed by Mostwin. Mostwin used the symbolic drawing of the family life space as part of a short-term multidimensional family intervention model cited by these authors. This technique can be used in the first therapeutic encounter in this fashion. A large circle is drawn by the therapist on a blackboard or standing easel. The family is told that everything inside this family circle represents what they feel is part of the family. Persons and institutions felt not to be part of their family are placed outside of the family circle in the environment. The family circle and the environment represent the family life space.

Each member of the family is asked in turn to come to the blackboard and place a small circle representing himself or herself within the family circle. The therapist's judgment and intuition determines the order of chosen family members. Even though there are no hard and fast rules, the order may shift from the identified patient to the family unit, but we recommend that the identified patient never be called to the blackboard first. We suggest that the most cooperative family member be asked to start and the rest of the family proceed as they seem free to do. Each family member then proceeds to place himself or herself in the circle in a position relative to other family members in the circle. For the sake of clarity, several different colors of marking pens or pieces of chalk are provided so that each family member can choose a different color. Immediate feedback is given by the therapist to the family member as he places himself in relation to others. At this point the therapist attempts to gain information about the family members' social network by asking the following questions: "Are there any other people who you feel are important enough to be included in this drawing?" Then the family members may place important others, for instance, absent family members or friends, deceased or living, somewhere within or outside the family circle. There may be disagreement among family members about the importance of absent family members. When the disagreement takes place, the therapist notes the perceptual differences diagrammatically by asking the dissenting family member to place the person where *he* feels the person should be in the drawing.

The therapist then asks each family member to place significant social institutions, schools, churches, and community elements in the environment. This means outside of the circle. After the family members have each come to the blackboard to place themselves and significant others, then the therapist instructs the family in the following way: "Now I would like to know how you feel you communicate with the people and institutions in this drawing. By communicate, I mean how you feel you can talk with another person, whether or not that person understands you. In other words, do you get your message across? You have three choices: If you feel that you have good communication with another person, draw a straight line from you to that person like this (and the therapist draws an example of an arrow from one person to another). If you feel that you have so-so communication with another person, sometimes good and sometimes not so good, draw a dotted arrow from you to that person. Finally, if you feel that you have poor communication with another person, draw an arrow slashed twice from you to that person like this (therapist draws an example). So you have three choices: good, so-so, and poor, or no communication at all." At this point the therapist calls each family member, usually in the same order as before, to indicate the quality of his or her communication with the other members of his family, significant others, and social institutions present in the drawing. A gained feedback is provided by the therapist to each family member by reflecting the quality of communication needed. This constant feedback and clarification of the family members' perceptions, coupled with their own diagrammatic presentations of their relationship engages the family actively in the process of self-observation.

Consequently, Geddes and Medway (1977) contend that the symbolic drawing of the family life space serves as: (1) a diagnostic source providing information regarding the structural configuration of the family; (2) a therapeutic tool gauging the degree of intrafamilial congruence, that is, agreement of perception of spatial position within the family, and agreement regarding quality of communication; and (3) a research device providing an effective means of measuring the change of family structure. They then proceed to give examples of symbolic family drawings from their work to illustrate the functions mentioned above. Consequently, the authors observed that this simple technique

> is an effective device for lowering anxiety and reducing blocks to communication, especially in the complex, initial diagnostic encounter. The task is interesting enough to grasp everyone's attention, yet does not require family members to perform or expose themselves prematurely. Its simplicity is one of its greatest assets, as children of 5 or 6 years of age have little difficulty in comprehending the directions. By giving the family an achievable and unthreatening task, use of the symbolic drawing of the family life space engages the family in therapy before they even realize it. (p. 226)

Family Art Therapy.   Sherr and Hicks (1973) presented the case where the use of family art therapy provided immediately highly significant diagnostic data not otherwise observable, and it served as a dramatic catalytic agent for constructive changes as evidenced by subsequent family sessions. The pioneer in family art therapy is Hanna Kwiatkowska (1967), who discussed the importance of this modality of treatment and pointed out that family art therapy sessions were distinguishable from other types of therapy by the fact that the entire family simultaneously became engaged in a form of nonverbal expressive behavior. She suggested that many of the usual inhibitions and defenses did not appear simply because of this new modality, since people did not know how to defend against the request of art therapy. This method uses easels with six drawing pages set up for each member of the family. Each member has chalks or crayons and is given six tasks to perform: (1) a continuous drawing, (2) a picture of the family, (3) an abstract picture of the family, (4) a free scribble drawing, (5) another drawing, and (6) a collaboration by the whole family on one of the scribbles, usually chosen by them, and, finally, (7) another continuous drawing. They are told to give a title to the picture they drew, and at the completion of each step, the entire group together with the therapist sit down and discusses the picture. Sherr and Hicks feel that drawings with families have enabled them to demonstrate the importance of this modality. They report about a family whose son had been treated for two years with drugs and whose parents had been in a parents' group without any significant changes in behavior. Consequently, family therapy was initiated with the inclusion of family art therapy. The question with this kind of case study is whether the same kind of results, if any, would have been obtained if another method had been used. This is a question that is relevant to all methods used in family therapy.

Puppetry.   At the Pittsburgh Child Guidance Clinic and Family Therapy Center of the Western Psychiatric Institute, a number of expressive modalities have been utilized in work with individual groups and families. In addition to the technique of family art used in the previous section, the family puppet interview (Irwin & Malloy, 1975) was used involving the family simultaneously. The family puppet interview generally lasts one-and-a-half hours and can be taped and used later with the family in ongoing therapy. To present the rationale and task of the puppet story, the therapist might say: "The purpose of our meeting is to get to know you as a family. One way to become better acquainted is to ask you to do something together. Sometimes it is difficult at first, especially for kids, to feel comfortable in talking directly about our problems and feelings. At this clinic we have found that this task is made easier when parents and children join together in an activity. So I am going to ask you as a family to play together for a while. Here is a basket of puppets. Take a few minutes to look through them and choose a few that interest you." After the family has chosen a puppet for themselves, the therapist observing the interactions and behaviors, the remainder of the puppets left by the family is put away. Now the following instructions are given:

Now I would like you to work together to make up a story using these puppets. I will go in the next room and watch through the window while you are playing. Just try to decide how this story might begin. It is important that this be a made-up story, not one that you have seen or read.

The therapist excuses himself and leaves (*some prompting and some encouragement may be necessary*), noting what goes on after the family has decided on a story. These stories with the puppets come to natural endings. Sometimes, however, a conflict emerges in the story and the family gets stuck, as in real life, demonstrating their inability to resolve the impasse. In such a situation the therapist can either intervene and help the family find a satisfactory ending, or explore alternative endings that each member may prefer. When the story is either completed or stopped, the therapist can continue the interaction by talking directly to the puppets or suggesting that certain puppets talk to each other about problem areas in the story. It happens sometimes that the family members become quite interested with the puppets and consequently insist that the story end in a certain way. The conflicts among various endings can be used as exploration for significant themes that may appear in the story. When the puppets are put away, the members return to the discussion, where they are encouraged to associate to the story they have just played. Each member might be asked to think of a title for the story, a theme, a moral, or a lesson that one might have learned from the story, the character each would most want to be, and the character each would least like to be, etc. To get some idea of the family's ability to observe, members are asked to comment on ways in which the planning of a story represents the family. The therapist may try to help the family connect the story with issues relevant to complicated areas for the family itself. At the end of each session, the family is thanked for its participation and encouraged to continue to share with each other additional feelings or ideas that may be related to the experience, particularly those that may fit with their own particular family pattern. Irwin and Malloy (1975) present quite a few case studies in which the puppet stories seem to do exactly or fulfill the functions that they want. The puppet stories seem to fit especially families that have difficulty in communicating verbally and that seem to respond with enthusiasm and pleasure to the invitation to play with appealing materials. The experience may afford relief from the usual demand to put things into words. Another kind of family that would seem to benefit by this kind of experience is the highly organized, intellectualized obsessive-compulsive family. In the defense against feeling strongly, members tend to ruminate and intellectualize and in this way their tendency toward play and action is minimum. Insistence on playing out cuts through the process of intellectualization and allows the therapist to get underneath the very strong defense. As Irwin and Malloy (1975) concluded: "The puppet play with its universal character types appears to be a useful procedure for families in lessening either controls or the usual defenses. In emphasizing the make-believe aspect of play, families can often be helped to play, fantasize, and look at family functioning in a non-threatening way."

Storytelling.   Fellner (1976) presented two general factors that have been singled out as being held in common by all types of psychotherapy: (1) educational, rational structure, often called *content*; and (2) a factor of the interrelationship between the therapist and the patient, often called *process*. In the field of family therapy, then, noneducational aspects of intervention are sometimes presented in the form of therapeutic paradoxical communication or in the therapy of the absurd. In this paper Fellner presents a form of therapeutic communication, the teaching stories, that embodies a unique mixture of both educational and paradoxical or absurd communication. Taking a suggestion from Sufi traditions, Fellner gives examples of quite a few stories told to families. Unfortunately, the stories to be told depend a good deal on the therapist herself, her level of sophistication, her knowledge, her inclinations, and her interests, since this use is selective and arbitrary. An example of a story to relate to a resistant family is given by Fellner:

> One evening a man was walking toward his home on the outskirts of the city. As he turned into a deserted street, he saw a group of men coming toward him. His imagination began to work, and he became afraid of what they would do to him— rob him, beat him up, or worse. His fear grew to the point where trying to escape, he jumped over a fence and stumbled into a building site. The men in their turn saw him jump, heard the commotion in the yard, became curious, and some went after him. They found him lying there, frozen in fear, and one said with concern: "What is wrong with you? Can we help you?" Our friend realized his mistake, his fears abated, he got up and started to think rationally again. He turned his attention now to the question of this man who had asked if he could help him. He bent over and said: "Well, it is more complicated than you assume. You see, I am here because of you; and you, you are here because of me."

Another example situation of stories for specific situations is when a certain problem is brought up repeatedly, and the therapist tries to come up with a device for its solution. The story told by Fellner (p. 430) is related to the Zen Master who received a monk who wanted to be enlightened by him. The Master's answer was: "Come again when there is nobody around and I will tell you what it is." The monk waited impatiently for an appropriate moment and sometime later came again to the Master and implored: "Now there is no one about, tell me the secret." The Master said, "Closer." When the monk did so, the Master whispered to him, "This is something that cannot be conveyed by word of mouth." Since there is no simple problem, it follows there is no easy solution, either. As Fellner realized, to share stories is a very personal and private contribution of the therapist. In terms of the distinction between methods and techniques, storytelling at this point falls into the category of techniques that could become a method if they are systematized.

Forced Holding

The purpose of this section is to present forced holding as a method of therapeutic intervention that will help to establish a clear, intergenerational chain of command in the family between the adults and children when such a chain is missing or is inadequate (Johnson, Weeks, & L'Abate, 1979). The technique helps parents reestablish the control and/or authority that has been given up and directed onto one or more children, usually the symptom bearer. This method is used to redistribute power and to make the generational boundaries firmer. It should be used when the therapist asks a child the question, "Who is the boss in the family?" and the child answers in one of the following ways: (1) "I am" or (2) reluctantly wavers between the parents, or (3) contradicts the appropriate verbal answers ("Daddy is") by laughing, making faces, rolling eyes, and by using other disqualifying signals.

Friedman (1970) and Friedman et al. (1978) followed up twenty-five children (twenty-one boys and four girls) where this technique was used, and these are their conclusions:

> (1) With some parents, the physical closeness of holding was either absent or a negative experience for both parent and child; for example, the nurturing aspect of the experience has been observed to increase physical affection between parent and child; (2) using of the holding technique is primarily a physical rather than a verbal experience; (3) although physical, the holding technique is nonpunitive; (4) it does not depend on the prior development of insight; (5) it is quick and decisive and cuts through rationalizations, intellectualizations, and other defenses; (6) it often is an immediate success and establishes a feeling of parental work; (7) it reduces anxiety, hyperactivity, and uncontrollable behavior; (8) it increases the child's verbalization; (9) it focuses responsiblity on the parent as the primary change agent and makes clear that it is the parent, rather than the therapist or the child, who is the key to establishing positive behaviors. This technique has also been described by Friedman (1972) and by Saposnek (1972).

Zaslow and Breger (1969, pp. 246–288) described a similar method for working with autistic children called the "rage reduction method." The cases that will be reported here are not as seriously disturbed as those described by them. In fact, some of the cases discussed by these researchers had previously been defined as hopeless. Zaslow and Breger emphasized the therapist working with the child, although they later found that the method was more effective when the parents continued treatment at home.

This method has been found especially useful in treating single-parent families when there is a power struggle between the remaining parent and one or more children. Typically, the power conflict within the single-parent family assumes one of two forms. First, the remaining parent may impose a "parentified" role onto a given child thereby relinquishing parental authority that is needed by the child (Boszormenyi-Nagy & Spark, 1973). The remaining parent may look to one or more children to assume a "parentified" role by becoming either a pseudospouse and/or pseudoparent in which the child becomes caretaker of the needs of the parent and of the other children. Second, the single parent, by virtue of being a solo parent, is more prone to become inconsistent and overburdened by parenting duties. In both instances, the power boundary between parent and child may become blurred or nonexistent, and the child may believe he or she is as powerful as the parent (Haley, 1976).

Forced holding involves having the child sit on the parent's lap with one of the parent's legs over the child's body to entrap it. The parent's arm should encircle the child's torso and grasp the child's hands. With older children, the child should lie face down on the floor and the parent should straddle the back of the child with the hands pressing firmly down on the shoulders or clasping the hands. In both cases, the area surrounding this activity should be unencumbered and no sharp or hard surfaces should be exposed. Glasses, pens, shoes, and other harmful objects should be removed before the process begins. With larger and stronger children it is advisable for the therapist to help the parent in maintaining control, usually by holding the legs down so that the parent appears to have the most control. Once the parent and child have assumed this position, the therapist has the parent ask the child the question: "Who is the boss?" repeatedly until the child can congruently respond that his parent is the boss. By congruent, it is meant: (1) eye contact is maintained with the parent; (2) the response is in the form of a complete sentence; and (3) there are no distractions or contradictions.

There are a number of procedures and guidelines which should be followed in employing the forced holding method. First, it should be employed early in the therapeutic process. When it is used later the child may feel that he has been betrayed by the therapist(s) and it will take longer to reestablish a trusting relationship with the child. Secondly, assuming that the parent is willing to try the technique, the child may resist sitting on the parent's lap or getting on the floor. A couple of paradoxical maneuvers may be used to get the child in position. One involves telling the child that you know he doesn't want to do what you have asked him, but that when his parent finds out what this is about (s)he will like it a lot less. The other maneuver is to provide a worse alternative to the child. For example, "OK, either you sit on your father's lap or I will pick you up and put you there." Thirdly, the family's first reaction to this method is that it is a game. As the process unfolds, both the child and parent become angry. The child should be encouraged to express his anger through struggling, screaming, crying, pounding fists on the floor, etc.

The parents' anger must be carefully monitored and controlled. The parent should not be permitted to hurt or abuse the child and should be encouraged to maintain a position of loving firmness and control. In the early phase of treatment, the parent should ask repeatedly, "Who is the boss?" Both parent and therapist may challenge the child by saying such things as, "If you are the boss, why can't you get up?" "How can your father do this to you if you are the boss?" When the child reaches the stage of anger and eventual exhaustion and giving up, the parent should shift from a strictly confronting stance (e.g., "Who is the boss?") to a supporting stance (e.g., "I expected you to fight and you're putting up a good one. It hurts me that I didn't settle this a long time ago. It is enough for you just to be responsible for you. I am the parent and I will start taking care or charge of both of us from now on. I want you to enjoy being a child and I will start taking responsibility for being in charge."). The therapist is essentially socializing the parent so that the child may assume the role of child, and the parent may assume the role of nurturing parent who can set limits. Fourthly, the entire process may take two, three, or more hours. The therapist should have adequate time to devote to the process and the parents should be questioned about any time restrictions before beginning. In addition, once the process has started it should not be stopped prematurely. Stopping would constitute a public victory for the child which would add to, rather than reduce, the problem. Finally, when the child does submit, the battle has been won, but the war may be far from over. The child may continue to test the parent's power both verbally and behaviorally. The parent should be aware that this testing will occur. In other words, the therapist should predict that the child will test the parent, perhaps pointing out ways he might do so. To facilitate the maintenance of the verbally established boundary, the family may be given a task (see Haley, 1976; Minuchin, 1974) which should reinforce the parent's position of being in charge.

Further, in the conclusion of the "boss" session, it should be emphasized to the child that he is the boss of himself and that this will take all of his energy. The child could also be congratulated for putting up a good fight and for his insight that his parent is the boss of the family. After finishing the procedure, it is important with intact families to have the father assert that in his absence the mother is the boss and that he backs her up in whatever she may choose to do.

We have used forced holding and found it to be very successful with families seen in therapy as well as in a structured intervention situation such as enrichment (L'Abate, 1976). We will present several cases illustrating when and how to use this method.

Case 1. A single-parent family consisting of a 38-year-old divorced mother and an 11-year-old daughter were seen in therapy. The mother presented the daughter's defiance against her as the main reason for entering therapy. The daughter's defiance was not only against her mother but also against her teachers and friends. Over the course of therapy, it was learned that the mother was inconsistent in setting limits with her daughter; gave in to her daughter's demands, for example, buying whatever she wanted at the grocery store and cooking whatever she wanted for breakfast; looked to her daughter to be an adult; and placated the ex-husband in front of their daughter whenever problems arose concerning the daughter. One of the mother's reported complaints was that her daughter respected her father and wanted to be with him more than her.

It became evident that the daughter saw herself to be as powerful, if not more so, than her mother and that reestablishing the mother's authority was necessary for this family. The question, "Who is the boss?" was asked of the daughter, who quickly answered her father. The question was asked again, except this time the question applied only to the relationship between the daughter and mother. The daughter answered that she was the boss of her mother. The daughter was asked to sit on her mother's lap. She refused the request. Then, she was asked to lie face down on the floor. She agreed, and the mother was instructed to straddle the daughter's back in accordance with the procedure described earlier.

The mother was instructed to ask repeatedly, "Who is the boss?" At first, the daughter treated the event as a game. Later, she began to fight back and at times cried to be released. One of the therapists had to support the mother's hold by securing the daughter's legs. The session lasted one-and-a-half hours before the daughter unequivocally stated that her mother was the boss.

After the daughter's release, the mother was asked to recapitulate her main feelings about her daughter for the first time in therapy. Also, the various ploys used by the daughter in the struggle (e.g., crying and other manipulative behaviors) were explored. From this, the mother began to realize that her daughter also used these same ploys in their relationship in order to get her way.

During the remainder of the session and for several sessions thereafter, the daughter continued to be angry and silent toward the therapists and her mother. Several follow-up sessions were conducted for the purpose of dealing with the daughter's anger toward her mother and discuss how she could assert her power with her daughter and ex-husband.

In this family forced holding marked a breakthrough and a new beginning. The mother began to assert her rightful power and authority so that her daughter could be free to be the child that she needed to be. Also, this method served as a vehicle for opening up the mother and child to a deeper expression of their feelings toward each other.

Case 2.   An adopted 5-year-old boy was referred by a pediatrician and a learning specialist for hyperactivity and inability to get along with other children in kindergarten. His parents were also referred for marital counseling and were seen for six sessions before the child was seen. The whole family suffered from a great many psychosomatic diseases—obesity, allergies, and skin conditions. The child, especially, suffered from the same allergies specific to his adoptive father. The mother, who was quite obese and suffered from an unidentified blood disease, had a history of extreme familial deprivation; for example, her mother had committed suicide in front of her in her teens. The father was a workaholic who spent seventy hours a week on the job. Before the child was seen, the parents were probed about who was the boss at home. They reported that the child had replied assuredly: "I am."

When the child came in, he started showing extreme negativism and hyperactivity by not sitting still in his chair and calling attention to himself repeatedly. His restlessness in the chair continued in spite of his adoptive father's repeated admonishments to "be quiet." He agreed to sit on his father's lap, but when questioned again about who was the boss, he started struggling, claiming that he "hurt" and that he could not "breathe." Once he saw that his father meant business and that he would hold him firmly and not release him, he started crying heavily with intermittent coughing. The crying continued for about fifteen minutes; then the child was able to whisper: "You, Daddy, are the boss." He was asked to say it louder for everybody to hear. After he complied with eye contact he was asked to acknowledge that mother was the boss when father was absent. After this acknowledgment, he sat quietly between the parents except for suddenly brightening up and getting up to pick up a red box beyond the back of the therapist. When the father said, "No," he started crying and sat back again between the parents.

Since the major complaint of the adoptive parents was one of not being heard by the child, they were instructed on how to use a time-out sequence procedure. Thus, if and when they said something to him that was not carried out, he would be asked to repeat what the parent(s) had just said, told to carry it out, and then go to his room for five minutes. He could get out of the room whenever the kitchen timer would ring at the end of five minutes. They were also given a time sheet to chart the frequency of these episodes. As these instructions were given in the therapy session, the child, who had been completely still, fell asleep and had to be awakened to leave. His negativism toward the therapists continued; for example, as he left, he refused to shake hands or to respond to their queries. The mother was worried that this time-out method had to be carried out to the letter without anger and that for the first four days she would find it very difficult to carry it out, since the child could try to defeat her.

An appointment with the parents alone was made within a week with the understanding that results and therapy with them would continue for some time. In subsequent sessions, the parents reported a considerable improvement in the child's behavior almost to the point of being "no problem" and "a pleasure."

Case 3. A single-parent family comprised of a 30-year-old professional mother with two boys, one nine and the other eight, were referred for therapy. The symptom carrier was the 8-year-old son, who had a history of sporadic encopresis, constant bedwetting since birth, and general hyperactivity and rebelliousness. Forced holding was instituted after three evaluation sessions.

During the session, the mother picked up immediately on the instructions and demanded in a very determined and assertive manner to know who was the boss. The child, who was being held in the position described earlier, replied laughingly but clearly to her question: "I am." The mother contradicted him, and a struggle ensued whereby the child eventually curled up on the floor with his mother pinning him down on his hands and sitting on him for about forty-five minutes. The child was determined to hold out for the whole hour, because he kept asking for the time from his brother, who eventually was told to be quiet and not to answer. During the struggle the therapists helped the mother in asserting that she was the boss. The mother was told that the child had to give the straightforward and complete message—"You, Mother, are the boss."

Also, the boy was told that he would need to be the boss of his body and that this responsibility would require all his efforts and energy. Eventually, he was able to give the required congruent message without hesitation, with eye contact, with clear voice, without contradictory facial signs, and seriously.

After his release, the matter of bedwetting was brought up, which up to this time had not been considered. He was given the choice of using a "buzzer pad" that would wake him up if and when he started to wet, or going to the bathroom before going to bed with his taking responsibility to remind himself that he needed to go just before going to bed. Some doubt was expressed by the therapists about whether he would be able to assume responsibility for his body. The boy called the next morning to report that he "did not do it," indicating that this was the first time in his life in which he had awakened to a dry bed. After two weeks of dry nights (except for one relapse), he was asked whether he could wet the bed again in order to earn a reward in money. He refused. After two follow-up sessions, therapy was terminated to everyone's satisfaction.

Case 4.   In this case, a 6-year-old boy was referred for bullying and "fomenting" a revolution with his peers in a private school. The father was a professional man in his early thirties, and the mother was a professional mental health worker. A younger 4-year-old sister completed the family. The mother spent a great deal of time in the initial session explaining how the boy had been raised according to the latest psychodynamic practices in which she had avoided "hurting the ego" of the child. During the session, it became clear that the parents were overpermissive and did not set limits on the child. Also, the father seemed cowed by his wife's superior knowledge of "psychodynamic practices" and seemed unable to establish his role as a father.

While the parents were talking, the boy kept distracting through such behaviors as getting up, moving around the room, and speaking out of turn. The boy was quite articulate and bright, and his school grades were excellent. When the boy was asked: "Who is the boss in this family?" he laughed loudly and vacillated between his parents. The boy was obviously using one parent to deny the power of the other through pointing and wavering between them: "You are; no, you are." The boy continued to treat the question as if it were a game.

At this point, the father was instructed on how to hold the child. The child willingly sat in his father's lap and the father was told to ask him the question again. As predicted, the boy laughed and started wiggling to break his father's hold. When he saw the father meant business and would not let go, he started crying, trying to get his mother to come to his rescue. She seemed too shocked to respond and said nothing, even though her eyes and facial features conveyed a pained expression of fear, anxiety, and protectiveness. Eventually, the boy stopped crying and was able to comply with the question by saying clearly and straightforwardly: "You, Daddy, are the boss." Next, the boy was told to acknowledge that when his father was gone, his mother would be the boss. After being released by his father, the boy sat quietly for the rest of the session.

On a second visit, the father was able to show that he was in control by clearly telling the boy to: "Sit down and be quiet, please. You can talk when mother and father are finished." The mother reported being greatly relieved from having to take so much responsibility for the child's behavior. A six-month follow-up indicated that the child's school problems had disappeared and everyone in the family was getting along fine.

Case 5. A single-parent family consisting of a 32-year-old, divorced, professional woman with two children—a girl aged ten and a boy aged seven—applied for family enrichment. The mother stated that she was concerned about frequent bickering between the children, about her son's attitude and emotional development because of not having a father in the home, and about communication. The mother had been divorced for several years.

During the course of enrichment, we observed that the mother was overpermissive with the children and was unable to establish a firm boundary between herself and both children. The mother especially allowed the boy privileges that infringed on the rights of her daughter. The daughter was expected to adopt an adult role and to be tolerant of her brother. The boy was observed to be hyperactive and demanding of his mother's attention, as he talked about himself continually and was very affectionate with his mother. It became apparent that the boy had more power than anyone else and that he was usually able to manipulate his mother to get whatever he wanted. When asked, he proudly admitted that he was the boss of the family, although his mother and sister protested.

During the fifth session, the subject of who was boss in the family was explored again. The boy maintained that he was still the boss. We asked him to sit in his mother's lap, which he did. The mother held both of his wrists while he continued to say that he was the boss. We told him that his mother would hold him until he told who was *really* boss in their family. The boy at first tried to kiss his mother. Later, he struggled more vigorously, although he was laughing in the process. Eventually, he began kicking, biting, pleading, and crying. The mother continued to wrestle with him and was surprised at his refusal to admit that she was boss. We continued to speak in a calm manner, saying, "Go ahead and tell her, so you can get loose. She knows who is the boss. It is hard to give up being boss when you have been in charge so long. It must be a hard job to be boss, why don't you just take a rest from it? Maybe you are afraid she won't love you, if you are not boss anymore." With this last statement, the boy shook his head in agreement with a deluge of tears. We also told him that he would see that his mom loved him because he was himself and not because he was smart or powerful.

In all, the struggle lasted about ninety minutes, placing us well beyond the limits we had set for the session. Finally, the boy tried to get away once more. He began hitting his mother with his fists, screaming, "You are, you are, you are!" His mother let him go. We suggested that he might enjoy being a 7-year-old again and knowing that he did not have to work so hard.

In a follow-up visit one month later, we asked each family member whether there had been any changes in the family since our last visit. The boy reported that he was no longer able to be the boss and gave several examples where he was complying with his mother's limits. The mother substantiated that her son was more cooperative and that the bickering between him and his sister had decreased. The boy also seemed very pleased to see the enrichers, and the mother reported that he saw us as friends.

Case 6.   A single parent family comprised of a mother aged twenty-eight and her 6-year-old twin daughters were seen in therapy. The mother was experiencing difficulty disciplining the children and complained about the constant fighting between the children. Although the children did not exhibit serious behavior problems in the therapy sessions, it was observed that they frequently did not mind their mother. When asked who the boss was in the family both children replied (with a burst of enthusiasm), "I am." On hearing the children's response mother giggled half-heartedly and acknowledged her lack of control and authority in the family.

At this point, the children were asked to lie on the floor and the mother straddled herself across both of them. All three family members responded initially by laughing at the "game" the therapist had them playing. After several minutes of laughing, the children began struggling to get up, but were unable to do so. When asked again who the boss was, both children replied that they were. The game-like quality of forced holding subsided as the children struggled harder and harder to get up, and mother exerted more and more energy to keep them down. Despite their inability to get free of mother's grasp, neither child would let go of the notion that they were boss. The struggling persisted and both children became quite upset, screaming and crying to be released, yet unwilling to acknowledge that mother was truly the boss in the family. After forty minutes of forced holding one of the twins gave in and acknowledged that mother was boss. A few minutes later her sister also submitted. Susie, the second twin to give in, was quite upset as the forced holding came to an end. She was crying a great deal and mother responded to her crying by holding and nurturing her. This was the most overt showing of nurturant mother behavior on the part of Mrs. J. in the therapy sessions. At the end of the session, one of the twins said she had to use the bathroom. Her sister responded by saying she knew where it was and would take her. Mrs. J. reacted by saying that they were to wait and that she would take them in a minute. Rather than objecting and putting up a fight, the children readily obeyed.

Mrs. J. was next seen alone six weeks later. She reported that for several weeks following the forced holding session the children had fought less with each other and were generally more obedient. However, Mrs. J. stated that after several weeks she began to interact less frequently with the children and to spend less time with them. This regression coincided with a return to the previous pattern of fighting and misbehaving in the twins.

Case 7. In this single-parent family forced holding was not successful. The family consisted of a mother, a teen-aged daughter, and a 12-year-old girl who was the symptom bearer. The mother refused to carry out the physical struggle as instructed, although the 12-year-old was sitting in her lap. Instead, the mother made verbal pleas rarely heeded by the daughter. The oldest daughter, who was the parentified child, assumed major responsibility for correcting her sister, corrections which resulted in a long series of bickering episodes that were helplessly watched by the mother. The mother refused physical involvement and confrontation with her daughter when the struggle became tough, because the mother said that she needed to behave like a "lady," and to her, a physical struggle was not "lady-like." Consequently a time-out procedure was instituted as a solution to the problems in this family.

This case serves as an example of how important it is to assess whether a parent wants to assume control and to be responsible as a parent. Forced holding will not be effective unless the parent is ready and well prepared to assume this responsibility.

Discussion

Forced holding is similar to methods used by Erickson (1962) and Zaslow and Breger (1969). Haley (1973) has also described in detail this technique as used by Erickson. However, there are differences between our technique and the others referenced here. For example, Erickson's case involved the rebellious behavior of an 8-year-old boy in a single-parent family (Haley, 1973). His basic technique is similar to ours, except that Erickson had the mother and son perform the technique at home, whereas we advocate that it is most effective when applied in the office where the therapist(s) can directly monitor the procedure. Using the technique in the office under the therapist's direction and support is especially applicable to single-parent families, since the parent may resist or waver in completing the method. Also, for physical reasons, such as with older children, the sole parent may not be able to restrain the child physically without the physical support of the therapist. Further, it has been our experience that forced holding often results in a deep emotional experience for the parent(s) and child. It is recommended that it can only be used safely in the presence of a therapist who can facilitate this emotional experience for the benefit of the entire family.

Another added benefit to using this method in the office is that it affords the opportunity for observing first-hand the interaction between the parent and child during their power struggle. For example, the child typically uses ploys, for example, crying and manipulative behaviors, in trying to outmaneuver the parent and therapist in order to get his or her own way. Exploring the reactions of the parent and child after the struggle and exploring the child's ploys during the struggle will increase the parent's awareness of how the child has been successful in winning past power struggles at home and in other situations.

Conclusion

Forced holding has been presented as a method of intervention for reestablishing intergenerational boundaries between parents and children where the child feels he or she is in charge or in power within the family. The method serves the function of rechanneling authority and power back to the parents, thus facilitating the children in assuming the role of children and the parents in assuming the role of parents. The conditions under which this method is to be applied were described and illustrated through seven case studies. Some of the conditions for application of this method were that it be used (1) in the presence of a therapist; (2) when it is indicated that the parent(s) wants and is capable of assuming parental responsibilities; and (3) when therapeutic follow-up support can be provided for assisting the parent(s) in maintaining authority.

CONTRACTUAL METHODS

Both major schools of therapy, that is, behavioral and dynamic, use contracts even though the nature of these contracts can be quite different, depending on the therapist's theoretical orientation. Firestone and Moschetta (1975) considered the use of behavioral contracts in family therapy and suggested that these contracts are especially important in dealing with adolescents and to help in the process of negotiation and renegotiation. They give a case example of a 15-year-old girl who had engaged in a constant struggle with both parents for the past three years. At the urging of school officials, both parents sought family counseling with Kathy because she was failing in five or six subjects in school and was often truant. She also repeatedly stole money and jewelry from her mother. She preferred the company of teenagers and demanded freedom from her parents that she could not handle appropriately. She was rebellious and argumentative and argued constantly with her mother, refusing to take responsibility for household chores. They were seen in family therapy for two evaluative sessions and some of the background of the parents in terms of their deprivations came out, and their inability to get close and to use positive methods of parenting, since none of these methods had been available to them as they grew up. In short, both parents were unable to meet Kathy's emotional needs.

Eventually the therapists were able to draw a contract between the parents and the adolescent girl which dealt with chores that Kathy would perform in exchange for receiving increases in allowance and permission to go out on week nights and participation in extracurricular activities, and extension in curfew times. The contract dealt with chores in the home, attendance in school, refraining from "borrowing" her mother's jewelry, and respecting all curfew hours. With the structure of the contract, the family was able to experience some success in changing old patterns of relating with each other for the first time in many years. Their success depended strongly on whether the family members felt strong enough to risk disclosing themselves more than they had thus far, especially as far as the parents were concerned in regard to their marriage.

As Firestone and Moschetta concluded: "Making therapeutic inroads where dysfunctional family systems are already established necessitates overcoming substantial resistance. The behavioral here and now orientation of the contracting process is less threatening to anxious family members frightened by the notion of "psychotherapy." Contracting sesions allow family members to experience the therapist as neutral and nonthreatening. If adequately fulfilling his role, the therapist is viewed as a guide or moderator providing a safe process for free expression." They add that timing is of the utmost importance in the use of any treatment technique, but that utilization of the contracting approach needs to take place during the initial phase of treatment in order to hook the family, especially in terms of hooking the resistant family, into treatment. Hence, contracting seems to be a relatively safe technique that can be introduced at the beginning.of treatment and will provide some change in the process of family therapy.

Group Composition

Among methods using group composition we recognize at least four independent categories: (1) three-generation families, where grandparents are included; (2) major social network including distant relatives, friends, and neighbors; (3) two or more families in therapy; and (4) multiple impact therapy, where various therapists work with different family members.

Three-Generation Families. This method is used so extensively that it is difficult to find specific references to it. The reader is referred to the work of Boszormenyi-Nagy and Sparks (1973) as an illustration of the theory and background of inclusion of grandparents *when available.*

Network Interventions. Rueveni (1979) presented one case story of a couple who initially sought help for marital problems, but continued in therapy by including their 16-year-old son and ended up with a network assembly of thirty-five members—relatives, friends, and neighbors—meeting at home to help solve the family's ongoing conflicts. The full network meetings provided the Kellys with a supportive group of concerned, active people, network activists whom they could begin to trust and with whom they could share some of the previously difficult relationships, concerns, and unrealistic expectations of each other. The Kellys' network continued meeting on their own for three months. Network news reports and telephone contacts with the family members indicated continued progress in the relationship between David and his mother, and less confrontation and more adequate communication among all family members.

Doldorf (1976) presented a study that investigated areas of stress and support using the structural model of social network. The social network model, which is borrowed from sociology and anthropology, is used to describe and quantify not only the individual's immediate family, but also all of those individuals with whom the individual maintains contact. In comparing the network of a sample of normal and schizophrenic males, Doldorf found a possible identified difference between their relationships in the social network, in the makeup of the networks themselves, and in the coping styles and recent histories of the subjects. The results of this study suggested that the network model can be used to investigate the larger social system from which the individuals interact, and secondly, it may be a valuable approach to the expansion of family research.

Erickson (1964) has generalized the concept of social network to the concept of personal network, which he feels is a major unifying framework in his clinical practice. After reviewing the developing trends of network practice, he examined some of the forms of characteristics of personal networks and considered theoretical and practical issues. He considered (1) network as a curative grouping, (2) network as a resource grouping, (3) network as interpreted by health-seeking behavior, and (4) network as mitigator of the effects of multiorganizational involvement. He then goes from social network to personal network. Erickson defined a personal network as:

> A flexibly bounded grouping of individuals comprising at least a focal person, everyone the focal person knows or interacts with, the set of relationships between those individuals and the focal person, the set of relationships that exist independently of the focal person. A minimal personal network in practice would contain (for a member of an intact nuclear family): (1) the focal person, a marital pair, a nuclear family, a bilateral extended grouping; in short, an unclear sector, (2) a number of friends, acquaintances, neighbors, workmates; what would be called a friendship sector, (3) a social worker, physician, clergyman, and others who stand in relationship to the focal person as a socially sanctioned helping person; in short, a serving or a caretaking sector. (p. 103)

In terms of advantages, the personal network, according to Erickson, offers the following immediate advantages: (1) a sufficiently large number of relationships is included as conflicts for understanding of behavior; (2) a number of intervention points can be envisaged within the network; (3) a number of compatible relationship theories and intervention strategies can be utilized; (4) large areas of social science can be integrated in the structure of the framework; and (5) the clinicians and other care givers are included in the network, and by including one or more organizations, their policies, and their programs are included as legitimate subjects of interest. The value of network analysis is its attempt to link together kinship, friendship, and care-giving systems rather than keeping these separate.

Multiple Family Group Therapy (MFGT)

According to Strelnick (1977) MFGT has been employed in a wide variety of settings and for many purposes. It has been used in general community hospitals, in state psychiatric hospitals, and in private psychiatric hospitals, community health centers, psychiatric base centers, prisons, with alcoholic couples, drug addicts, chronic schizophrenics, families of hemodialysis and intensive care patients, in child guidance clinics, inpatient schools, and growth groups.

As Strelnick reports,

> several attempts to evaluate outcome through questionnaires, clinical impressions, or family self-evaluation. Few attempt to assess variables in outcome more rigorously. Almost all ignore the existing literature on family process and therapy and on MFGT, so many observations are repetitious and/or unvalidated. Few questions on the indications for therapy have been raised, and few problems for research have been outlined. In general, the field is in a primitive state of development with only a major single contributor (Laqueur) and no empirical studies on process or outcome despite the scope of clinical and descriptive studies (p. 323).

One question that needs to be answered has to do with the relationship between network intervention and multiple family therapy.

One of the important components of this method is the composition of the families making up a whole group. Should these models be open regardless of age or socioeconomic background? Should they be heterogeneous? Should they be homogeneous as far as any variables of socioeconomic background or age? Methods used have been role playing and psychodrama and enactment of concrete family situations with commentary reactions in behavioral alternatives coming from the group. The therapist's responsibilities and goals vary with each author, and there is no uniformity of practice in most of the literature. The group seems to go through various stages of development. One is the pregroup stage when the group, meeting together, is still dominated by an external order rather than an organization of its own. Initially, the focus is on the scapegoat patient as the problem and keeping the problem inside the patient. Patients are usually quiet, compliant, and separate from families. The parents usually carry the burden of interruption, and the communication at this point is fairly superficial and trivial. Parents and children do not communicate. The second stage is reached when more group support emerges, and by the third to the fifth meeting there is an organization in development or role and power struggles within the family, even though parental conflicts are still denied. The division between "sick" and "well" members is beginning to fade out. The third stage is a working period characterized by significant group interaction. Finally, there are exchanges between parents and across generational lines, and marital problems and role expectations begin to emerge. The final stage of consolidation-termination-decreased anxiety is characterized by a family's organization in an alternate state of homeostasis.

The goals of MFGT are essentially to get the patient well and integrated into the family and to improve family communication. A later goal is to increase the awareness of interaction and communication taking place in the family. A fourth goal is the clarification of family and marital roles. MFGT has been employed for a wide variety of populations and settings where families are involved in the treatment process, whether voluntarily or otherwise. Methods used to promote the working group have been borrowed heavily from group therapy and include therapist modeling, role playing, and psychodrama. The composition of the group and the definition of the relevant family members or significant others who should participate vary with the design and purpose of specific groups. No consensus on co-therapist roles exists, although their communication is emphasized.

Discussions on the process of MFGT usually center on both the parenting and family role expectations, the marital climate of families, the relation of the family to the mental health of its members, and the relationship among dependents in individuation, separation, and differentiation. The most common theme is family communication on all levels.

In a review of the literature on multiple family therapy systems, Benningfield (1978) gives a basic historical development of this method, as well as reports of multiple family therapy groups found in the literature. The characteristics of this treatment method are delineated with special attention to the elements of change attributed to it and each stage of development. Some implications for research are outlined, indicating that this method is lacking in adequate validation as a treatment modality. Possible advantages inherent in multiple family therapy systems which have been suggested by Laquer's clinical findings are also reported. It is clear that a great deal of the outcome of the process still rests in the personality and techniques of the therapist.

Multiple Impact Therapy (MIT)

Multiple impact therapy is an approach that was used by the Outpatient Psychiatric Clinic for Adolescents at the University of Texas Medical Branch Hospital at Galveston, Texas. It is a diagnostic and therapeutic intervention using the entire time and facilities of a psychiatric team in different combinations with a family for two-and-a-half days (McGregor, Ritchie, Serrano, & Schuster, 1974).

This is a final report of a clinical project using families who consult a child guidance clinic and live a great distance away. They are housed in a hospital for two-and-a-half days and treated in this way.

MISCELLANEOUS METHODS

Among methods that cannot be clarified within the three previous categories we can consider: (1) home visits and (2) activities like camping, hiking, sports, etc.

Home visits were made by Prosky (1974) in which she gave a verbatim account. Sperekas (1974) described the experience of a mental health team as part of the Denver General Hospital's Community Mental Health Center, delivering direct treatment services to families in the homes. This team had professionals and paraprofessionals on their staff. The goals of the team were (1) to relate history evaluation to the formulation of the strengths and weaknesses of a family; (2) increase reality testing with respect to the true focus of the family problems; (3) find out if home-based therapy experience is more comfortable for the families; (4) explore the intense involvement of the therapist required in the home. "Occasionally we found it imperative to have a family come to the clinic for its sessions," Sperekas noted. "Sometimes the home setting was just too chaotic. There were too many interruptions or sometimes a family played quite expertly the game of uproar, making so much noise that the therapist could not hear himself think. The clinic, in these cases, allowed us to establish some sense of order, whereupon we were able to move back to the home." Sperekas noted that the unusual nature of the team involvement with the clients in the home made it difficult to prevent reinforcement of a certain degree of family dependency. Besides complicating the treatment process, this tendency made it difficult to do time-limited therapy. Termination became a complex and painful process and the family had difficulty in accepting the termination of a friendly relationship. In the clinic the family leaves the clinician, while in the home the clinician leaves the family. This termination sometimes increased the feelings of rejection on the part of the family. In short-term cases the decision was to have the therapy in the clinic. This study fails to indicate any advantage of the home visit over the family's going to the clinic. The exception would be when a medical problem precludes one or more client from going to the clinic. In these cases treatment in the home allows the clinician to become more involved with the broader spectrums of the family's home life, forcing the therapist to share the problems and to participate directly in the therapeutic process. It clearly makes the treatment more realistic.

Tooley (1975) suggested the home visit as a diagnostic and training method to sensitize trainees to the details of family life that are discussed in consultation and supervision.

CONCLUSION

In this chapter we have reviewed briefly the promising miscellaneous methods of family therapy that are easily *replicable*. The major issues with these methods lie in their replicability and their selective usage, (i.e., when can they best be used with what kind of families?). The field of family therapy does not lack for methods but it *does* lack for tested *methods*.

12

The Goals of Family Therapy

Toward a Negotiated Life Style

The purpose of this chapter is (1) to argue that improved negotiation skills among family members is the ultimate goal of therapy, and (2) to present an eclectic model for negotiation that can be applied to most families in trouble.

THE GOALS OF FAMILY THERAPY

Freeman (1981, pp. 9–15) considered the goal-setting process an important therapeutic endeavor. These goals should be specific and clearly defined. He defined at least four levels of goal setting: (1) individual, (2) familial, (3) command, and (4) therapeutic. The family simultaneously works for seemingly contradictory goals: (1) the autonomy and competence of its members, and (2) loyalties and commitments to the family, which Freeman (as well as others) maintain are present in all families, both clinical and nonclinical.

It is important, according to Freeman, to distinguish short-term from long-term goals. An immediate goal may be to obtain symptomatic relief, while long-term goals would be to (1) improve communications; (2) feel accepted as individuals; (3) relieve the symptom-bearer from his or her role; (4) develop more flexible assumption of leadership by any family member as situations require; (5) improve empathy and understanding; (6) improve ability to deal with and accept differences; (7) improve individual and family problem-solving abilities; (8) decrease externalization and victimization; (9) improve sensitivity to its internal functioning; (10) improve autonomy and individuation; and (11) develop a functional balance between individual autonomy and family solidarity.

Grosser and Paul (1964) considered nine specific goals of family therapy. These goals related to unconscious fantasies and effects, empathy, reality testing, frustration tolerance, internal and external relationships, and the eventual loss of the therapist at termination.

Of course, for Bowen (1966) the major goal of therapy lies in the differentiation of self within the family, with all the implications that this term implies. According to Speck and Attneave (1973), the goals of network therapy are to (1) activate latent strengths; (2) change attachments; and (3) clarify communications.

According to Bell (1975), the family should be led to use its own value system to erect its own goals with the therapist assuming the role of facilitator, but not introducer of the family's goal setting. At the other extreme of the activity continuum, Haley (1976) is very clear about *avoiding leaving goals unformulated:*

> It is often more difficult to formulate goals for marital problems than for other kinds. Yet, out of negotiations with the couple should come goals. If a therapist does not have a destination, his path to get there is likely to meander. (p. 166)

The goal setting should be done by the family, even though its staging is started by the therapist, according to Haley.

Rabiner, Molinski, and Gralnick (1962) were the first to consider the goals of family therapy in an inpatient setting, the last of which was to alter family communication patterns to make the discharge a constructive process. Ranz and Ferber (1972) see the goals of therapy as an amalgam of what the family and therapist wish they could change.

In their assessment of the goals of family therapy, Sprenkle and Fisher (1980) found that goals enunciated or ranked by 316 clinical members of AAMFT reflected no single "school" of family therapy, and most of them included encouraging family members to relate to each other caringly, responsibly, and creatively in *negotiating* (underlining ours!) their differences. Thus, even though these common goals were identified, how are therapists and families to achieve them? Haphazardly? Chaotically? Hysterically? Many therapists, one ventures to assert, do not even know how the process of negotiation takes place in their own lives let alone in the lives of the couples and families they seek to help.

Lewis (1980) listed fourteen interactional variables associated with family competence. One of these is what he called *goal-directed negotiation*; that is, the manner in which families solve problems. "Efficient negotiation involves the exploration of each member's opinions and feelings, the search for a consensus, or the ability to compromise." (p. 14).

Boszormenyi-Nagy and Spark (1973) agree with Freeman (1980) that individual and family goals are inseparable from each other. The therapist should consider the family's goals rather than his own. To specify the difference between goals of therapists and goals of families we need to separate and use the distinction between content and process; that is, a family needs to concern itself with what is negotiated, which is its own private business. Therapists, on the other hand, need to concern themselves with *how* issues are negotiated (or failed to be negotiated) within each family. Thus, families are responsible for *content*; therapists are responsible for the *process*. This distinction, then, allows us to reconcile the goals of therapy for therapists and families.

The work of Waring (1980a, b) and of Reiss (1981) consistently points out that one of the major deficiencies present in dysfunctional couples and families lies in problem solving, that is, they do not have skills to initiate and carry out over a prolonged period of time decision making, bargaining, and negotiating. These consistent findings support the position taken by Alexander and Parsons (1982) that interventions could be clarified according to a crisis-oriented therapy in a beginning phase, skill-oriented and educationally based training in a second phase, and thirdly a termination phase. In other words, the field of family therapy could stand some infusion of skill-training programs (L'Abate, 1981) that would enhance, complement, and supplement the effects of therapy. Such a combination is possible, as demonstrated by work in our laboratory (L'Abate, 1977; L'Abate & Rupp, 1981). We all need to learn how to negotiate, since many of us never had an opportunity to learn.

Thus, the goals of therapy are two-fold: (1) on the therapist's side, to teach couples and families the skills of negotiation (process); while (2) couples and families need to focus on the issues they need to negotiate about (content). We need to teach the *how*; they, the family, need to settle on the *what*. These skills need to transcend the therapy office and need to be practiced in the kitchen, the bedroom, and the dining table.

An important advantage of reduction of therapy to negotiation lies in the fact that negotiation can be studied experimentally, while therapy as a whole cannot. This is the main *raison d'etre* for this review.

NEGOTIATION

Mace and Mace (1980) stressed the importance of negotiation in enriching marriages:

> Negotiation is the key word. All human conflict at any level is the same basically, whether it is the kids squabbling in the background, or a husband and a wife, or labor and management, or the impending strike, or a war. The process is always the same and the process is negotiation.
> It may be, in fact, that in learning how to negotiate in marriage it is more important and will have longer range beneficial effects than the outcomes of specific negotiations. (p. 105)

One would add that learning how to negotiate would be beneficial for whole families, even though admittedly children will learn to negotiate to the extent that their parents do (or don't). The variety of descriptions of processes in negotiations will be summarized later on in a table where the various stages described by different sources can be located (Table 12-1).

Definitions

Aldous (1971, p. 279) defined problem solving as synonymous with the process of negotiation, presenting a six-step framework in interaction with family characteristics (age and sex structure, ongoing group maintenance, communication structure, affective structure, and power structure).

The concept of negotiation has two other similar terms which are related to it. They are bargaining and problem solving. Here negotiation will be considered as a process that may start with bargaining as the beginning point ending toward problem solving. Thus, bargaining and problem solving are seen as the beginning and the end of the negotiating process, respectively.

Rubin and Brown (1975) defined bargaining as "the process whereby two or more parties attempt to settle what each shall give and take, or perform and receive, in a transaction between them" (p. 2). The give and take usually concerns "division or exchange of one or more specific resources and/or resolution of one or more intangible issues among the parties or among those whom they represent" (p. 10). Proposals and counterproposals and evaluation of each in terms of cost and rewards is part of the process of bargaining. Rubin & Brown also summarized the individual differences in bargainers.

Hayes-Roth (1981) performed five experiments that confirmed that (1) people can adopt different strategies in the allocation of cognitive resources during problem solving; (2) people can learn new strategies from explicit instructions or from experience; (3) problem characteristics can influence which strategy people adopt; and (4) adopted strategy interacts with problem characteristics to determine planning time, number, and importance of planned sessions. But what is negotiated? Among other things, power!

POWER, DECISION MAKING, AND NEGOTIATION

There have been a variety of definitions of power as in interpersonal context (Schopler, 1965). Power has been equated to energy in the physical realm and, as such, it is difficult to define and to assess. Some people suggest that this concept could be done away with completely as being too vague and too difficult to assess, while others consider it the basic ingredient of decision making (French & Raven, 1959; Haley, 1976). Perhaps this construct would become useful if we were to define power in terms of two components: authority and responsibility. Authority refers to who has the power to make decisions, and responsibility refers to who has the power to carry out those decisions. Thus, authority is the process of decision making, while responsibility is the process of implementing such decisions. Oftentimes, both authority and responsibility reside in the same individual, if and when that individual makes strictly self-relating decisions. On the other hand, a variety of decisions involve more than one person. More specifically, in marriage there are a variety of decisions that need to be carried out, like, for instance, house-cleaning, cooking, child-caring, and finances. Oftentimes, under such circumstances, authority and responsibility may become split, that is, one individual may have all the decision-making powers while the other has all the responsibility to carry out decisions. Furthermore, the spouse who has the authority but not the responsibility is the one who wants to retain such an arrangement. Under these conditions, the marriage becomes a boss-servant relationship rather than a partnership. Depending on how ingrained and rigid this arrangement may be, it may or may not be functional for the parties involved. While the split between authority and responsibility is commonly seen in spouses, it can be found also in parent-child relationships, where the parent wants the authority, and the child takes or refuses responsibility depending on the extent to which he or she conforms to the parental decision making. However, if the authority is inconsistent, coercive, or rigid, the child may develop oppositional or rebellious behaviors that question the parental authority. Hence, a vague construct like power can be reduced to specific visible processes of decision making (authority) and carrying out or implementing decisions (responsibility). Dysfunctionality takes place whenever both processes are not satisfactorily negotiated.

Authority supposedly should be commensurate to responsibility. However, this is not always the case, especially in intimate relationships. Oftentimes (L'Abate, 1975c) fathers want the authority but not the responsibility and some wives collude with them in this arrangement. By the same token, some men relinquish decision-making authority to avoid assuming responsibility. This may result in conflict and dysfunctionality if the conflict is not resolved.

Thus, power becomes a highly visible and observable concept when it is reduced to who makes the decisions more often about what issues (authority) and who carries out and translates such decisions into tasks and chores. For instance, in analyses of house chores many supposedly egalitarian couples claim equal responsibility. However, when one observes who does what, it often becomes apparent that the woman is still more likely the one who completes these chores. The issue here is that power, like most anything else in life, needs to be negotiated.

NEGOTIATIONS: THE SHARING OF POWER

Despite the large amount of research literature on the issue of power in the family (Cromwell & Olson, 1975; Alkire, 1972; Bahr, Bowerman, & Gecas, 1974; Bowerman & Bahr, 1973; Swingle, 1976; McDonald, 1980) and the importance of this concept in family functioning and decision making (Haber, 1976), very little of this literature has filtered into the everyday language of family therapists. The reasons for such a neglect may be multiple and perhaps irrelevant to the issue at hand, and that is: *Whatever power may be in the family, it needs to be negotiated. In order to be negotiated, it needs to be shared by everybody in the family.* To achieve this end a clear definition of power needs to be given as being split into two important but conceptually and practically separate concepts: authority, who makes the decisions; and responsibility, who carries out the decisions.

Inability to negotiate derives from feelings of inadequacy, powerlessness, and a genuine lack of appropriate skills. Consequently, this inability is the outcome of prolonged social deviance and/or isolation that has produced poor motivation to negotiate and inadequate negotiating skills. Thus, Negotiation Potential (NP) in this model is the outcome of the following multiplicative factors: Health × Ability × Motivation (NP = Ill × Skill × Will). This model of NP involves at least three characteristics as being the minimum necessary conditions to start the process of negotiation: (1) the degree of health-functionality (Ill) existing at the time, which also is related to (2) the number of skills available, and (3) the degree of motivation (Will) necessary to want to negotiate. Thus, negotiation cannot take place unless a certain degree of functionality (as yet unknown), a certain number of skills (also unknown), and a certain degree of motivation are available in the system.

In addition, Levin (1976) differentiated two levels of power based on the importance and frequency of decisions. Rule-setting decisions that determine the family life style were defined as *orchestration* level. Frequent administrative decisions necessary for the ongoing life of the family were defined as *instrumentation* level. In terms of the analysis of 140 couples interviewed through a specially derived questionnaire, Levin found that the partner who had the greater ratio of resources had the greater authority to make orchestration decisions and to relegate such an authority. Orchestration-level decisions were found to be male dominant while instrumentation-level decisions were female dominant. Levin's differentation yields a model to understand the sharing of power in the family:

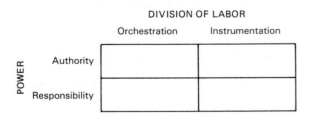

DIVISION OF LABOR

	Orchestration	Instrumentation
Authority		
Responsibility		

POWER

FIGURE 12-1   A Model of Power Sharing in the Family

A third aspect of this model lies in the structure of the task or issue at hand; to decide about moving or buying a home may be a different issue than going to a movie or to a restaurant. Very likely dysfunctional families may find it difficult to participate at all levels of decision making and become upset by minor decisions as much as major ones. Functional families may be upset (in addition to Negotiation Potential, division of labor, and levels of power sharing) more by major than by minor decisions. Furthermore, functional families would be clearer on issues of authority versus responsibility and of orchestration versus instrumentation; so that no one member is stuck in any one role. In dysfunctional families rules governing who decides what may be more rigid and less flexible, while in functional families greater confusion would arise about who does what and when (L'Abate, 1986).

Most models of conflict resolution appear substantially and substantively similar to most models of decision making and problem solving (Keeney, 1982).

THE PROCESS OF NEGOTIATION

Various models of negotiation are available in the literature on social skills training (L'Abate, 1981) and in couples communication frequency (Miller, Nunnally, & Wackman, 1975). Very little about negotiation can be found in the general family therapy literature (Gurman & Kniskern, 1981).

The McMaster model of family functioning (Epstein, Bishop, & Levin, 1978) considers the model of negotiation as consisting of seven stages: (1) identification of the problem; (2) communication of the problem to the appropriate source(s); (3) development of action alternatives; (4) decision of one alternative; (5) action; (6) monitor the course that action is taking; and (7) evaluation of success.

Harrell and Guerney (1976) developed a behavioral exchange program designed to teach couples conflict negotiation skills. This program is based on the following steps: (1) listening carefully; (2) locating a relationship issue; (3) identifying one's contributions to the issue; (4) identifying alternative solutions; (5) evaluating alternative solutions; (6) making an exchange; (7) determining conditions for the exchange; (8) implementing the behavioral exchange contract; and (9) renegotiation of the behavioral exchange contract. They report positive results through the use of various self-report measures and assessment of valid and negative behaviors.

As Kent (1967) has shown, bargaining with threats is designed "to make the threatened party's welfare level for the non-agreement outcome lower than it would be if no threat is issued" (p. 108). Threats and defeats are really designed to keep the interaction the same and the distance between both parties constant (L'Abate & Farr, 1981).

Hanan, Cribbin, and Bessian (1977) classified "negative" leadership patterns in negotiations as being: (1) aggressive; (2) manipulative; (3) interpretive patterns. Even though they may have considered these negative and positive patterns in business sales, their classification is extremely relevant to an understanding of individual styles in negotiation.

Scanzoni and Polanko (1980) proposed a three-stage model for explicit marital negotiation made up by: (1) *Social context variables* grouped into four different clusters: (I) composition of demographic and temporal factors; (II) resources (like education, status, abilities, instrumental skills, etc; (III) orientations toward bargaining power, like self-esteem, sex-role preferences, stakes in the outcome of the issue, salience and importance of the issue; and (IV) orientations toward cooperative bargaining, trust, equitability and fairness of individual styles, understanding and communication, and amount of resentment over past issues; (2) *Bargaining processes* varying from one-shot to repetitive sequential or serial sessions; and (3) *Outcomes* resulting in consensus or dissensus.

In addition to a relevant review of the pertinent literature on negotiation, Scanzoni and Polanko considered various problems that arise from disparities in social context variables, differences in bargaining styles, and expectations of outcomes. This article points out very well where negotiation theory and application could become a fertile meeting ground for researchers and clinicians alike where a confluence of both behavioral and nonbehavioral approaches could be integrated.

Olson, Sprenkle, and Russell (1979) considered negotiation as one aspect of many family adaptability dimensions (assertiveness, control, discipline, roles, rules, and system feedback). They characterized chaotic families as showing endless negotiation and poor problem solving, while flexible and structured families would show good negotiation and problem solving. Rigid families would show limited negotiation and poor problem solving.

Scanzoni and Szinovacz (1981) in their developmental sex-role model of family decision making considered the influence of prior decisions, current context factors, and decisioning processes like consensus, conflict, discussions, etc. They identified at least four major dimensions in which the past impinges on the present (pp. 34–40): (1) cooperativeness, (2) trust, (3) fairness or equity, and (4) empathy. Of course, a great deal of therapy time is spent on bringing about a positive resolution of those four aspects, which in the present model would enter under the rubric of Emotionality, the first step toward negotiation. There is a great deal to recommend in Scanzoni and Szinovacz's view that is relevant to the purposes of the present discussion. However, space limits referring to it in a more extensive fashion.

Ginsburg (1980) in reviewing the papers at the Wolfson College symposium (Brenner, 1980) found that one of the themes of this symposium was the communicative act and, more specifically, the meanings of communicative acts and actions, concluding:

> Thus, the creation of the framework of shared social reality is an active process which may involve *negotiation* (underline, ours) of meanings between the interactors.

The shared frameworks, as a continuing intersection of meanings, is a product of joint action and cannot be explained or understood in terms of either person alone. (p. 338)

Adler (1977) suggested a framework for negotiation that is based on an "assertive" view of conflict management: (1) identify ownership of problem; (2) present problem to the other person using "I" language in terms of how the problem bothers you and how experience affects how each individual experiences the feelings that result from the issue at hand; (3) persist until the other individual has assured you that the problem has been understood; (4) produce a proposal and allow room for counterproposals, or suggest various alternatives available, asking the other individual to generate additional alternatives; (5) from the various alternatives find the one which has the highest rewards and least costs for both individuals; (6) plan another meeting to evaluate progress.

Capell (1978) outlined a nine-step human systems change process that follows the same general path as negotiations and problem solving: (1) analyze situation, (2) assess change potential, (3) set outcome criteria, (4) generate alternative solutions, (5) make decision (on which solution to follow), (6) develop plan (of action), (7) implement plan, (8) evaluate performance, (9) reward performance (or consider other alternatives if performance does not reach original outcome criteria or change criteria). To assess change potential Capell uses a 3 x 3 criterion grid based on an assessment of motivation, skill, and power with three degrees of intensity (low, medium, and high). As Capell observed (1979, p. 85), the process of negotiation between spouses is not too "unlike labor-management negotiations." He distinguished seven different levels of intervention: (1) intrapersonal, (2) interpersonal (or marriage), (3) group (or family), (4) intergroup, (5) organization, (6) interorganization, and (7) community. It is clear that therapists intervene most of the time at the first three levels, but that the process of change or failure to change is similar at all levels since all of them are living systems where the same processes operate even though the content may be different.

Levi (1980) boiled down the process of negotiation to six steps: (1) analyze the situation, (2) decide on your goals and alternatives, (3) evaluate your adversary, (4) strategize (sic) your approach, (5) do your homework, and (6) apply the tactics that will get you where you want to be. Even though Levin thought in terms of adversary procedures, he suggested a variety of useful strategies: (1) "You have to understand what it is your opponent wants and what you are willing to give. Otherwise you will just have a stalemate" (p. 36); (2) to get what you want and deserve in life, you have to let people know that you expect to be treated well (but you need to treat them in the way you want to be treated); (3) the more time available, the more talk will take place. The more talk goes on, the less effective it becomes. Deadlines increase the momentum of any discussion (this is why it is important that a time be set before the beginning of any serious conference); (4) trade-offs, (i.e., alternatives or proposals and counterproposals); and (5) solutions should be temporary, delayed, conditional, limited, or postponed if either party is unclear or uncomfortable about the final agreement; (6) once a conclusion is reached, put it in writing. This step is crucial if one wants to achieve clarity in the process. Without a written document (L'Abate & L'Abate, 1977) both parties tend to forget, distort, or omit parts of the whole agreement.

Karrass (1970) produced a very readable summary of various experimental findings from social psychology combining it with Maslow need hierarchy and other fields of study. He used a model where goal setting is the first step but where power both in its perception and source is shared within five different types of negotiations. To maximize goal satisfaction both parties need to go through various steps of (1) share-bargaining pertaining to issues of divisions of labor, goals, and status; (2) problem-solving, which involves understanding in both partners of what is necessary to solve a problem; (3) attitudinal bargaining, which deals with the emotional climate of the process and consideration of costs and rewards involved in at least five different modes of conflict resolution (extreme aggression, mild aggression for deterent purposes, mutual accommodation, open cooperation, and direct collusion; (4) personal bargaining involving what each part is willing to give and take; and (5) in-group bargaining which is the reconciliation of the various needs and goals in the two parties. Karrass applied his model to business and political negotiations as well as marriage, ending his presentation with a proposal to negotiate that contains most of the components of his approach.

As Nierenberg (1971) suggested:

> The idea that everyone wins in a successful negotiation is not being presented here solely on ethical grounds. In actuality it is considered simply good business. It is a matter of receiving long range objections instead of short-term advantages. Negotiation solutions are likely to be longer lasting when each party has gained and has a stake in maintaining the conclusion. (p. 14)

Nierenberg (1971) started a process of creative negotiation with a recognition of needs continuing Maslow need hierarchy with Murray's list to deal with the issue of motivation. The first step, therefore, is one of recognizing one's wants and needs. A second step consists of recognizing shortcomings of an alternative to a win/lose approach (p. 48) within a climate of supportive rather than defensive maneuvers. A third step involves engaging in joint fact finding, essentially differentiating between needs, wants, and realistic goals that can be achieved. A fourth step consists of creating as many possible and realistic alternatives for mutual accommodation (even though one would not want to leave out seemingly outlandish possibilities).

Another way of proceeding in this step is to suggest that parties learn to propose and to counterpropose. For instance, in one couple separated for two months the husband wanted her and their child to come home and "everything will be all right." The wife refused categorically to come back home for good. However, she left the door open for possible weekend trial visits. She proposed to visit from 6 P.M. on Saturdays to 6 P.M. on Tuesdays. He counterproposed from 6 P.M. on Fridays to 6 P.M. Sundays. This length was excessive and unacceptable to the wife, but she agreed to follow a schedule from 6 P.M. Fridays to 10 A.M. on Sundays with the child being left with the father for the rest of the day on alternate Sundays. Nierenberg (1971) provided a whole series of questions (pp. 86–90) that could become part of the armamentarium of any therapist.

Kessler (1978) proposed a model of creative conflict resolution that finds its origin in divorce mediation. She defined negotiation as the process where "disrupting persons work out their own settlement" without outside help. Mediation instead involves the involvement of a third party to facilitate the process. Hence, therapists perform the role of mediators, but even more importantly, as teachers of how negotiation should (ought, must) take place.

She reviewed the advantages and disadvantages of two dysfunctional modes of conflict resolution (fight versus flight), proposing a creative alternative of the "fix" based on (1) compromise, (2) creative alternatives, (3) full disclosure, and (4) mutual gain rather than win/lose outcome. She followed some of Nierenberg's (1971) techniques in suggesting successful and unsuccessful methods of approach.

Craddock (1980) found out that marital problem solving between heterogeneous and homogeneous couples was a function of authority role expectations and value systems in interaction with sex and situational variables. Welk and Henley (1969) examined social contracts between sexes, spouses, parents and children, siblings, in-laws, friends, bosses and teachers, and doctor-patient, giving easy to follow instructions at a very simple and concrete level. Peterson, Frederiksen, and Rosenbaum (1981) followed a four-step sequence of negotiation based on: (1) statement of position, (2) statement of differences, (3) suggestion of alternatives, and (4) evaluation of alternatives.

The behavioral literature usually equates negotiation with contracting (Weiss, 1978). Gurman (1978), on the other hand, criticized behaviorists for focusing too much on the content and too little on the process (p. 495). Some of the models reviewed in this section are summarized in Table 12-1.

On the basis of the foregoing review we can conclude that negotiation takes place according to an invariant sequence of steps:

1. Confronting the issue(s), expressing feelings related to them
2. Discussing and discovering ways of dealing with issues—considering response alternatives and focusing on one approach that is agreeable to both parties
3. Implementing the approach
4. Evaluating the approach and deciding how to keep, change, or vary from the original approach.
5. Achieving an awareness of the whole context within which this transaction is taking place.

On the basis of this review of the literature on negotiation, we are led to conclude that this whole area has been sorely neglected by marriage and family therapists, while it has been considered mainly in politics (Belson, 1980), business (Cohen, 1980; Nierenberg, 1971), labor relations (Karrass, 1970), and even hijacking (Zartman, 1978).

Resistance to Negotiating

Oftentimes, by asking couples and families to start the negotiating process, one is able to flush out the most resistant members as well as resistance games most couples and families play. In fact, one should contract *from the beginning of therapy* that couples and families spend at least one hour at home as they spend in the therapy office. By setting this contract up from the outset one is starting already to see or set up the process of resistance, no matter how useful and money-saving such a procedure may be claimed to be by the therapist. Chaotic families, of course, have the most difficult time in even starting, so that the degree of functionality can be gauged by how well or poorly a couple or family fulfills this assignment.

What about if one partner or a family member refuses to negotiate? You can lead a horse to water but . . . of course, this avoidance takes place quite often in the course of therapy. Then one needs to understand what the goals of individual family members are. Usually we have found that negotiation avoiders need to *defeat* the system to protect it from change. Hence, they should be actively complimented for all of the energy and efforts that they put in protecting the system from change. More active ways of dealing with their defeating efforts is to write letters of congratulations and support for all the caring and responsibility taken to keep the *status quo* (Chapter 6).

Are there nonnegotiable issues? Of course there are. Each individual should be able to state clearly what his or her nonnegotiable issues are, if he or she can. Oftentimes, there are individuals who see a reality where "everything is negotiable." Such a stance is as dangerous and perhaps more slippery and difficult to deal with than the avoidance of negotiation. A great deal of effort needs to be put into dealing with such a position toward finding what each individual wants and does not want, likes and does not like, and where they want to draw a line.

NEGOTIATION: BARGAINING AND PROBLEM SOLVING

On the basis of the foregoing review the process of negotiation can be divided into two major phases. The first phase, bargaining, includes the first three steps (consideration of issue, explanation of feelings related to it, and facilitation of alternative solutions). The second phase, problem solving, involves the following four steps: implementation of agreed upon solutions, monitoring and evaluation

TABLE 12-1   Summary of Different Models of Negotiation, Bargaining, and Problem Solving

SOURCES	Stages		
	1	2	3
Adler (1977)	Identify ownership of problem	Present problem	Produce proposal and consider counterproposals
Aldous (1971)	Identification and definition	Collection of information	Production of alternative solutions
Glass, Holyoak, & Santer (1979)	Understanding the problem		Planning a solution
L'Abate (1986)	Emotionality: 1) Confronting issue 2) Expressing feelings related to it		Rationality: 1) Discovering ways of dealing with issue 2) Focusing on one approach agreeable to both parties
Scanzoni & Polonko (1980)	Social context		
Spivack, Platt, & Shure (1976)	Bringing up the problem	Clarifying the problem	Presenting solutions

of solution, continuation of original solution, or implementation of a second alternative.

The two first steps of the bargaining phase can be broken down into at least five separate but sequential steps (Goldstein & Rosenbaum, 1982): (1) state your position; (2) state your understanding of the other person's position; (3) ask if the other person agrees with your statement of his or her position; (4) listen openly to his or her response; and (5) propose a compromise. Additional points would consist of (6) an elaboration and support of one's proposal (rationale, pros and cons, etc); (7) asking for a counterproposal; and (8) integrating both proposals into one that is satisfactory to both parties.

An issue of disagreement about how long to negotiate pertains to time limits. Our instructions to couples rigidly demand that no longer than one hour at a time be spent negotiating and that negotiation be then continued at another date with a reasonable time in between to allow for reflection of the process and alternatives. The rationale for such rigid time limits is based on the experience that setting time limits and following them is a form of control. Consequently

Stages			
4	5	6	7
Select more acceptable alternative		Evaluate	
Deciding among alternatives	Taking action	Evaluation of action (taken)	
	Carrying out solution		
	Activity: Words Deeds	Evaluation of approach (Awareness) Feedback	Context (Spatial and Temporal): Deciding on whether to keep or change approach
Processes			Outcomes
Discussion of feasibility	Role playing of solution		

we want our couples to learn temporal boundaries, with a clear distinction of when they are negotiating and when they are not.

Goldstein and Rosenbaum (1982, p. 56) on the other hand, take the completely opposite position ("If possible, try to avoid time limits"). Their position is based on the rationale that "time pressures . . . have a mixed effect on the outcome of negotiation." They feel that time pressures cause: (1) a lowering of goals; (2) an increase in demands; and (3) an increase in bluffing and other nonconstructive communications. Consequently, they recommend that negotiations take as long as it is necessary to reach a satisfactory compromise.

To reconcile these seemingly contrasting positions, we suggest that time limits be set and maintained when and if the process of negotiation is negative and nonconstructive. If and when the process is smooth, positive, and constructive, then all the time necessary can be taken at will.

To implement the first step, the suggestions by Miller et al. (1975) seem very useful, that is: (1) disclosures of discomfort about one or many issues; (2) checking out of message being received ("Did you hear me? Did you understand me? What did I say? What did you get from what I said?"); (3) importance of self and others and avoidance of discounting.

IMPLICATIONS

Why has this area been neglected by marriage and family therapists in spite of its apparent relevance to the fact that we deal with the same processes of conflict resolution and management? It is hard to find the answer to this question. All that one can say is that we can make up for such an oversight by incorporating in our work models and methods of negotiation that can be applied to couples and families (as well as in our lives!)

The important characteristic of negotiation is that, regardless of its theoretical source/systems (behavioral, humanistic) or field of application (labor relations, business, politics, organizations, etc), the general agreement on the sequence of steps necessary to find an agreement and to generate a feasible solution seems to be immutable and constant in most instances. However, in stressed and distressed couples and families the major issue is to get them together to even begin to negotiate! Most of the time there is no motivation to do so; in fact, there is negative motivation to thwart and defeat the process of change! Thus, the first step of getting the interested parties to the bargaining table is usually the most difficult.

One important issue is how much do marriage and family therapists know about negotiation processes and outcome. The literature in this regard may be bare but this bareness does not in and by itself imply ignorance. On the other hand, if negotiation procedures are used in therapy, why are they not talked about? Thus, the field of negotiation can and should become the meeting grounds between therapists and social skills trainers (L'Abate, 1980, 1981) who up to now have been separate from each other.

Negotiation therapy therefore draws its theoretical and empirical roots from social psychology (Rubin & Brown, 1975; Swingle, 1970), economics (Young, 1975), sociology (Aldous, 1971), behavioral methodology (Liberman, 1970), social skills training (Miller et al, 1975), and, of course, psychology (Spivak et al., 1976).

TOWARD A MORE ACTIVE (AND CONDUCTIVE) THERAPEUTIC STANCE

Teaching negotiation skills and steps to couples and families implies a much more active role than some therapists are willing to assume. Levenson (1972) predicted that:

> A new therapy is emerging, along with a new therapist and new patient, oriented more to participation than understanding, sensitivity and design rather than to

insight and formulation. Psychoanalysis, to remain an enterprise of true sensibility, must be a bit ahead of its time, seeing into the future and embracing it. This is not mere modishness, although it moves toward it, but rather a quite necessary vitality. *What "works" pragmatically in one period will not work in the next.* (pp. 222–223)

The polarities of active and inactive have been aptly summarized by Levenson (1972):

The extreme intrapsychic position, at its best, predicates a respect for the patient's own growth processes and dictates a policy of noninterference. At its worst, it permits a passive, omniscient posture on the part of the therapist. Moreover, he never fails to cure; the patient fails to be treatable. At the other extreme, the interpersonal position predicates the cure on the experience with the therapist. At its best, it permits an authentic engagement, a nonauthoritarian meeting with respect for the patient's humanity rather than his pathology. Nosological diagnosis, a mainstay of intrapsychic psychiatry, becomes name-calling in the interpersonal sphere. At its worst, it degenerates into a "laying on of hands," a curing through the evangelistic power of the therapist. The patient is never unsuitable: the therapist has failed to cure. The range is from insight to experience: at one end, the patient learns himself in relative isolation; at the other, he learns the Other interaction. (pp. 17–18)

Garfield (1981) in commenting on changing phases in psychotherapy felt that shorter and more active therapies may be one of these trends. He mentioned Herzberg (1946) and Thorne (1946) as two of the pioneers in this area. Herzberg (1946) was one of the first therapists to indicate how to exert direct influence on the patient's personal environment through removal or transfer. He also assigned tasks directed against: (1) impulses maintaining the neurosis, (2) obstacles to satisfaction, (3) essential predispositions (to failure), (4) (secondary) gains, (5) delaying factors.

THE E-R-A-Aw-C MODEL AS A DIAGNOSTIC INDICATOR OF A LIFE CYCLE DESCRIPTOR OR A THERAPEUTIC GOAL

If the goal of family therapy is to improve the negotiating competence of a family, we need to know more about the process of negotiation and its components. Unfortunately, existing models of negotiation, decision making, and problem solving are either incomplete (they do not include emotions as a component, for instance), irrelevant (because they are applied to short-lived and contrived situations), or ineffective (because they are applied to homogeneous groups of managers and not to heterogeneous groups like the family). In the search for a relevant and effective model of negotiation the senior writer developed the E-R-A-Aw-C model, (L'Abate, 1983, 1986), which allows us to separate the components of the negotiation process, including giving a diagnostic notion of the process as it breaks down and how it applies to clinical and non-clinical families.

THE FUNCTIONS OF A NEGOTIATION MODEL

The E-R-A-Aw-C model (Table 12–1) has a variety of functions: (1) It synthesizes and integrates a wide range of knowledge, schools and theories, showing how each school, theory, or approach impinges and emphasizes one particular component of an information processing chain; (2) this model not only outlines the steps of a negotiation process but deals with specific competencies that are needed to negotiate; that is, a deficit in any one of the five areas can break down the whole process; (3) these components are relevant to a life cycle view of negotiation, identifying: (I) personal career (emotionality and awareness), (II) educational career (self-concept); (III) occupational career (activity); and (IV) contextual careers (in-laws, children, siblings, friends, neighbors, etc.). How this model applies to the actual teaching of negotiation can be found in L'Abate (1981) concerning the role of family conferences as a step toward learning negotiation skills. Actual guidelines for negotiation and family conferences appear in Appendix A.

CONCLUSION

On the basis of our review of the literature we conclude that: (1) most family therapy literature has not paid the necessary attention to the steps and sequences of negotiation; (2) negotiation is an invariant process that colors a great part of our lives. However, most of us, personally and professionally, have had little experience in it; (3) power, defined here in terms of authority and responsibility, needs to be negotiated in the family (as well as outside of it); (4) a model of power sharing and negotiation is submitted to identify and clarify component steps of the process. We hope that family therapists will be able to use and implement the information from this chapter (and this book).

Appendix A

Guidelines for Family Conferences

Dear Family Members:

These guidelines have been found useful in helping families to conduct the business of living. Without a structure such as Family Conferences, families flounder and fail. The Family Conference is what most families need to learn if they are to accomplish their goals.

The Family Conference is one, perhaps the only, major vehicle through which family members can learn how to negotiate and how to give and take. The guidelines assume that the family does eat the evening meal together at least two to three times a week. During one of these times, preferably Fridays, after the evening meal, the conference should be held under the following specified conditions (unless told or agreed otherwise).

1. Announce plans for the conference at least one week in advance, at a time when everybody is present; for example, "Next Friday we are going to have a Family Conference right after supper so all of us will need to be there." If other plans have been made, you may make the following changes:
   a. another evening more suitable to everybody;
   b. change the time of the evening meal to an earlier hour to allow the meal and the conference to take place. Plan about one hour for the meal (sometimes one-half hour may be sufficient) and one hour for the conference.

2. Do not conduct "business," or matters to be considered at the conference, during the meal (or any meal) unless the matter is urgent (this could happen during meals during the week but not during the meal prior to the conference).

3. Make sure that dishes are cleared from the table so that the table is clear of everything except usual decorations and notepaper.

4. Set time (clock or whatever) to one hour and make it very clear from the outset that the conference will last one hour and that whatever business has not been dealt with during this conference will be dealt with during the next conference. It is imperative—absolutely mandatory—that the conference not last longer than the stated time.

5. Set general rules of conduct during the conference if you need to, for example:
   a. Speak as long as necessary to the point being considered.
   b. Do not interrupt whoever is speaking.
   c. Follow general Robert's rules of order concerning consideration, decisions, agreements, tabling of matters, and voting.

6. Give everyone ample freedom to talk and to have their say without interruptions, ridicule, or distractions. Distractions may be dealt with as the family becomes aware that distractions, as much as withdrawals, may demonstrate how the family as a whole functions or fails to function.

7. Avoid and help others to avoid use of the pronoun *you*. Ban the pronoun *you* from conversation. As long as the pronoun *you* is used, the family will get nowhere. Do use and encourage the use of the pronouns *I* and *we*; that is, I feel, I think, I am aware, I wonder, I am afraid.

8. Start by generally encouraging everybody to share good, positive feelings about themselves and the family (e.g., "I feel good about . . ."). Do insist that each member come up with at least one positive about him- or herself or others. If positives cannot be found, the family may have become immersed in a quagmire of negativity.

9. After positives, encourage everybody to voice complaints, beefs, displeasures, anger, and so on. Allow feelings to be expressed as long as these feelings are not confused with actions or with accusations. Make notes of these complaints and who made them. Use "I" statements; avoid "you" statements.

10. When everybody has had his or her say, lead the discussion toward whichever matter, by family consensus, should be considered first (i.e., what is most urgent to most family members). List these topics by priority.

11. When a decision has been reached about what matters the most to the family as a whole, discuss freely the pros and cons of *all* possible solutions, including implications, ramifications, costs and reward, and consequences. Do discuss and encourage discussion of all possibilities, no matter how outlandish they may appear at first blush. Do not allow put-downs or belittlement of any viewpoint expressed.

12. If the discussion gets out of hand—to the point of chaos and uproar—so that mutual give-and-take cannot take place, give the family a choice: "We either calm down and resume discussion, or we will need to end this conference today and go on next week to deal with the same matters."

13. If one or more members seem committed to sabotaging (distracting, etc.) the regular course of events, do bring up the issue of change: "Does this family want to stay the same?" or "As long as we cannot conduct our affairs properly, we can neither start nor end anything we need to do among ourselves."

14. Conduct yourselves as leaders, not dictators, tyrants, or tycoons. Remember that you are part of the system and that no member of a family is any better than the so-called "worst" member. Avoid ganging up on anybody and avoid scapegoating anyone in the family.

References

ACKERMAN, N. W. (1967). Prejudice and scapegoating in the family. In G. H. Zuk & I. Bo-szormeyi-Nagy (Eds.), *Family therapy and disturbed families.* Palo Alto, CA: Science and Behavior Books.

ADLER, R. B. (1977). *Talking straight: Assertion without aggression.* New York: Holt, Rinehart & Winston.

AHRONS, C., & PERLMUTTER, M. (1982). The relationship between former spouses: A fundamental subsystem in the remarriage family. In L. Messinger (Ed.), *Therapy with remarriage families* (pp. 31–46). Rockville, MD: Aspen Systems Corporation.

ALBEE, G. W. (1979). A competency model must replace the defect model. In L. Bowd & J. Rosen (Eds.), *The primary prevention of psychopathology: Promoting social competence and coping in adulthood.* Hanover, NH: The University Press of New England.

ALBERTI, R., & EMMONS, M. (1975). *Stand up, speak out, talk back.* New York: Pocket Books.

ALDOUS, J. (1971). A framework for the analysis of family problem solving. In J. Aldous, T. Condon, R. Hill, M. Strauss, & I. Tallman (Eds.), *Family problem solving: A symposium on theoretical methodological and substantive concerns.* Hinsdale, IL: The Dryden Press.

ALEXANDER, C. N., & SCRIVEN, G. D. (1977). Role playing: An essential component of experimentation. *Personality and Social Psychology Bulletin, 3,* 455–466.

ALEXANDER, J. & PARSONS, B. (1982). *Functional family therapy.* Monterey, CA: Brooks/Cole.

ALGER, I. (1976). Integrating immediate video playback in family therapy. In P. J. Guerin, Jr. (Ed.), *Family Therapy: Theory and Practice.* New York: Gardner Press.

ALKIRE, A. A. (1972). Enactment of social power and role behavior in families of disturbed and condisturbed preadolescents. *Developmental Psychology, 7,* 270–276.

ALLOY, L., & ABRAMSON, L. (1979). Judgment of contingency in depressed students: Sadder but wiser? *Journal of Experimental Psychology: General, 108,* 441–485.

ALLPORT, G. (1968). The open system in personality therapy. In W. Budkley (Ed.), *Modern systems research for the behavioral scientist.* Chicago: Aldine.

ANDERSON, C. M., & MALLOY, E. S. (1976). Family photographs in treatment and training. *Family Process, 15,* 259–264.

ANDOLFI, M. (1979). *Family therapy: An interactional approach.* New York: Plenum.

ANDOLFI, M. (1980). Prescribing the family's own dysfunctional rules as a therapeutic strategy. *Journal of Marriage and Family Therapy, 6,* 29–41.

ANDOLFI, M., ANGELO, C., MENGHI, P., & NICOLO-CORIGLIANO, A. M. (1983). *Behind the family mask: Therapeutic change in rigid family systems.* New York: Brunner/Mazel.

ANDREWS, E. S. (1972, April). *Experiential role-play in the training of family therapists.* Paper presented at the 49th Annual Conference of the American Ortho-Psychiatric Association, Detroit, Michigan.

ARGYLE, M. (1980). Interaction skills and social competence. In M. P. Feldman & J. Oxford (Eds.), *Psychological problems: The social context* (pp. 123–150). New York: John Wiley.

ATKINSON, M. B. (1977). The effect of complementary and noncomplementary dyadic situation and level of assertiveness on role-played behaviors. *Dissertation Abstracts International, 37,* 3591B–3592B.

BACH, G., & WYDEN P. (1970). *The intimate enemy.* New York: Avon Books.

BAHR, S. J., BOWERMAN, D. E., & GECAS, V. (1974). Adolescent perceptions of conjugal power. *Social Forces, 52,* 357–367.

BANDLER, R., & GRINDER, J. (1975). *Patterns of the hypnotic techniques of Milton H. Erickson, M.D.I.* Cupertino, CA: Meta Publications.

BANDLER, R., & GRINDER, J. (1982). *Reframing: Neuro-linguistic programming and the transformation of meaning.* Moab, UT: Real People Press.

BARNHILL, L. R. (1979). Healthy family systems. *The Family Coordinator, 28,* 94–100.

BARTON, C., & ALEXANDER, J. (1983, October). *The anatomy of therapeutic directives: A framework for effecting change in families.* Workshop presented at the Association for Marriage and Family Therapy, Annual Meeting, Washington, DC.

BATESON, G. (1979). *Mind and nature: A necessary unity.* New York: Bantam Books.

BATESON, G., JACKSON, D. O., HALEY, J., & WEAKLAND, J. (1956). Toward a theory of schizophrenia. *Behavioral Science, 1*(4), 251–264.

BATESON, G., & RUESCH (1951). *Communication: The Matrix of Psychiatry.* New York: W. W. Norton.

BEAVERS, W. (1977). *Psychotherapy and growth: A family systems perspective.* New York: Brunner/Mazel.

BEAVERS, W. R. (1982). Healthy mid-range and severely dysfunctional families. In F. Walsh (Ed.), *Normal family processes.* New York: The Guilford Press.

BELL, J. E. (1975). *Family Therapy.* New York: Jason Arouson.

BELSON, R. (1980). International politics and family systems: Some observations on tactics. *International Journal of Family Therapy, 2,* 212–229.

BEM, D. J. (1972). Self-perception theory. In L. Berkowitz (Ed.), *Advances in experimental psychology* (Vol. 6). New York: John Wiley.

BENNINGFIELD, N. B. (1978). Multiple family therapy systems. *Journal of Marriage and Family Counseling, 4,* 25–34.

BERGMAN, J. S. (1980). The use of paradox in a community home for the chronically disturbed and retarded. *Family Process, 19,* 65–72.

BIDDLE, B. J. (1979). *Role theory: Expectations, identities, and behaviors.* New York: Academic Press.

BIRCHLER, G. (1979). Communication skills in married couples. In M. Hersen and A. S. Bellak (Eds.), *Research and practice in social skills training.* New York: Plenum.

BIRDWHISTLE, R. (1971). *Kinesics and context.* London: Penguin.

BOHART, A. C. (1972). Role playing and the reduction of interpersonal conflict. *Dissertation Abstracts International, 33,* 435B–436B.

BOLES, K. G. (1972). Role playing as a behavior change technique: Review of the empirical literature. *Psychotherapy: Theory, Research and Practice, 9,* 185–192.

BOSZORMENYI-NAGY, I., & SPARK, G. (1973). *Invisible loyalties: Reciprocity in intergenerational family therapy.* Hagerstown, MD: Harper & Row, Pub.

BOWEN, M. (1966). The use of family theory in clinical practice. *Comprehensive Psychiatry, 7,* 345–374.

BOWEN, M. (1978). *Family therapy in clinical practice.* New York: Aronson.

BOWERMAN, C. D., & BAHR, S. J. (1973). Conjugal power and adolescent identification with parents. *Sociometry, 36,* 366–377.

BRENNER, M. (Ed.) (1980). *The Structure of Action.* New York: St. Martin's Press.

BROSS, A. (Ed.) (1982). *Family therapy: Principles of strategic practice.* New York: Guilford.

BUCHLER, J. (1961). *The concept of method.* New York: Columbia University Press.

BURKES, O. J. (1970). Determinants and consequences of toughness. In P. Swingle (Ed.), *The structure of conflict* (pp. 45–68). New York: Academic Press.

CAILLE, P. (1982). The evaluation phase of systemic family therapy. *Journal of Marital and Family Therapy*, 8, 29–39.

CALONICO, J. M., & THOMAS, D. L. (1973). Role-taking as a function of value similarity and affect in the nuclear family. *Journal of Marriage and the Family, 35*, 655–666.

CAPELL, R. G. (1979). *Changing human systems.* Toronto, Ontario: International Human Systems Institute.

CARKHUFF, R. (1969a). *Helping and human relations. Vol. I: Selection and training.* New York: Holt, Reinhart & Winston.

CARKHUFF, R. (1969b). *Helping and human relations. Volume II: Practice and research.* New York: Holt, Reinhart & Winston.

CARROLL, J. (1956). *Language, thought, and reality. Selected writings of Benjamine Lee Whorf.* Cambridge, MA: MIT Press.

CARTER, E. A., & MCGOLDRICK, M. (Eds.) (1980). *The family life cycle: A framework for family therapy.* New York: Gardner Press.

CARTER, R., & THOMAS, E. (1975). Modification of problematic marital communication. In A. S. Gurman & D. Rice (Eds.), *Couples in conflict.* New York: Jason Aronson.

COHEN, H. (1980). *You can negotiate anything: How to get what you want.* New York: Lyle Stuart.

COMMONER, D. (1971). *The closing circle.* New York: Knopf.

CONSTANTINE, L. (1978). Family sculpture and relationship mapping techniques. *Journal of Marriage and Family Counseling, 4*(2), 13–23.

COOPER, J. (1976). Deception and role-playing: On telling the good guys from the bad guys. *American Psychologist, 31*, 605–610.

COOPER, W. (March 3, 1974). Use of Hypnosis in obstetrics. West Virginia, University Hospital.

COOPERSMITH, E. E. (1981). Developmental reframing. *Journal of Strategic and Systemic Therapies, 1*, 1–8.

CORSINI, R. J., & CARDONE, S. (1966). *Roleplaying in psychotherapy: A manual.* Chicago: Aldine.

CRADDOCK, A. E. (1980). Marital problem-solving as a function of couples' marital power expectations and marital value systems. *Journal of Marriage and the Family, 42*, 185–196.

CROMWELL, R. E., OLSON, D. H. L., & FOURNIER, D. G. (1976). Diagnosis and evaluation in marital family counseling. In D. H. L. Olson (Ed.) *Treating Relationships.* Lalse Mills, Iowa: Graphic Publishing.

CRONEN, V., JOHNSON, K., & LANNAMANN, J. (1982). Paradoxes, double binds, and reflexive loops: An alternative theoretical perspective. *Family Process. 21,* 91–112.

DABBS, J. M., & HELMREICH, R. L. (1972). Fear, anxiety, and affiliation following a role-played accident. *Journal of Social Psychology, 86,* 269–278.

DAITZMAN, R. J. (1977). Methods of self-confrontation in family therapy. *Journal of Marriage and Family Counseling, 3,* 3–9.

DELL, T. (1980). Researching the family theories of schizophrenia: An exercise in epistemological confusion. *Family Process, 4,* 19, 321–335.

de SHAZER, S. (1982). *Patterns of brief family therapy: An ecosystemic approach.* New York: Guilford Press.

de SHAZER, S., & MOLNAR, A. (1984). Four useful interventions in brief family therapy. *Journal of Marital and Family Therapy, 10,* 297–304.

DREYER, P. H. (1978). Family environment scale. In O. K. Buros (Ed.), *The eighth mental measurements yearbook,* (Vol. I). Highland Park, NJ: The Gryphon Press.

DRUCKMAN, P. (Ed.) (1977). *Negotiations: Social psychological perspectives.* Beverly Hills, CA: Sage Publication, Inc.

DUHL, F., & DUHL, B. (1982, October). *Training for trainers in systems: Learning from the inside out.* Workshop presented at the Annual Meeting, American Association for Marriage and Family Therapy, Dallas, Texas.

DUHL, F., KANTOR, D., & DUHL, B. (1973). Learning, space, and action in family therapy. In D. Bloch (Ed.), *Techniques of family psychotherapy: A primer.* New York: Grune & Stratton.

D'ZURILLA, T., & GOLDFRIED, M. (1971). Problem solving and behavior modification. *Journal of Abnormal Psychology, 78*(1), 107–126.

EISENBERG, L. (1977). Psychiatry and society: A sociobiologic synthesis. *New England Journal of Medicine, 296,* 903–910.

ELLIS, A. (1963). *Reason and emotion in psychotherapy.* New York: Lyle Stuart.

EPSTEIN, N., BISHOP, D., & LEVINE, S. (1978). The McMaster model of family functioning. *Journal of Marriage and Family Counseling, 6,* 19–31.

EPSTEIN, N. B., BISHOP, D. S., & BALDWIN, L. M. (1982). McMaster model of family functioning: A view of the normal family. In F. Walsh (Ed.), *Normal family processes.* New York: Guilford Press.

ERICKSON, M. (1964). The confusion technique in hypnosis. *American Journal of Clinical Hypnosis, 6,* 183–207.

ERICKSON, M. H., & ROSSI, E. L. (1981). *Experiencing hypnosis.* New York: Irvington Publishers.

FAGAN, J., & SHEPHERD, I. L. (1970). *Gestalt therapy now.* New York: Harper Colophon Books.

FELLNER, C. (1976). The use of teaching stories in conjoint family therapy. *Family Process, 15,* 427–433.

FEYNES, C. (1976). Kiss the frog: A therapeutic intervention for reframing family rules. *Family Therapy, 3,* 123–128.

FIRESTONE, E., & MOSCHETTEA, P. (1975). Behaviorial Counteracting in Family Therapy, *Journal of Family Counseling, 3,* 27–31.

FISCH, R., WEAKLAND, J. H., & SEGAL, L. (1983). *The tactics of change: Doing therapy briefly.* San Francisco: Jossey-Bass.

FISHER, J., RYTTING, M., & HESLIN, R. (1976). Hands touching hands: Affective and evaluative effects of an interpersonal touch. *Sociometry, 39*(4), 416–421.

FISHER, L. (1977). On the classification of families: A progress report. *Archives of General Psychiatry, 34,* 424–433.

FISHER, L. F. (1976). Dimensions of family assessment: A critical review. *Journal of Marriage and Family Counseling, 2,* 367–382.

FOGARTY, T. F. (1976). System concepts and the dimension of self. In P. J. Guerin, Jr. (Ed.), *Family Therapy: Theory and Practice.* New York: Gardner Press.

FOREHAND, R. L., & McMAHON, R. J. (1981). *Helping the noncompliant child.* New York: Guilford Press.

FREEDMAN, J. (1969). Role playing: Psychology by consensus. *Journal of Personality and Social Psychology, 13,* 107–114.

FREEMAN, D. (1981). *Techniques of family therapy.* New York: Jason Aronson.

FRENCH, J. R. P., JR., & RAVEN, B. (1959). The bases of social power. In D. Cartwright (Ed.), *Studies in social power.* Ann Arbor: University of Michigan, Institute for Social Research.

FRENCH, A. P. (1977). *Disturbed children and their families: innovations in evaluation and treatment.* New York: Human Sciences Press.

FRIEDMAN, P. H. (1972). The effects of modeling, role-playing and participation on behavior change. In B. A. Maher (Ed.), *Progress in experimental personality research,* (Vol. 6). New York: Academic Press.

FRIEDMAN, R. (1970). A "rage-reduction" diagnostic technique with young children. *Child Psychiatry and Human Development, 1,* 112–125.

FRIEDMAN, R., DREIZENK, K., HARRIS, L., SCHOEU, P., & SHULMAN, P. (1978). Parent Power: A Holding Technique in the treatment of Omnipotent Children. *International Journal of Family Counseling, 6,* 66–75.

FUHR, R., MOOS, R. H., & DISHOTSKY, N. (1981). The use of family assessment and feedback in ongoing family therapy. *American Journal of Family Therapy, 9,* 24–36.

GANAHL, G. (1982). *Effects of client, treatment, and therapist variables on the outcome of structured marital enrichment.* Unpublished doctoral dissertation, Georgia State University, 1981. *Dissertations Abstracts International, 42,* (11), 4576B.

GANAHL, G. (1983). Interviewing and intervening in the Milanese style. Workshop 105. *Forty-first Annual American Association of Marriage and Family Therapy Conference.* Osborne Highland, IN: Creative Audio, 1983.

GARFIELD, R. (1982). Mourning and its resolution for spouses in marital separation. In L. Messinger (Ed.), *Therapy with remarriage families,* pp. 1–15. Rockville, MD: Aspen Systems Corporation.

GARFIELD, S. L. (1981). Psychotherapy: An 80-year appraisal. *American Psychologist, 36,* 174–183.

GARFIELD, S. L., & BERGIN, A. E. (Eds.) (1978). *Handbook of psychotherapy and behavior change.* New York: John Wiley.

GEDDES, M., & MEDWAY, J. (1977). The symbolic drawing of the family life space. *Family Process, 16,* 219–228.

GINSBURG, G. P. (1980). Epilogue: A conception of situated action. In M. Brenner (Ed.), *The structure of action* (pp. 313–350). New York: St. Martin's Press.

GLASS, A. L., HOLYOAK, K. J., & SANTER, J. L. (1979). *Cognition.* Reading, MA: Addison-Wesley.

GLICK, I. D., & KESSLER, D. R. (1974). *Marital and family therapy.* New York: Grune & Stratton.

GOFFMAN, E. (1974a). *Frame Analysis.* New York: Harper & Row, Pub.

GOLDHABER, G. M. (1979). *Organizational communication* (2nd Ed.). Dubuque, IA: William C. Brown Company.

GOLDIN, S. E., & HAYES, R. B. (1981). Individual differences in planning processes. *JSBS Catalog of Selected Documents in Psychology,* Ms. 2254.

GOLDSTEIN, A. P., & ROSENBAUM, A. (1982). *Aggress-less: How to turn anger and aggression into positive action.* Englewood Cliffs, NJ: Prentice-Hall.

GORDON, T. (1970). *Parent effectiveness training.* New York: D. McKay.

GOTTMAN, J. M. (1979). *Marital interaction: Experimental investigations.* New York: Academic Press.

GOTTMAN, J. M., GONSO, J., NOTARIUS, C., & MARKMAN, N. (1976). *A couple's guide to communication.* Champagne, IL: Research Press.

GREEN, S. B., BURKHART, B. R., & HARRISON, W. H. (1979). Personality correlates of self-report, role-playing, and in vivo measures of assertiveness. *Journal of Consulting and Clinical Psychology, 47,* 16–24.

GREENBERG, M. S. (1967). Role playing, an alternative to deception. *Journal of Abnormal and Social Psychology, 7,* 152–157.

GROSSER, G. H., & PAUL, N. L. (1964). Ethical issues in family group therapy. *American Journal of Orthopsychiatry, 34,* 875–885.

GRUNEBAUM, H., & CHASIN, R. (1978). Relabeling and reframing reconsidered: The beneficial effects of a pathological label. *Family Process, 17,* 449–455.

GUERIN, P. J., JR. (1976). The use of the arts in family therapy: I never sang for my father. In P. J. Guerin, Jr. (Ed.), *Family Therapy: Theory and practice* (pp. 480–500). New York: Gardner Press.

GUERIN, P. J., JR., & PENDAGAST, M. A. (1976). Evaluation of family system and genogram. In P. J. Guerin, Jr. (Ed.), *Family therapy: Theory and practice.* New York: Gardner Press.

GUERNEY, B. G. (1977). *Relationship enhancement.* San Francisco: Jossey-Bass.

GURMAN, A. S., & KNISKERN, S. P. (1978). Research on marital and family therapy: Progress, perspective and prospect. In S. L. Garfield & A. E. Bergin (Eds.), *Handbook of Psychotherapy and Behavior Change.* New York: John Wiley.

GURMAN, A. S., & KNISKERN, D. P. (1981). *Handbook of family therapy.* New York: Brunner/Nagel.

GUTSKEY, S., and SRODES, C. (March 3, 1984). Management of acute and chronic pain. West Virginia Conference on Hypnosis. Morgantown, WV: West Virginia University Hospital.

HALEY, J. (1963). *Strategies of psychotherapy.* New York: Grune & Stratton.

HALEY, J. (1973). *Uncommon therapy: The psychiatric techniques of Milton H. Erickson.* New York: Norton.

HALEY, J. (1976). *Problem-solving therapy.* San Francisco: Jossey-Bass.

HALEY, J. (1984). *Ordeal therapy.* San Francisco: Jossey-Bass.

HALL, E. (1959). *The silent language.* New York: Doubleday.

HANAN, M., CRIBBIN, J., & BESSIAN, H. (1977). *Sales negotiation strategies.* New York: AMA-COM.

HARREL, J., & GUERNEY, B. G., JR. (1976). Training married couples in conflict negotiation skills. In D. H. L. Olson (Ed.), *Treating relationships* (pp. 151–165). Lake Mills, IA: Graphic.

HARRELL, J. E. (1975). Efficacy of a behavioral exchange program for teaching conflict negotiation skills to enhance marital relationships. *Dissertation Abstracts International, 36,* 4063A.

HAYES-ROTH, B. (1981). Flexibility in executive strategies. *JSBS Catalog of Selected Documents in Psychology,* Ms. 2254.

HENDRICK, C. (1977a). Role-playing as a method for social research: A symposium. *Personality and Social Psychology Bulletin, 3,* 454–458.

HENDRICK, C. (1977b). Role-taking, role-playing, and the laboratory experiment. *Personality and Social Psychology Bulletin, 3,* 457–478.

HERZBERG, A. (1946). *Active psychotherapy.* New York: Grune & Stratton.

HILL, R. (1970). *Family development in three generations.* Cambridge, MA: Schenkman.

HOFFMAN, L. (1976). Breaking the homeostatic cycle. In P. Guerin (Ed.), *Family therapy: Theory and practice.* New York: Garden Press.

HOFFMAN, L. (1981). *Foundations of family therapy.* New York: Basic Books.

HUNT, J. M. (1984). Orval Hobart Mowrer (1907–1982). *American Psychologist, 39,* 912–914.

HUNTINGTON, D. S. (1982). Attachment, loss and divorce: A reconsideration of concepts. In L. Messinger (Ed.), *Therapy with remarriage familes* (pp. 17–29). Rockville, MD: Aspen Systems Corporation.

IRWIN, E. C., & MALLOY, E. S. (1975). Family puppet interview. *Family Process, 14,* 179–191.

IVEY, A. E. (1971). *Microcounseling: Innovations in interview training.* Springfield, IL: Charles C. Thomas.

JACKSON, D., & WEAKLAND, J. (1971). Conjoint family therapy: Some considerations on theory, techniques, and results. In J. Haley (Ed.), *Changing Families.* New York: Grune & Stratton.

JACKSON, D. D. (1965). The study of the family. *Family Process, 4,* 1–20.

JACOBSON, N. S. (1978). A review of the research on the effectiveness of marital therapy. In T. J. Paolino & B. S. McCrady (Eds.), *Marriage and marital therapy.* New York: Brunner/Mazel.

JEFFERSON, C. (1978). Some notes on the use of family sculpture in therapy. *Family Process, 17,* 69–76.

JOHNSON, D. W. (1971). Role reversal: A summary and review of the research. *International Journal of Group Tensions, 1,* 318–334.

JOHNSON, F. L. (1977). Role-taking and referential communication abilities in first- and third-grade children. *Human Communications Research, 3,* 135–145.

JOHNSON, J., WEEKS, G. R., & L'ABATE, L. (1979). Forced holding: A technique for treating parentified children. *Family Therapy, 6,* 124–132.

JONES, C. W. (1983). Reframing: A clinical strategy for transforming meaning. Unpublished manuscript, Georgia State University.

KADZIN, A. E., & MASCITELLI, S. (1982a). Behavioral rehearsal, self-instruction, and homework practice in developing assertiveness. *Behavior Therapy, 13,* 346–360.

KADZIN, A. E., & MASCITELLI, S. (1982b). Covert and overt rehearsal and homework practice in developing assertiveness. *Journal of Consulting and Clinical Psychology, 50,* 250–258.

KANTOR, D., & LEHR, W. (1975). *Inside the family: Toward a theory of family process.* San Francisco: Jossey-Bass.

KANTOR, D., & VICKERS, M. (1983). Divorce along the family life cycle. In H. A. Liddle (Ed.), *The family life cycle: Implications for therapy* (pp. 78–99). Rockville, MD: Aspen Systems Corporation.

KARPEL, M. (1976). Individuation: From fusion to dialogue. *Family Process, 15,* 65–82.

KARPMAN, S. (1968). Fairy tales and script drama analysis. *Transactional Analysis Bulletin, 7,* 38–43.

KARRASS, C. L. (1970). *The negotiation game.* New York: The World Publishing Co.

KATES-JULIUS, E. (1978). Family sculpting: A pilot program for a schizophrenic group. *Journal of Marriage and Family Counseling, 4*(3), 19–24.

KEENEY, B. (1983). *The aesthetics of change.* New York: Guilford Press.

KENNEY, B. P. (1979). Ecosystemic epistemology: An alternative paradigm for diagnosis. *Family Process, 18,* 117–129.

KENNEY, W. (1982). Interrelating theoretical models of conflict resolution. *Peace and Change, 8,* 43–54.

KELMAN, H. C. (1967). Human use of human subjects: The problem of deception in social psychological experiments. *Psychological Bulletin, 67,* 1–11.

KENT, C. (1967). *The effect of threats.* Columbus, OH: Ohio State University Press.

KESSLER, S. (1978). *Creative conflict resolutions: Mediation.* Atlanta, GA: National Institute for Professional Training.

KLEIN, D. M., & HILL, R. (1979). Determinants of family problem-solving effectiveness. In W. R. Burr, R. Hill, F. I. Nye, & I. L. Reiss (Eds.), *Contemporary theories about the family, Vol I: Research-based theories.* New York: Free Press.

KOESTLER, A. (1978). *Janus, a summing up.* New York: Random House.

KRUPAT, E. (1977). A re-assessment of role-playing as a technique in social psychology. *Personality and Social Psychology Bulletin, 3,* 498–504.

KWIATKOWSKA, H. Y. (1978). *Family therapy and evaluation through art.* Springfield, IL: C.C. Thomas.

L'ABATE, L. (1973). Psychodynamic interventions: A personal statement. In R. H. Woody & J. D. Woody (Eds.), *Sexual, marital, and family problems: Therapeutic interventions for professional helping.* Springfield, IL: C.C. Thomas.

L'ABATE, L. (1975a). *Manual: Family enrichment programs.* Atlanta, Georgia: Social Research Laboratories.

L'ABATE, L. (1975b). A positive approach to marital and family intervention. In L. Wolberg & M. Aronson (Eds.), *Group therapy 1975—An overview.* New York: Stratton Intercontintental Medical Book Corporation.

L'ABATE, L. (1975c). Pathogenic role rigidity in fathers: Some observations. *Journal of Marriage and Family Counseling, 1,* 69–79.

L'ABATE, L. (1976). *Understanding and helping the individual in the family.* New York: Grune & Stratton.

L'ABATE, L. (1977). *Enrichment: Structured interventions for couples, families, and groups.* Washington, DC: University Press of America.

L'ABATE, L. (1981a). The role of family conferences in family therapy. *Family Therapy, 9,* 33–38.

L'ABATE, L. (1981b). Skill training programs for couples and families. A. S. Gurman & D. P. Kniskern (Eds.), *Handbook of family therapy* (pp. 631–661). New York: Brunner/Nagel.

L'ABATE, L. (1983). *Family Psychology: Theory, therapy and Training.* Warlington, N.C.: University Press of America.

L'ABATE, L. (1986). *Systematic family therapy.* New York: Brunner/Mazel.

L'ABATE, L., BAGGETT, M. S., & ANDERSON, J. S. (1984). Linear and circular interventions with families of children with school-related problems. In B. F. Okun (Ed.), *Family therapy with school-related problems.* Rockville, MD: Aspen Publications.

L'ABATE, L., & FARR, L. (1981). Coping with defeating patterns. *Family Therapy, 8,* 91–103.

L'ABATE, L., & L'ABATE, B. L. (1977). *How to Avoid Divorce's Help for Troubled Marriages.* Atlanta, GA: John Knox Press.

L'ABATE, L., & RUPP, G. (1981). *Enrichment: Skills training for family life.* Washington, DC: University Press of America.

L'ABATE, L., & SAMPLES, G. (1983). Intimacy letters: invariable prescriptions for closeness-avoidant couples. *Family Therapy, 10,* 37–45.

L'ABATE, L., & WAGNER, V. (1985). Theory-derived, family oriented test-batteries. In L. L. L'Abate (Ed.), *Handbook of family psychology and therapy.* Homewood, IL: Dorsey Press.

L'ABATE, L., WEEKS, G. R., & WEEKS, K. (1979). Of scapegoats, strawmen, and scarecrows. *International Journal of Family Therapy, 1,* 86–93.

L'ABATE, L., WILDMAN, R. W., II, O'CALLAGHAN, J. B., SIMON, S. J., ALLISON, M., KAHN, G., & RAINWATER, N. (1975). The laboratory evaluation and enrichment of couples: Applications and some preliminary results. *Journal of Marriage and Family Counseling, 1,* 351–358.

LAING, R. D. (1965). Mystification, confusion, and conflict. In I. Boszormenyi-Nagy & J. L. Framo (Eds.), *Intensive family therapy.* New York: Harper & Row, Pub.

LAING, R. D., PHILLIPSON, H., & LEE, A. R. (1966). *Interpersonal perception: A theory and a method of research.* New York: Harper & Row, Pub.

LANDFIELD, A. (1975). The complaint: A confrontation of personal urgency and professional construction. In D. Bannister (Ed.), *Issues and approaches in psychological therapies.* New York: John Wiley.

LANGE, A., & VAN DER HART, O. (1983). *Directive family therapy.* New York: Brunner/Mazel.

LAQUEUR, H. P., LaBURT, H. A., & MORONG, E. (1964). Multiple family therapy. *Mental Hygiene, 48,* 544–551.

LEDERER, W. J., & JACKSON, D. D. (1968). *The mirages of marriage.* New York: W. W. Norton.

LeFAVE, M. K. (1980). Correlates of engagement in family therapy. *Journal of Marital and Family Therapy, 6,* 75–81.

LESTER, G. W., BECKMAN, E., & BAUCOM, D. H. (1980). Implementation of behavioral marital therapy. *Journal of Marital and Family Therapy, 61,* 189–199.

LEVANT, R. F. (1983). Diagnostic perspectives on the family: Process, structural and historical contextual models. *The American Journal of Family Therapy, 11*(2), 3–10.

LEVENSON, E. A. (1972). *The fallacy of understanding: An inquiry into the changing structure of psychoanalysis.* New York: Basic Books.

LEVI, E. (1980). *Levi's laws: Tactics for winning without intimidation.* New York: M. Evans and Company, Inc.

LEVIN, E. L. (1976). *The marital power structure.* Unpublished doctoral dissertation, Georgia State University, Atlanta.

LEWIS, J. M. (1980). The family matrix in health and disease. In M. C. K. Holling & J. M. Lewis (Eds.), *The family: Evaluation and treatment* (pp. 5–44). New York:Brunner/Mazel.

LEWIS, J. M., BEAVERS, W. R., GOSSETT, J. T., & PHILLIPS, V. A. (1976). *No single thread: Psychological health in family systems.* New York: Brunner/Mazel.

LIBERMAN, R. (1970). Behavioral approaches to family and couple theory. *American Journal of Orthopsychiatry, 40,* 106–118.

LOFTUS, E. F. (1979). *Eyewitness and testimony.* Cambridge, MA: Harvard University Press.

LOFTUS, E. F., & PALMER, J. C. (1974). Reconstruction of automobile destruction: An example of the interaction between language and memory. *Journal of Verbal Learning and Verbal Behavior, 13,* 585.

LUTHMAN, S. G., & KIRSCHENBAUM, M. (1974). *The dynamic family.* Palo Alto, CA: Science and Behavior Books.

McDONALD, G. W. (1980). Family power: The assessment of a decade of theory and research, 1970–1979. *Journal of Marriage and the Family, 42,* 841–854.

MACE, D., & MACE, V. (1980). Enriching marriages: The foundation stone of family strengths. In N. S. Stinnett, B. Chesser, J. DeFrain, & P. Knaube (Eds.), *Family strengths: Positive models for family life* (pp. 89–100). Lincoln, NE: University of Nebraska Press.

MacGREGOR, R., RITCHIE, A. M., SERRANO, A. C., & SCHUSTER, F. P. (1964). *Multiple impact therapy with families.* New York: McGraw-Hill.

MADANES, C. (1984). *Behind the one-way mirror: Advances in the practice of strategic therapy.* San Francisco: Jossey-Bass.

MADANES, C. (1980). Protection, paradox, and pretending. *Family Process, 19,* 73–85.

MAULTSBY, M. C. (1971). Systematic, written homework in psychotherapy. *Psychotherapy: Theory, Research and Practice, 8,* 195–198.

McGINNIS, A. L. (1979). *The friendship factor.* Minneapolis: Augsburg Publishing House.

McGOLDRICK, M., & CARTER, E. A. (1982). The family life cycle. In F. Walsh (Ed.), *Normal family processes* (pp. 167–195). New York: Guilford Press.

MEICHENBAUM, D. (1974). *Cognitive behavior modification.* Morristown, NY: General Learning Press.

MESSINGER, L. (Ed.) (1982). *Therapy with remarriage families.* Rockville, MD: Aspen Systems Corporation.

MILLER, S., NUNNALLY, E. W., & WACKMAN, D. B. (1975). *Alive and aware: Improving communication in relationships.* Minneapolis: Interpersonal Communication Programs, Inc.

MINUCHIN, S. (1974). *Families and family therapy.* Cambridge, MA: Harvard University Press.

MINUCHIN, S. (1979). *Anorexia is a Greek word* [Videotape]. Brookline, MA: Boston Family Institute.

MINUCHIN, S., MONTALVO, B., GUERNEY, B., ROSMAN, B., & SCHUMMER, F. (1967). *Families of the slums: An exploration of their structure.* Cambridge, MA: Harvard University Press.

MITCHELL, E. V., KAUL, T. J., & PEPINSKY, H. B. (1977). The limited role of psychology in the roleplaying controversy. *Personality and Social Psychology Bulletin, 3,* 514–518.

MOSTWIN, D. (1972). *Involving the family in the treatment of school phobia: A team approach to family casework.* Unpublished paper.

MOVAHEDI, S. (1977). Role playing: An alternative to what? *Personality and Social Psychology Bulletin, 3,* 489–497.

MURNIGHAM, J. K. (1978). Models of a coalition behavior: Game theoretic, social psychological, and political perspectives. *Psychological Bulletin, 85,* 1130–1153.

MURPHY, D. C., & MENDELSON, L. A. (1973). Communication and adjustment in marriage: Investigating the relationship. *Family Process, 12,* 317–326.

NAPIER, A. Y. (1978). The rejection-intrusion pattern: A central family dynamic. *Journal of Marriage and Family Counseling, 4*(1), 5–12.

NAVRAN, L. (1967). Communication and adjustment in marriage. *Family Process, 6,* 173–184.

NELSON, J. C. (1983). *Family treatment: An integrative approach.* Englewood Cliffs, NJ: Prentice-Hall, Inc.

NICHOLS, M. (1984). *Family therapy: Concepts and methods.* New York: Gardner Press.

NIERENBERG, G. I. (1971). *Creative business negotiating: Skills and successful strategies.* New York: Hawthorne.

OLSON, D. H., BELL, R., & PORTNER, J. (1983). *Faces II.* St. Paul, MN: Family Social Science.

OLSON, D. H., RUSSELL, C. S., & SPRENKLE, D. H. (1983). Circumplex Model VI: Theoretical update. *Family Process, 22,* 69–83.

OLSON, D., SPRENKLE, D., & RUSSELL, C. (1979). Circumplex model of marital and family systems: I. Cohesion and adaptability dimensions, family types, and clinical applications. *Family Process, 18*(1), 3–28.

OXFORD, J., & FELDMAN, M. (1980). Overview and implications: Towards an applied social and community psychology. In M. P. Feldman & J. Oxford (Eds.), *Psychological problems: The social context* (pp. 367–379). New York: John Wiley.

PALAZZOLI, M. S., CECCHIN, G., BOSCOLO, L., & PRATA, G. (1978). *Paradox and counterparadox.* New York: Jason Aronson.

PAPP, P. (1976). Family choreography. In P. J. Guerin (Ed.), *Family therapy: Theory and practice.* New York: Garner Press.

PAPP, P., SILVERSTEIN, O., & CARTER, E. (1973). Family sculpting in preventive work with families. *Family Process, 12,* 197–212.

PATTERSON, G. R., & REID, J. B. (1970). Reciprocity and coercion: Two facets of social systems. In C. Neuringer & J. L. Michael (Eds.), *Behavior modification in clinical psychology.* New York: Appleton-Century-Crofts.

PAUL, N. L., & PAUL, B. D. (1975). *A marital puzzle: Transgenerational analysis in marriage counseling.* New York: Norton.

PEARSON, L. (Ed.) (1965). *The use of written communication in psychotherapy.* Springfield, IL: Charles C Thomas.

PERLS, F. (1973). *The gestalt approach and eye witness to therapy.* Palo Alto, CA: Science and Behavior Books.

PETERSON, G. L., FREDERICKSEN, L. W., & ROSENBAUM, M. S. (1981). Developing behavioral competencies in distressed marital couples. *American Journal of Family Therapy, 9,* 13–23.

PHILLIPS, E. L. (1978). *The social skills basis of psychopathology.* New York: Grune & Stratton.

PINSOFF, W. (1983). Integrative problem-centered therapy: Toward the synthesis of family and individual psychotherapies. *Journal of Marital and Family Therapy, 9,* 19–35.

POLLACK, A. (1981). Personal Communication. Carmel, NY: Carmel Mental Health Center.

PROSKY, P. (1974). Pitfalls of a home visit-or-the mad tea party. *Family Therapy, 1,* 193–209.

PROSKY, P. (1981, April). *Intuitive family therapy.* Workshop presented at Hudson River Psychiatric Center, Poughkeepsie, NY.

QUARTON, R. J. (1976). *The development of social cognition: Role-taking.* Unpublished doctoral dissertation, Pennsylvania State University, University Park, PA.

RABINER, E. L., MOLINSKI, H., & GRALNICK, A. (1962). Conjoint family therapy in the inpatient setting. *American Journal of Psychotherapy, 16,* 618–631.

RABKIN, R. (1967). Uncoordinated communication between marriage partners. *Family Process, 6,* 10–15.

RANZ, J., & FERBER, A. (1972). How to succeed in family therapy. In L. A. Ferber, J. Mendelsohn, & A. Napier (Eds.), *The book of family therapy.* New York: Academic Press.

REID, W. J., & EPSTEIN, L. (1972). *Task-centered casework.* New York: Columbia University Press.

REISS, D., (1981). *The Family's Construction of Reality.* Cambridge, MA: Harvard University Press.

REISS, D., COSTELL, R., JONES, C., & BERKMAN, H. (1980). The family meets the hospital. *Archives of General Psychiatry, 37,* 141–154.

RUBEN, A. G. (1978). The family picture. *Journal of Marriage and Family Counseling, 4*(3), 25–27.

RUBIN, J., & BROWN, B. (1975). The Social Psychology of *Bargaining and Negotiation.* New York: Academic Press.

RUBIN, K. H. (1978). Role-taking in childhood: Some methodological considerations. *Child Development, 49,* 428–433.

RUBINSTEIN, D. (1980). Self-confrontation techniques in family therapy. In L. R. Wolberg & M. L. Aronson (Eds.), *Group and family therapy 1980* (pp. 345–356). New York: Brunner/Mazel.

RUESCH, J., & BATESON, G. (1968). *Communication, the social matrix of psychiatry.* New York: W. W. Norton.

RUEVENI, V. (1979). *Networking families in crisis.* New York: Human Services Press.

RUTLEDGE, A. L. (1962). Husband-wife conferences in the home. *Marriage and Family Living, 24,* 151–154.

SAPOSNEK, D. T. (1972). An experimental study of rage-reduction treatment of autistic children. *Child Psychiatry and Human Development, 3,* 50–61.

SATIR, V. (1967). *Conjoint family therapy* (Rev. ed.). Palo Alto, CA: Science and Behavior Books.

SATIR, V. (1972). *Peoplemaking.* Palo Alto, CA: Science and Behavior Books.

SCANZONI, J., & POLONKO, K. (1980). A conceptual approach to explicit marital negotiation. *Journal of Marriage and the Family, 42,* 31–44.

SCANZONI, J., & SZINORACZ, M. (1981). *Family decision making: A developmental sex role model.* Beverly Hills, CA: Sage Publications, Inc.

SCHACTER, S. (1964). The detection of cognitive and physiological determinants of emotional states. In L. Berkowitz (Ed.), *Advances in experimental social psychology* (Vol. 1). New York: Academic Press.

SCHOPLER, J. (1965). Social power. In L. Berkowitz (Ed.), *Advances in experimental social psychology* (Vol. 2). New York: Academic Press.

SCHULMAN, G. L. (1979). The changing American family: For better or worse. *International Journal of Psychotherapy, 1,* 9–21.

SELVINI-PALAZZOLI, M., BOSCOLO, L., CECCHIN, G., & PRATA, G. (1978). *Paradox and counterparadox: The family in schizophrenic transaction.* New York: Jason Aronson.

SHELTON, J. L. (1979). Instigation therapy using therapeutic homework to promote treatment gains. In A. P. Goldstein & F. H. Kanfer (Eds.), *Maximizing treatment gains: Transfer enhancement in psychotherapy* (pp. 225–245). New York: Academic Press.

SHELTON, J. L., & LEVY, R. L. (1981). A survey of the reported use of assigned homework activities in contemporary behavior therapy literature. *The Behavior Therapist, 4,* 13–14.

SHEPHERD, G. (1980). The treatment of social difficulties in special environments. In M. P. Feldman & J. Oxford (Eds.), *Psychological problems: The social context* (pp. 249–278). New York: John Wiley.

SHERR, C., & HICKS, H. (1973). Family drawings as a diagnostic and therapeutic technique. *Family Process, 12,* 439–460.

SIMON, R. M. (1972). Sculpting the family. *Family Process, 2,* 49–57.

SINGER, M. T., & WYNNE, L. (1965). Thought disorder and family relations, IV: Results and implications. *Archives of General Psychiatry, 12*(2), 201–212.

SLUZKI, C. (1978). Marital therapy from a systems theory perspective. In T. J. Paolino & B. S. McCrady (Eds.) *Marriage and marital therapy.* New York: Brunner/Mazel.

SMITH, G. W., & PHILLIPS, A. I. (1971). *Me, you, and us.* New York: Peter H. Wyden.

SMITH, M. (1975). *When I say no I feel guilty.* New York: Bantam Books.

SMYE, M. D. (1978). Behavioral and cognitive assessment through role-playing. *Psychology, 15,* 35–48.

SOLOMON, M. (1973). A developmental conceptual premise for family therapy. *Family Process, 12,* 179–188.

SPECK, R., & ATTNEAVE, C. (1972). Network therapy. In M. A. Ferber, M. Mendel-John, & A. Napier (Eds.), *The book of family therapy* (pp. 637–665). New York: Science House.

SPENCER, C. D. (1978). Two types of role playing: Threats to internal and external validity. *American Psychologist, 33,* 265–268.

SPEREKAS, N. B. (1974). Home visiting in family therapy. *Family Therapy, 1,* 171–178.

SPIEGEL, J. (1971). *Transactions: The interplay between individual, family and society.* New York: Science House.

SPIVACK, G., PLATT, J., & SHURE, M. B. (1976). *The problem-solving approach to adjustment.* San Francisco, CA: Jossey-Bass.

SPRENKEL, D. H., & FISHER, B. (1980). An empirical assessment of the goals of family therapy. *Journal of Marital and Family Therapy, 6,* 131–139.

STANTON, M. D., & TODD, T. ET AL. (1982). *The family therapy of drug abuse.* New York: Guilford Press.

STEINGLASS, P. (1978). The conceptualization of marriage from a systems theory perspective. In T. J. Paolino & B. S. McCrady (Eds.), *Marriage and marital therapy: Psychoanalytic, behavioral and systems perspectives.* New York: Brunner/Mazel.

STIERLIN, H. (1974). *Separating parents and adolescents.* New York: The New York Times Book Co., Quadrangle Books.

STINNETT, N. (1979). Introduction. In N. Stinnet, B. Chesser, & J. DeFrain (Eds.), *Building family strengths: Blueprints for action.* Lincoln, NE: University of Nebraska Press.

STRELNICK, A. H. (1977). Multiple family group therapy: A review of the literature. *Family Process 16,* 307–325.

STRUPP, H. H. (1976). Themes in psychotherapy research. In J. L. Claghorn (Ed.), *Successful psychotherapy,* pp. 3–23. New York: Brunner/Mazel.

STUART, R. B. (1983). *Couple's therapy workbook: Behavior change systems.* Salt Lake City: University of Utah.

SWINPLE, P. G. (1976). *The management of power.* Hillsdale, NJ: Lawrence Erlbaum & Associates.

SWINGLE, P. (Ed.) (1970). *The structure of conflict.* New York: Academic Press.

STRAUS, M. A., & BROWN, B. W. (1978). *Family Measurement Techniques: Abstracts of published instruments, 1935–1974.* Minneapolis, MN: University of Minnesota Press.

TENNEN, H., ROHRBAUGH, J., PRESS, S., & WHITE, L. (1981). Compliance, defiance, and therapeutic paradox: Guidelines for strategic use of paradoxical interventions. *American Journal of Orthopsychiatry, 51*(3), 454–467.

THOMAS, D. L., FRANKS, D. D., & CALONICO, J. M. (1972). Role-taking and power in social psychology. *American Sociological Review, 37,* 605–614.

THORNE, F. C. (1946). Directive psychotherapy, VI: The techniques of psychological palliation. *Journal of clinical psychology, 2,* 68–79.

TODD, T. C. (1982). Paradoxical prescriptions. *Journal of Strategic and Systemic Therapies, 1*(1), 28–44.

TOMAN, W. (1969). *Family constellation: Its effects on personality and social behavior* (2nd ed.). New York: Springer.

TOOLEY, K. (1975). The diagnostic home visit: on aid in training and case consultations. *Journal of Marriage and Family Counseling. 1,* 317–321.

TSOI-HOMMAND, L. (1976). Marital therapy: An integrative behavioral learning model. *Journal of Marriage and Family Counseling, 2*(1), 179–191.

VALINS, S., & NISBETT, R. E. (1972). Attribution processes in the development and treatment of emotional disorders. In E. E. Jones et al. (Eds.) *Attribution, perceiving the causes of behavior.* Morristown, NY: General Learning Press.

VAN DER VEEN, F., HUEBNER B., JORGENS, B., & NEJA, P., JR. (1964). Relationships between the parents' concept of the family and family adjustment. *American Journal of Orthopsychiatry, 34,* 45–55.

VENEMA, H. B. (1976). Marriage enrichment: A comparison of the behavioral exchange negotiation and communication models. *Dissertation Abstracts International, 36,* 4148–4185.

VIARO, M. (1980). Case report: Smuggling family therapy through. *Family Process, 19,* 35–44.

VOSS, J. R., ARRICK, M. C., & RIMM, D. C. (1978). Behavior rehearsal, modeling, and coaching in assertive training. *Behavior Therapy, 9,* 970–971.

WAGNER, V., & L'ABATE, L. (1977). Enrichment and written homework assignments with couples. In L. L'Abate (Ed.), *Enrichment: Structured interventions with couples, families, and groups.* Washington, DC: University Press of America.

WAHLROOS, S. (1974). *Family communication.* New York: Macmillan.

WALSH, F. (1980). The family in later life. In E. A. Carter & M. McGoldrick (Eds.), *The family life cycle: A framework for family therapy.* New York: Gardner Press.

WARING, E. M. (1980). Marital intimacy, psychosomatic symptoms and cognitive therapy. *Psychosomatics, 21,* 595–601.

WATZLAWICK, P. (1964). *An anthology of human communication.* Palo Alto, CA: Science and Behavior Books.

WATZLAWICK, P. (1976). The psychotherapeutic technique of "reframing." In J. L. Claghorn (Ed.), *Successful psychotherapy* (pp. 119–127). New York: Brunner/Mazel.

WATZLAWICK, P., BEAVIN, J. H., & JACKSON, D. D. (1967). *Pragmatics of human communication: A study of interactional patterns, pathologies and paradoxes.* New York: W. W. Norton.

WATZLAWICK, P., WEAKLAND, J. H., & FISCH, R. (1974). *Change: Principles of problem formation and problem resolution.* New York: W. W. Norton.

WEAKLAND, J. (1976). Communication theory and clinical change. In P. Guerin (Ed.), *Family therapy: Theory and practice.* New York: Garner Press.

WEEKS, G. (1977). Towards a diaelectical approach to intervention. *Human Development, 20,* 277–292.

WEEKS, G., WAGNER, V., & L'ABATE, L. (1979). Enrichment and written messages with couples. *American Journal of Family Therapy, 8,* 36–44.

WEEKS, G. R., & L'ABATE, L. (1982). *Paradoxical psychotherapy: Theory and practice with individuals, couples, and families.* New York: Brunner/Mazel.

WEISS, R. L. (1978). The conceptualization of marriage from a behavioral perspective. In T. J. Paolino & M. S. McGrady (Eds.), *Marriage and Family Therapy* (pp. 165–238). New York: Brunner/Mazel.

WELK, R. L., & HENLEY, A. (1969). *Yes power.* New York: Peter H. Wyden.

WELLS, R., & FIGUREL, J. (1978). *Structured communication training with conflicted marital couples: A demonstration* [Videotape]. Pittsburgh, PA: University of Pittsburgh, Center for Instructional Resources.

WHITAKER, C. (1975). Psychotherapy of the absurd with special emphasis on the psychology of aggression. *Family Process, 14,* 1–16.

WHITAKER, C. (1982, June). Carl Whitaker Workshop. Pittsburgh, PA.

WHITESIDE, M. (1983). Families of remarriage: The weaving of many life-cycle threads. In H. A. Liddle (Ed.), *The family life cycle: Implications for therapy* (pp. 100–119). Rockville MD: Aspen Systems Corporation.

WILHELM, R., & JUNG, C. G. (1970). *The secret of the golden flower. A Chinese book of life.* San Diego: Harcourt Brace Javanovich, Inc.

WOLBERG, A. R. (1976). The contributions of Jacob Moreno. In L. R. Wolberg & M. L. Aronson (Eds.), *Group therapy 1976: An overview* (pp. 1–15). New York: Stratton Intercontinental Medical Book Corporation.

WYNNE, L. C., & SINGER, M. T. (1963). Thought disorder and family relations of schizophrenics, II: Classification of forms of thinking. *Archives of General Psychiatry, 9*(3), 33–40.

YABLONSKY, L. (1976). *Psychodrama: Resolving emotional problems through role playing.* New York: Basic Books.

YOUNG, O. R. (Ed.) (1975). *Bargaining: Formal theories of negotiation.* Urban, IL: University of Illinois Press.

ZARTMAN, I. W. (Ed.) (1978). *The negotiation process: Theories and applications.* Beverly Hills: Sage Publications, Inc.

ZASLOW, R., & BREGER, L. (1969). Theory and treatment of autism. In L. Berger (Ed.), *Clinical cognitive psychology: Models and integrations* (pp. 246–291). Englewood Cliffs, NJ: Prentice-Hall.

ZUK, G. H. (1978). The three crises in family therapy. *International Journal of Family Therapy, 1,* 1–5.

Author Index

Subject Index